I0129568

Rebuilding European Democracy

Rebuilding European Democracy

Resistance and Renewal in an Illiberal Age

Richard Youngs

I.B. TAURIS

LONDON • NEW YORK • OXFORD • NEW DELHI • SYDNEY

I.B. TAURIS
Bloomsbury Publishing Plc
50 Bedford Square, London, WC1B 3DP, UK
1385 Broadway, New York, NY 10018, USA
29 Earlsfort Terrace, Dublin 2, Ireland

BLOOMSBURY, I.B. TAURIS and the I.B. Tauris logo are trademarks of
Bloomsbury Publishing Plc

First published in Great Britain 2022

Copyright © Richard Youngs, 2022

Richard Youngs has asserted his right under the Copyright, Designs and
Patents Act, 1988, to be identified as Author of this work.

Cover design: Holly Bell

All rights reserved. No part of this publication may be reproduced or transmitted
in any form or by any means, electronic or mechanical, including photocopying,
recording, or any information storage or retrieval system, without prior
permission in writing from the publishers.

Bloomsbury Publishing Plc does not have any control over, or responsibility for,
any third-party websites referred to or in this book. All internet addresses given
in this book were correct at the time of going to press. The author and publisher
regret any inconvenience caused if addresses have changed or sites have ceased
to exist, but can accept no responsibility for any such changes.

A catalogue record for this book is available from the British Library.

A catalog record for this book is available from the Library of Congress.

ISBN: HB: 978-0-7556-3971-7
PB: 978-0-7556-3972-4
ePDF: 978-0-7556-3974-8
eBook: 978-0-7556-3973-1

Typeset by Newgen KnowledgeWorks Pvt. Ltd., Chennai, India

To find out more about our authors and books visit www.bloomsbury.com
and sign up for our newsletters

Contents

Illustrations

Figures

Tables

Preface

After a decade of worryingly adverse trends in democracy, this book goes somewhat against the analytical grain in exploring efforts to uphold and improve European democratic processes. It hopes to show that these initiatives of democratic resistance and renewal have become significant counterpoints to the many ways in which democracy has been threatened and diluted in recent years. To rebut an immediate objection, the book does not paint a rosy picture of the state of European democracy, and it does not breezily idealize or celebrate these pro-democratic actions. Yet it does start from the conviction that pro-democratic strategies have gathered a momentum that merits serious attention. A rather all-consuming focus on Europe's populist surge and its implications for democracy has arguably diverted attention away from the many other important political trends and developments that have unfolded in recent years.

These themes have been central to the author's work at the Carnegie Europe think tank for several years. The book developed in particular out of a project on Reshaping European Democracy run from Carnegie's Brussels office. I am grateful for support from the Carnegie team for this and other projects and to the wide range of colleagues in Brussels who have been involved in these endeavours. Our regular off-the-record seminars with policymakers ignited many of the concerns and reflections that are explored though the book. The Covid-19 pandemic complicated this project work and also presented difficult substantive questions for the book's main themes; yet we were fortunate in Carnegie to count on wide-ranging participation in online debates during 2020 that helped shine a light on how democracy strategies were adapting to the crisis.

A number of people helped prepare the text and offered inputs to its different chapters, including Alberto Alemanno, Ozlem Atikcan, Cristina Buzasu, Thomas Carothers, Fernando Casal Bértoa, Katherine

Chapanionek, Steve Feldstein, Nita Gegeshidze, Agata Gostyńska-Jakubowska, Heather Grabbe, Poonam Joshi, Maarten de Groot, Maria Koomen, Hans Kundnani, Sarah Manney, Pawel Marczewski, Giada Negri, Elene Panchulidze, Nicole Pofcher, Mike Saward, Magdalene Segre, Louisa Slavkova, Victoria Stoiciu and Richard Wilson. At Bloomsbury, Tomasz Hoskins and Nayiri Kendir provided invaluable support in advancing the text. My work has benefited in recent years from the support that several foundations have provided to the Carnegie Endowment for International Peace for work relating to democracy and democratic activism. They include the Ford Foundation, the Hewlett Foundation and the Charles Stewart Mott Foundation. I am grateful for this support but of course remain solely responsible for the views expressed in this book.

This book is not a rallying cry for democracy and is not pitched as a series of recommendations for what governments and other actors should and should not do to preserve democracy. Rather, it is a close and critical analysis of real-life reform efforts. The book's basic tenor is to engage seriously with democratic actions and ask, in constructively critical fashion, how they might become more dynamic and innovative in the future. While developing a critique of these reforms' shortcomings to date, the book is written in sympathy with and great admiration for the effort of countless citizens, civic organizations, politicians, parties and officials working hard to ensure that Europe's democratic weaknesses do not develop into a deeper or even fatal crisis for the continent's most precious attributes of political freedom. Conversations and cooperation with many scores of these reformers inspired and informed the text. If the book helps in any way change the terms of debate over European democracy, it would be a testament to their commitment.

Introduction

During the 2010s, serious concerns emerged over the state of European democracy. Indices measuring democratic quality reported year-on-year declines across countries of the European Union (EU). Governments began chipping away at civic freedoms and democratic checks and balances. In a small number of European countries, overtly authoritarian dynamics took root and illiberal populist parties gained ground. Polls regularly suggested that voters came to question democratic norms more seriously than they had for many decades. The EU faced a series of crises that accentuated citizens' feeling that they had little democratic sway over decisions made in Brussels. Cutting across all these developments, digital technology increasingly appeared to be more of a threat than an enabler of personal freedom and democratic vitality.

Against this unsettling backdrop, many analysts, journalists and politicians stressed the danger of Europe descending into an era of conflict, driven by xenophobic nationalism and nativist authoritarians slowly dismantling liberal democratic rights. In 2020, the Covid-19 pandemic intensified these fears as the emergency led governments to take on far-reaching executive powers and restrict many democratic freedoms. While most of these restrictions were temporary and clearly justified in the fight against the virus, this new crisis raised the spectre of further damage to European democracy. In short, for many years perspectives on European democracy have been strikingly downbeat.

There is another side of the democratic equation, however. Citizens, civil society organizations, political parties, governments and EU institutions have gradually begun to push back in defence of democracy.

Many governmental, political and social actors have developed responses to Europe's democratic malaise at multiple levels – from the local through to the national and EU levels. Europe's democracy problems have been grave and far-reaching. Yet, a spirit of democratic resistance has slowly taken shape.

This book argues that the pro-democratic fight back may be belated, but it is real and has assumed significant traction. Efforts to rebuild European democracy have emerged at several different levels. Civic movements, national and subnational authorities, political parties and EU policymakers have all moved to upgrade their formal commitments to defend and rethink democracy. Many of them have redoubled such efforts in the wake of Covid-19. These different initiatives have not been strong or effective enough entirely to quell Europe's political ill health, but they offer the promise of meaningful democratic renewal. The book argues that this needs to be advanced further in particular through more ambitious citizen-oriented political innovation.

Beyond democratic pessimism

The book examines the different forms this democratic rebuilding has taken and assesses their significance. It proceeds from the belief that a focus on democratic responses is essential to move current debate into a necessary next stage of analysis. For many years, analysts have focused mainly on stressing the scale of Europe's democratic weaknesses. From the mid-2010s a raft of books and articles appeared dissecting what experts feared was democracy's imminent collapse, its terminal crisis, its de-consolidation, its defeat to a forbidding return of nationalist authoritarianism across Europe. On an almost daily basis, articles and opinion pieces have appeared lamenting the precarious state of European democracy. [1]

A whole cluster of different trends combined to unleash this wave of writings and fretful warnings. Hungary has moved incrementally from democracy to illiberal democracy and in the last several years towards outright authoritarianism. Since 2015, the Polish government has in a similar vein overturned several core areas of democratic politics. Though these two cases are the most visible and dramatic face of European democratic erosion, political illiberalism has also taken root across other parts of Europe. Chaotic and splenetic politics in the UK led analysts to couch Brexit as another part of European democratic meltdown. Polling seemed to suggest that European citizens have lost faith in democratic values, while external actors have also menaced democracy through digital means. Most recently, the Covid-19 emergency has clearly put additional strains on democratic systems as European governments have struggled to devise effective medical, economic and social responses.

As the political and analytical conversation has been mainly about the defensive fragility of Europe's democracy, the next stage of analysis needs to shift to the question of how different actors across Europe have sought to address the threats to democracy. Experts have exhaustively mapped out the extent of the problems; more systematic attention also needs to be given to responses. After all, despite so many apocalyptically dire predictions, European democracy has in most countries largely stood its ground. In some ways, European politics have even taken their

---

[1] Amongst the many volumes and articles along these lines, some of the most widely cited are L. Diamond, *Ill Winds: Saving Democracy from Russian Rage, Chinese Ambition and American Complacency* (London: Penguin, 2019); S. Levitsky and G. Ziblatt, *How Democracies Die* (London: Penguin, 2018); R. Foa and Y. Mounck, 'The signs of deconsolidation', *Journal of Democracy*, 28/1, 5–16; S. Berman *Democracy and Dictatorship in Europe* (Oxford: Oxford University Press, 2018); T. Snyder, *The Road to Unfreedom* (London: Vintage, 2019); Y. Mounck *The People versus Democracy* (Cambridge: Harvard University Press, 2018); D. Runciman, *How Democracy Ends* (London: Profile, 2019) ; J. Keane, *The New Despotism* (Cambridge: Harvard University Press, 2020); A. Appelbaum, *The Twilight of Democracy: The Seductive Lure of Authoritarianism* (London: Doubleday, 2020).

first, tentative steps along a path of healthy democratic renovation. The book asks whether these efforts have been sufficient to turn democracy's tide in a more favourable direction.

Mapping democratic renovation

This book offers an overview of these efforts to rebuild democracy across Europe; its geographical scope is EU member states and the UK (an EU member until 2020). The aim is to uncover emergent democratic practices and critically assess them. I categorically do not mean to suggest that democratic regression has run its course, nor do I minimize its ongoing reach and gravity. The goal is to ask what is being done to counter democratic decay and what these reform efforts portend for the future of European democracy.

The analysis distinguishes between two slightly different democratic dynamics. One dynamic can be defined as *democratic resistance*: new strategies that seek to defend core democratic norms against overtly non-democratic threats. The other can be termed *democratic renewal*: policies and initiatives aiming to change and improve democracy in a more qualitative sense. The book defines the overall agenda of rebuilding democracy as encompassing these two separate but overlapping dynamics. Actors have pursued a combination of the two as they try both to defend and rethink democratic practices across Europe. The different chapters examine the balance and complex relationship between these two dynamics of resistance and renewal.

Conceptually, the book seeks to add analytical ordering to the study of democratic resistance and renewal. Experts have devised analytical frameworks to describe and explain democratic decay – this has become one of the richest fields of endeavour in political science in recent years. This book seeks an equivalent kind of *analytical typology* for the inverse dynamics of democratic resistance and renewal. The underlying premise is that something of an analytical paradigm shift is due. For years, theorists debated competing models of democratization;

in the current era, they moved into theorizing democratic backsliding. Looking to the future, work will also be needed that begins thinking analytically about democratic resistance and renewal.

I adopt a multiple-level analytical framework that covers the various ways in which democratic practice is conceived and pursued. The approach is *actor-centred* as it examines the policies and strategies that have lately been adopted by a range of different actors across Europe – in effect, disaggregating the different levels at which democratic efforts have emerged. The successive chapters centre on actors' different visions, preferences and calculations of self-interest in the democratic strategies they pursue rather than assuming that democratic improvement is a matter of neutral, procedural change. I work upwards from this granular look at how different bodies are enacting democratic resistance and renewal to reflect on higher-level conceptual concerns over democracy.

The book examines in turn six emerging dimensions of democratic renovation, moving upwards from the grassroots through to the European level:

- citizens' mobilization to defend and reinvent democracy;
- European governments' initiatives for democratic consultation and participation;
- political parties' efforts to renew their contribution to European democracy;
- different actors' strategies to restore the democratic potential of the digital sphere;
- the EU's moves to take firmer action against systemic threats to democracy; and
- different actors' efforts to open up new routes to European-level democratic accountability.

Combining these different strands, the book offers a *composite* picture of European democracy. It understands democracy to include liberal, representative, participative, deliberative, direct, digital and transnational dimensions; it understands that countries move along a continuum of *democratic quality* that encompasses these multiple dimensions.[2] Analysts and practitioners most commonly focus on one bit of the democracy puzzle. Some are concerned with party systems and the growth of new political parties, some monitor EU level mechanisms relating to the rule of law, some home in on the mechanics of deliberative forums and others are preoccupied with digital issues. This book aims at a more all-inclusive understanding of trends in European democracy. It explores different levels of democratic rebuilding within a single account and sets them analytically alongside each other.

The book is concerned with mapping what is happening at the level of practical action rather than making the abstract case for one particular kind of democracy; it is not a work of normative political theory. My angle is mainly to explore how different actors themselves conceive and articulate their reform efforts. The book asks whether current reform initiatives offer ways of adding valuable mass-participative, civic, deliberative, direct, digital and supranational elements to existing democratic practice. In assessing these efforts, it works largely within the template of liberal-representative democracy; it does not foreground radical, non-liberal forms of democracy within its understanding of resistance and renewal (Chapter 2 unpacks the complex relationship between illiberalism and wider democratic trends). Having said this, the book charts ambitious efforts at far-reaching democratic renewal, and a central theme running through the chapters is that a blurred line often exists between a desire to improve existing democratic practices and an aim more deeply to challenge these.

The focus is very specifically on strategies that different actors have developed directly to defend or enhance democracy. This follows suggestions that analytical debate must do more to understand constantly unfolding channels of democratic change rather than simply comparing fixed end-state political ideals.[3] The book is not a generic call for deeper democracy, but a measured look at the good and bad

---

[2] Following the Varieties of Democracy definitions on these dimensions or strands of democratic politics, see V-Dem, *Structure of V-Dem Indices, Components and Indicators* (Gothenburg: University of Gothenburg, 2021).

[3] D. Runciman, 'How to fix British democracy', Talking Politics podcast, 3 January 2021.

in already-existing attempts to mitigate democratic decay. It does not cover every area of policy change connected to democratic quality, and its remit is not the question of what drives illiberal populism, as this has already received exhaustive attention in recent years. Rather, the focus is on policies and initiatives more directly related to democratic renewal. In short, I look at changes to democratic process not particular policies: that is, to the input not output side of European democracy.

What potential for rebuilding European democracy?

The book finds that efforts to rebuild European democracy have gained significant traction in recent years. This incipient democratic renovation has taken shape at multiple levels: mobilized citizens, civil society organizations, political parties, local authorities, national governments and EU institutions have all made contributions to holding democracy's depletion at bay. Of these different levels of change, the most resolute, dynamic and innovative strategies have come from Europe's civic sphere.

While the chapters uncover these varied and wide-ranging elements of democratic resistance and renewal, they also reveal the limits to reform. The book adopts a critical perspective in suggesting that many of Europe's emerging strategies of democratic fight back remain modest in their scale, ambition and impact. All levels and types of reform have displayed serious shortcomings and none has fulfilled its potential. In particular, many formal governmental reforms have been cautious and more cosmetic than democratically transformational. Leftist, centrist and rightist political forces have all been guilty of limiting or undermining reform efforts. The book notes a *democratic paradox* in the fact that populism's rise has both spurred and discouraged reform. Likewise, the Covid-19 pandemic has both galvanized many pro-democratic initiatives and undercut some of the momentum behind Europe's democratic renewal. Overall, democratic resistance and renewal have gathered much momentum but are still tentative in many areas.

The concluding chapter weighs the achievements and merits of each type of democratic rebuilding. It argues that less restrained forms of democratic resistance and renewal are needed beyond the reforms that have occurred in recent years. These need, in particular, to build in more innovative and unfettered forms of citizen participation, although in a way that adds to existing liberal-representative dynamics rather than subverting these. This form of democratic rebuilding requires above all that the different levels of resistance and renewal work in closer harmony with each other than has been the case to date. The book's composite analytical framework helps reveal the need to connect together different sites of democratic regeneration. Without such joined-up reform efforts, Europe's democratic rejuvenation will remain partial and incomplete – and the forces of democratic erosion and democratic renewal will continue to clash in uncertain ways.

2

Measuring the challenges to European democracy

Many measurements of democracy have given cause for serious concern in recent years. This chapter examines the state of play in European democracy by presenting a range of empirical information measuring different areas of democratic quality. Overall, the evidence uncovers mixed trends, some negative for democracy, others more reassuring. The chapter's purpose is to dissect recent trends relevant to European democracy as a baseline for assessing the different strategies of democratic resistance and renewal that have emerged in response. It shows the precise ways in which European democracy stands compromised, while also offering a more eclectic assessment of some political trends.

The data offered here paints the context within which ongoing reform efforts must be understood. The chapter summarizes indices of general democratic quality, data in the specific areas of rule of law and civil liberties, trends in populism, information on voters' changing values, developments related to other elements of democratic politics like political parties and elections, and rising digital concerns. The matter of how to define good quality democracy is itself contested and different measurements raise difficult questions in this regard. Still, taken as a whole this selection of data suffices to show the multiple levels at which European democracy has struggled in recent years, with threats coming from both so-called mainstream democratic governments as well as illiberal populists. This reality underpins the core argument that unfolds through the book: deeper and less conventional methods of democratic resistance and renewal still need freer rein across Europe.

Overall trend lines

Several indices and surveys measure the state of European democracy. While these focus on different indicators and produce slightly contrasting outcomes, they all point broadly in the same direction. According to their measurements, the quality of democracy in Europe began to deteriorate after the late 2000s. While there were concerns about democracy's health and de facto hollowing-out earlier than that, there was from this moment a downward inflection point in democratic quality. Overall, the decline has not been uniformly dramatic and trend lines have varied notably between European states. While the decline began to flatten out in most countries towards the end of the 2010s, EU member states as a whole have not recovered previous levels of democratic quality.

In the Economist Intelligence Unit's (EIU's) Democracy Index, democracy scores for Western and Eastern Europe stood at a lower level by 2020 than when the survey began in the mid-2000s. These scores declined notably in 2016, 2017 and 2018, before flattening out with unchanged scores for 2019. For 2019, the index ranked twelve out of twenty-seven EU member states (and the UK) as 'full democracies' and the rest as 'flawed democracies', with all Eastern European member states falling in this latter category. It ranked Romania lowest of all EU states and Sweden the highest. According to the EIU scoring, democratic quality has declined more in Europe than in any other region in the last decade (although its Europe category is wider than EU member states).[1]

The EIU's scores show some notable variations. Significant declines in Hungary, Poland and some other Eastern European states contrast with relatively constant scores in Germany and Scandinavia. In Poland and Hungary, government attacks on the media, courts, electoral bodies and civil society dragged scores sharply downwards into 2019. France fell from being a full to flawed democracy in 2017 before

---

[1] Economist Intelligence Unit, *Democracy Index 2018* (London: EIU, 2019).

recovering its score in 2019. Similarly, the scores for Portugal and Spain worsened in 2016 and 2017 before improving in 2019, while the 2018 and 2019 scores for Italy and Malta worsened significantly. Scores for the UK remained largely unchanged, with executive attempts to curtail parliamentary oversight of the Brexit process offset by improvements on other indicators, like local-level democracy.[2]

Successive Varieties of Democracy (or V-Dem) annual reports in the late 2010s showed similar trends. In V-Dem's ranking covering 2019, thirteen of the most democratic twenty states globally were EU states, with Denmark, Estonia and Sweden occupying the top three slots. Yet over the decade from 2009 to 2019, the democracy scores of twenty-three EU member states worsened, while only Denmark, Estonia, Luxembourg and Italy slightly improved. Most states' declines were modest, but the Czech Republic, Croatia, Poland, Bulgaria, Romania and Hungary suffered significant falls. The scale of Hungary's decline was the worst and Poland's the third worst in the world. Over this decade, the Czech Republic, Lithuania, Slovakia and Poland descended from being 'liberal democracies' to what V-Dem categorizes as more limited 'electoral democracies', while Bulgaria, Croatia, Malta and Romania remained in this latter category. V-Dem downgraded Hungary to what it defines as an 'electoral autocracy'. No EU government, whether from the left, centre or right, moved their country up a category over the 2010s decade. Figure 2.1 shows the slight decline in overall EU liberal democracy scores.[3]

The International Institute for Democracy and Electoral Assistance's (IDEA's) Global State of Democracy reports show similar trends, drawing on V-Dem but also on other data. From 2012 to 2017, the number of European countries suffering declines in democratic

[2] Economist Intelligence Unit, *Democracy Index 2017* (London: EIU, 2018); Economist Intelligence Unit, *Democracy Index 2018* (London: EIU, 2019); Economist Intelligence Unit, *Democracy Index 2019* (London: EIU, 2020).

[3] Varieties of Democracy, *Annual Democracy Report 2020* (Gothenburg: University of Gothenburg, 2020); Varieties of Democracy, *Annual Democracy Report 2019* (Gothenburg: University of Gothenburg, 2019); Varieties of Democracy, *Annual Democracy Report 2018* (Gothenburg: University of Gothenburg, 2018) .

Liberal Democracy Index

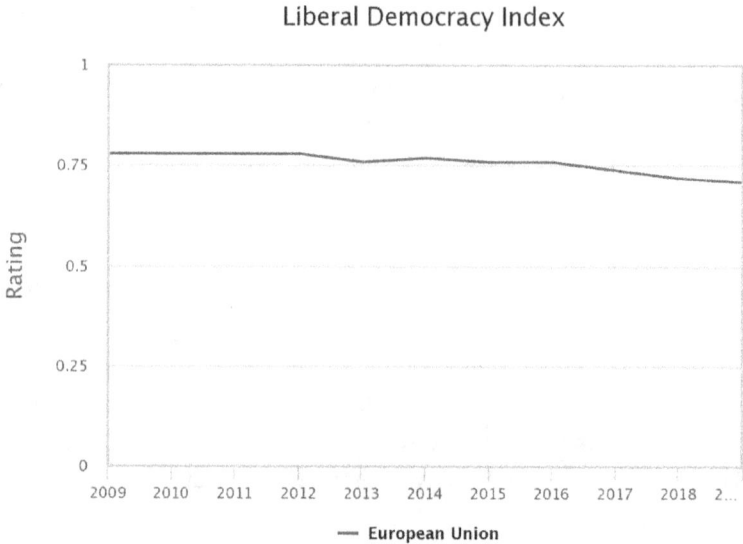

Figure 2.1 V-Dem Liberal Democracy Index

quality was more than double the number registering improvements.[4] International IDEA's 2019 Global State of Democracy index reported a flattening out of these declines, with further decreases in a select number of indicators – especially on civil liberties and checks against executives – offset by increases in others and with contrasting trends across different countries rather than any single dynamic.[5]

Freedom House scores for 2019 showed the fourteenth consecutive year of decline in the overall level of global democracy, with scores for Europe as a whole worsening in all categories of measurement in this time span – as shown in Figure 2.2. In the decade between 2009 and 2019, sixteen member states' scores worsened – with the biggest falls in Hungary, Poland, Malta, France and Spain – and only five states

---

[4] International IDEA, *Global State of Democracy 2018* (Stockholm: International IDEA, 2019).
[5] International IDEA, *Global State of Democracy 2019* (Stockholm: International IDEA, 2020).

Table 2.1 Freedom House aggregate scores 2009–19

2019, in order	Country	2009	2009–19 change	
100	Finland	100	No change	
100	Sweden	100	No change	
99	Netherlands	99	No change	
98	Luxembourg	100	Down 2	
97	Denmark	96	Up 1	
97	Ireland	97	No change	
96	Belgium	98	Down 2	
96	Portugal	97	Down 1	
94	Cyprus	94	No change	
94	Estonia	95	Down 1	
94	Germany	96	Down 2	
94	Slovenia	91	Up 3	
94	UK	96	Down 2	
93	Austria	97	Down 4	
92	Spain	97	Down 5	
91	Czech Republic	95	Down 4	
91	Lithuania	90	Up 1	
90	France	96	Down 6	
90	Malta	97	Down 7	
89	Italy	89	No change	
89	Latvia	86	Up 3	
88	Greece	86	Up 2	
88	Slovakia	90	Down 2	
85	Croatia	86	Down 1	
84	Poland	93	Down 9	
83	Romania	83	No change	
80	Bulgaria	82	Down 2	
70	Hungary	91	Down 21	(**16 down, 5 up**)

Freedom House Aggregate Scores

■ Change from 2009 to 2019

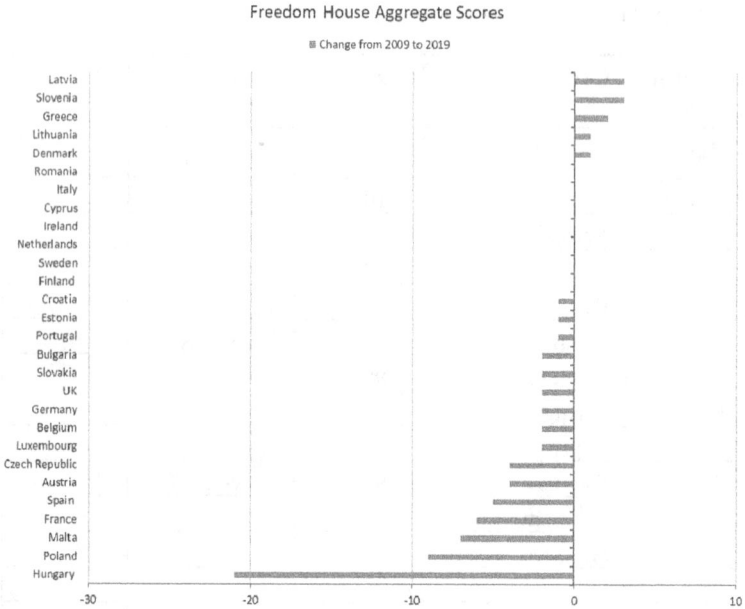

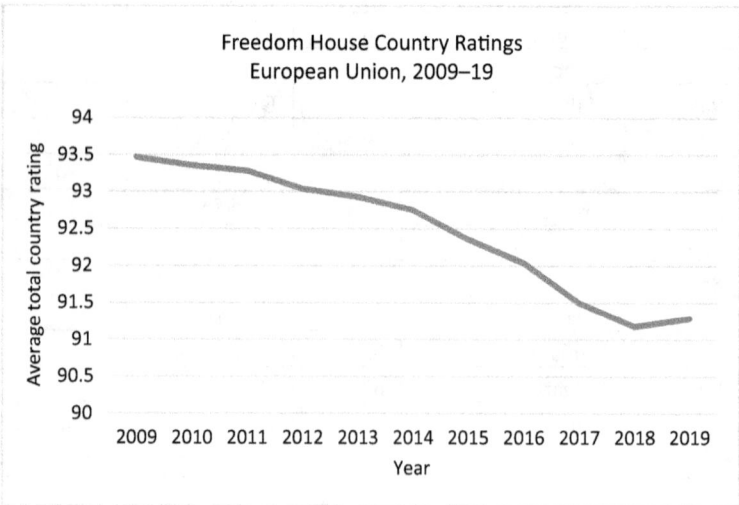

Figure 2.2 Freedom House country ratings European Union, 2009–19

improved (see Table 2.1). Freedom House's 2019 scoring was notable in downgrading Hungary to only 'partly free'.[6]

Freedom House's more specific 2020 report on Central and Eastern Europe suggested that Hungary was what it calls a 'hybrid regime' not a democracy of any kind, while Poland had fallen out of its 'consolidated democracy' category into a 'semi-consolidated democracy' grouping – with Bulgaria, Croatia and Romania also still stuck in this category. Of all Central and Eastern European EU states from 2010 to 2020, only Estonia registered an improved score while all others' democracy scores declined – in general modestly, except for the more dramatic falls in Hungary and Poland.[7] Table 2.2 summarizes these changes.

Indices need to be used with some caution as they miss many qualitative political trends and often reach contestable judgements. While assessment of their respective methodological nuances lies beyond this book's scope, taken together the indices are broadly in line with each other in painting a picture of moderate declines in democratic quality across Europe over the last decade and with significant variation between countries. In a small number of states, democratic erosion has been relatively dramatic: Hungary, Poland and some other Central and Eastern European states. In Western Europe, the fall in democracy scores has been gentler but real. All indices record a small number of modest democratic improvements in some EU member states, although they differ on exactly where these are to be found.

In 2020, government responses to the Covid-19 pandemic cast an uncertain shadow over this general state of EU democracy. To help manage the health emergency, European governments assumed extraordinary executive powers that curtailed democratic freedoms; administrations on both the left and right adopted such measures. Governments in thirteen states declared a state of emergency of some kind, while others acted through more specific legislation. Eleven EU states put off elections.[8] The Polish government sought self-servingly to keep the presidential election on schedule but was forced to push

[6] Freedom House, *Freedom in the World 2020: A Leaderless Struggle for Democracy*, p. 12.
[7] Freedom House, *Nations in Transit 2020* (Washington, DC: Freedom House, 2020)
[8] International Foundation for Electoral Systems, 'Elections postponed due to COVID-19', 25 August 2020.

Table 2.2   Freedom House democracy scores, Central Europe

Country	2010	2020
Bulgaria	4.96	4.54
Czech Republic	5.79	5.64
Estonia	6.04	6.07
Hungary	5.61	3.96
Latvia	5.82	5.79
Lithuania	5.75	5.64
Poland	5.68	4.93
Romania	4.54	4.43
Slovakia	5.32	5.29
Slovenia	6.07	5.93

Source: Freedom House, *Nations in Transit 2020*, p. 25.

the contest back until conditions allowed for a more competitive campaign. In Hungary, the government's new powers to rule by decree clearly deepened the country's autocratic dynamics, as Prime Minister Viktor Orbán used measures to force through measures unrelated to the pandemic, detain critical journalists and cut funds to opposition parties. His government rescinded the emergency measures in June 2020, although it retained many additional executive powers.

Elsewhere the impact was less dramatic, as Covid-19 measures were generally time-limited, kept within constitutional parameters, subject to review and supported by opposition parties. By July 2020, most governments had withdrawn the most draconian state-of-emergency restrictions on democratic rights, although nearly all retained at least some of their enhanced powers.[9] Parliaments kept operating in some form and several parliamentary committees opened enquiries into the crisis that kept governments under scrutiny.[10] Covid-19's second wave in

---

[9]   Democracy Reporting International, *Phase Two of Covid Responses across the EU: The Rule of Law Stress Test, Continued* (Berlin: DRI, 2020).

[10]   In the UK, one enquiry looked specifically at the human rights dimensions of government responses: UK Parliament, 'The Government's response to COVID-19: Human rights implications', UK Parliament Committees, 2020.

late 2020 caused European governments to reimpose some restrictions, although more selectively than in the first wave. At this point many parliaments and regional administrations insisted on having increased say over new emergency measures and in management of the crisis. Across the whole of 2020, Freedom House slightly downgraded democracy scores for Bulgaria, Greece, Hungary, Lithuania, Luxembourg, the Netherlands, Poland, Spain and the UK.[11] The EIU index recorded a very slight decrease in Europe's overall democracy score in 2020, with eighteen states in the region registering modest declines and France and Portugal slipping down a category to 'flawed democracies'.[12] V-Dem data did not change radically due to the pandemic, registering minor infringements of core democratic norms in all EU states other than Hungary and Poland, where problems were more serious.[13] Still, the pandemic presented challenges at a deeper level: the risk that its economic impacts might prevent parts of the population from effectively exercising their formal democratic rights, the question of how accountability should be exerted over the rising influence of health experts and scientists, the puzzle of Covid-19 apparently revealing both an excess and insufficiency of executive-state reach, and how the crisis seemed to reveal a more fragile communitarian ethos in Europe than in the Asian democracies that contained the virus more effectively.[14]

Civil liberties and the rule of law

Beyond the overarching rankings of democracy scores, it is instructive to break down trends affecting different arenas of democratic quality.

---

[11] Freedom House, *Freedom in the World 2020* (Washington, DC: Freedom House, 2021)
[12] Economist Intelligence Unit, *Democracy Index 2020*, (London: EUI, 2021) p. 51.
[13] See V-Dem's data under 'Pandemic Backsliding', at https://www.v-dem.net/en/our-work/research-projects/pandemic-backsliding/.
[14] These kinds of more indirect ramifications and issues are the subject of M. Maduro and P. Kahn (eds), *Democracy in Times of Pandemic* (Cambridge: Cambridge University Press, 2020).

A cluster of particular concerns across Europe has taken shape around the rule of law and the protection of civil liberties. We will see during the book that as these have had a notable impact on democracy trends, they have been prominent issues in different actors' democratic-rebuilding strategies.

Rule of Law. Some of the most worrying trends have occurred with regard to the rule of law. The European Commission's 2016 Justice Scoreboard found that in fourteen member states, less than half the population had confidence in the independence of the judiciary. This low-confidence group was made up of Central and Eastern European states along with Italy, Portugal and Spain. The Scoreboard's 2019 edition reported that in five member states more than 40 per cent of citizens thought there was 'interference or pressure from politicians' over the judiciary: Croatia, Bulgaria, Slovakia, Spain and Slovenia. The 2020 survey showed a slight increase in the share of populations perceiving their country's judiciary to be independent, but with under 50 per cent of people still judging this independence to be 'fairly good' or 'very good' in twelve states.[15]

More reassuringly, the World Justice Report Rule of Law Index for 2019 showed that in relative terms the rule of law remained relatively robust in Europe, with EU states occupying eight of the top ten spots. Lower scoring EU member states outside the global top twenty were Spain, Portugal, Slovenia, Poland, Italy, Romania, Greece, Croatia, Bulgaria and Hungary.[16] During the 2010s several governments promised to reduce political influence over judicial appointments but failed to follow through. In some countries, courts undertook more meaningful action against political corruption and governments lost office in several European states because of corruption, including in Spain and Romania. A Legatum Index reported that EU states' scores

---

[15] European Commission, *Justice Scoreboard 2016* (Brussels: Commission, 2016), pp. 44–5; European Commission, *Justice Scoreboard 2019* (Brussels: Commission, 2019), pp. 45–6; European Commission, *Justice Scoreboard 2020* (Brussels: Commission, 2020), p. 47.
[16] World Justice Report. *Rule of Law Index 2019* (Washington, DC, 2020), pp. 19–22.

on the less specific measure of government integrity improved slightly after 2017.[17]

The most drastic deteriorations in the rule of law have occurred in Hungary and Poland. The Hungarian government moved to exert almost complete political control over the judiciary by the mid-2010s. The Law and Justice (PiS in its Polish initials) government that took office in Poland in 2015 moved in incremental steps to remove independent-minded judges, replace these with its own supporters and set up a supine judicial body to challenge the Supreme Court. In both Hungary and Poland, government attacks on the rule of law have progressively widened into an assault on democracy more generally with laws in both countries being used to undermine independent electoral bodies, for example. In another serious case, the Romanian Social Democratic government increasingly tightened its control over legal bodies and sacked the head of the country's anti-corruption agency before being forced out of office prematurely in 2019.

In Spain, both sides of ongoing conflict over Catalonia's status have accused the other of breaching rule of law standards. International bodies criticized the government's detention and trial of Catalan separatist leaders.[18] Political leaders in Madrid insisted their hard line upheld the rule of law against Catalan secessionism. The conflict also shone a spotlight on the political basis of appointments to the country's high judicial council.[19] In Britain, from 2009 the new Supreme Court ensured a more rigorous separation of executive and judiciary, and at the end of the 2010s the court twice stopped the Conservative government from

---

[17] Legatum Institute, *Prosperity Index 2019* (London, 2019). See improvement in the 'Governance' pillar scores on p. 22 and for 'Government integrity' on p. 47.

[18] These bodies included the International Commission of Jurists and the United Nations Human Rights Council. The Spanish civic organization Judges for Democracy has detailed these concerns: www.juecesdemocracia.es. See also United Nations General Assembly, Human Rights Council Working Group on the Universal Periodic Review, Compilation of Information, A/HRC/WG.6/35/ESP/2, 18 November 2019 and I. Sanchez-Cuenca, 'A vueltas con España (y su democracia)', *Revista CTXT*, Numero 214, 27 March 2019. Also see reports by the civic group International Trial Watch, 'Spain: The right to protest in Spanish Courts', www.internationaltrialwatch.org.

[19] 'Spain's Sanchez in storm over judicial appointments bill', *EUobserver*, 19 October 2020.

circumventing parliament as it sought to expedite Brexit.[20] Still, when Prime Minister Boris Johnson promised a Constitution, Democracy and Rights Commission and opened an inquiry into judicial review in July 2020, many detected a desire to clip the court's wings. More specifically, the government's key Brexit legislation in autumn 2020 sat uneasily with several rule of law principles.

Restrictions on civil liberties. The worsening of liberal personal rights has been an especially notable aspect of Europe's democratic erosion. The EIU Index and V-Dem scores show their largest declines on indicators for freedom of expression and association and press freedom.[21] The 2019 Civicus monitoring report of global civil society ranked only half of EU member states as now having 'open' civil societies, with thirteen having 'narrowed' civic spaces (Austria, Bulgaria, Croatia, France, Greece, Italy, Latvia, Malta, Poland, Romania, Slovakia, Spain and the UK) and one 'obstructed' (Hungary). The EU's Fundamental Rights Agency published a report in 2018 that uncovered an extensive range of emerging restrictions on civil society organizations (CSOs) in virtually every member state. Nearly all EU governments have cut funds to domestic civil society bodies, while favouring more pliable CSOs.[22] In several member states, new laws have restricted NGOs from showing solidarity with migrants and refugees.[23]

The most brazen attacks on CSOs have been seen in Hungary and Poland. The PiS government created a new body to control civil society funding coming into the country. The Hungarian government advanced legislation severely restricting non-governmental organizations and moved to close down one of Hungary's most prestigious, independent universities, the Central European University. Beyond these most serious cases, restrictions have tightened in Western Europe too. The

---

[20] P. Dunleavy, A. Park and R. Taylor (eds), *UK Democratic Audit 2018* (London: LSE Press), p. 428.

[21] V-Dem, *Annual Democracy Report 2018* (Gothenburg: University of Gothenburg),p. 28.

[22] Fundamental Rights Agency, *Challenges Facing Civil Society Organizations Working on Human Rights in the EU* (Vienna: Fundamental Rights Agency, 2018).

[23] Civil Society Europe, *Report on Civic Space in Europe 2017* (Brussels, 2018).

Greek government raised complicated registration barriers for CSOs working on refugees. In the UK and Germany, state authorities and some legal rulings have constricted CSOs deemed to be engaged in 'political' campaigning. The French, Dutch and other governments have used tax and financial disclosure laws against CSOs and made their access to foreign funds more onerous.

After 2010, European states introduced new antiterror provisions that restricted civil liberties and weakened democratic control over security and intelligence services.[24] Repression and police assaults against protestors and arrests of activists have increased under these security laws, as has state digital surveillance of many civic groups. French CSOs and social movements in particular were caught in the net of antiterrorism laws; after terror attacks in November 2020, the French government moved to close or curtail the operations of many CSOs working with Muslim communities.[25] In the wake of several terror attacks, the British government gave security forces a number of human-rights exemptions. Spain's 2015 'citizen security law', colloquially labelled the *ley mordaza* or gag law, included highly restrictive measures against the freedom of expression, while a 2020 decree narrowed online freedom of information. Criticism mounted as high-profile artists were detained under these laws, and in early 2021 the Spanish government introduced proposals to relax some of the restrictions.[26]

It was in the area of civil liberties that governments' Covid-19 measures bit hardest. The pandemic contributed to a surge in restrictions against freedom of assembly and association. Many governments extended these beyond conditions strictly related to Covid-19 and used disproportionately heavy enforcement tactics. Governments of the left, centre and right maintained self-serving bans on political protests even as other areas of life reopened; exceptions were made on a somewhat

---

[24] Amnesty International, *Dangerously Disproportionate: The Ever-Expanding National Security State in Europe* (London: Amnesty International, 2017).

[25] O. Roy, 'French battle against Islamist "separatism" is at odds with commitment to liberty', *Financial Times*, 9 November 2020.

[26] Article 19, 'Spain: The Digital Royal Decree may give government powers to censor and takedown online content', 11 February 2020.

sporadic and ad hoc basis. By 2021, there were legislative proposals at various stages of preparation or review in Denmark, Greece, Italy, France, Poland, Spain and the UK aimed at placing longer-term limits on protests. Some governments infringed freedom of information rules in an attempt to control the pandemic story.[27]

Populism and the far-right

Much of the analytical focus in recent years has been on far-right populists' menace to European democracy.[28] What analysts classify as 'populist' parties have risen to account for around a fifth of the vote in European countries and have had some involvement in government in around half of EU states.[29] In Austria, the far-right Freedom Party entered a coalition with the Conservative People's Party in December 2017. In Italy, the Lega party formed a government with the Five Star Movement in 2018. In both cases, the parties pushed measures against migrants' rights and critical media outlets. Estonia's elections in March 2019 saw far-right party EKRE jump from 8 to 18 per cent of the vote and enter into coalition government. The rise of these parties has been underpinned by a growth in far-right pan-European social movements like Les Identitaires.[30] Table 2.3 shows vote shares that right-wing populist parties obtained in their respective countries' most recent elections.

[27]   G. Negri, 'Civic space under lockdown', in *European Civic Space Watch 2020: Stories from the Lockdown* (Brussels: European Civic Forum,2020), p. 27 and pp. 32–4; A. Narsee, 'Europe's right to protest under threat', Carnegie Europe, 27 January 2021; Civil Liberties Union for Europe and Greenpeace, *Locking Down Critical Voices* (The Hague: Civil Liberties Union for Europe, 2020).

[28]   J. Kyle and Y. Mounk, *The Populist Harm to Democracy: An Empirical Assessment* (London: Institute for Global Change, 2018); M. Eiermann, Y. Mounk and L. Gultchin, *European Populism: Trends, Threats and Future Prospects* (London: Institute for Global Change, 2017).

[29]   TIMBRO, *Authoritarian Populism Index* (Stockholm: TIMBRO, 2019) Data is online at https://populismindex.com/about/.

[30]   Counter Extremism Project, *Europe Ethno-Nationalist and White Supremacy Groups* (London/Berlin: CEP, 2019).

Some trends suggest the populist wave might have abated somewhat even if it has not definitively crested. Austrian Prime Minister Sebastian Kurz ended his power-sharing pact with the Freedom Party in May 2019; the party then fell by 10 per cent in the ensuing elections. Alternative for Germany (AfD) has slipped back from its 2018 high point of reaching 20 per cent and second place in opinion polls, supplanted by the Greens as Germany's fast-rising party. In 2019 elections, the Danish People's Party slumped, Golden Dawn lost all its seats in the Greek parliament, the PiS lost control of the Polish senate, ruling-party Fidesz lost control of several cities in Hungary, including the mayoralty of Budapest, and in Slovakia liberal anti-corruption campaigner Zuzanna Čaputová defeated populists on the right and left to become president. A corruption scandal in early 2021 cost EKRE its place in the Estonian government. The Covid-19 crisis undercut some populist parties like the AfD, although others retained their levels of support. The Lega lost support but found its way back into government as part of the national-unity administration that formed under Mario Draghi in February 2021, while the even more hard-line Brothers of Italy rose fast.

Debate has persisted over many years about how populism should be both defined and explained. Some writers have defined populism as intrinsically anti-democratic or suggest that the term should be applied only to those parties that fundamentally challenge core democratic norms.[31] One difficulty is that many commentators have come to use the term 'populism' very loosely as a label for positions that challenge any part of a liberal consensus. Other writers suggest that populism has a more ambivalent relationship to democracy; it is in many ways a threat to existing democratic practice but also in some cases a possible corrective of its limitations.[32] Its surge can be linked to the inverse

---

[31] J. W. Mueller, *What is Populism?* (Pennsylvania: University of Pennsylvania Press, 2016); T. Pappas, 'Populists in power', *Journal of Democracy*, 30/2 (2019), 70–84.

[32] C. Mudde and C. Kaltwasser 'Studying populism in comparative perspective: Reflections on the contemporary and future research agenda', *Comparative Political Studies*, 51/13 (2018), 1667–93.

Table 2.3 Right-wing populist party vote shares, most recent elections

Country	Party	Vote share
Hungary	Fidesz	49% in 2018
Poland	PiS	44% in 2019
Switzerland	SVP	29% in 2015
Slovenia	SDS	25% in 2018
Hungary	Jobbik	19% in 2018
Estonia	EKRE	18% in 2018
Sweden	Sw. Democrats	18% in 2018
Finland	Finns (PS)	17% in 2019
Italy	Lega	17% in 2018
Spain	Vox	16% in 2019
Austria	FPÖ	16% in 2019
Norway	FrP	15% in 2017
Latvia	KPV	14% in 2018
France	Front National	13% in 2017
Germany	AfD	13% in 2018
Belgium	VB	12% in 2019
The Netherlands	PVV	11% in 2021
Lithuania	NA	11% in 2018
Denmark	DPP	9% in 2019
Romania	Unity of Romanians	9% in 2020

problem of technocratic politics depriving citizens of meaningful political choice; one significant example of this is seen in the EU's democratic deficit that will be picked up later in the book. The threat to democracy comes more from the rise of the far-right than populism as such; leftist populism has had quite different implications for liberal democracy, as a number of examples will show in subsequent chapters.

In practice, the European parties routinely defined as populist have exhibited a range of positions on democracy; in many cases, their identities have also fluctuated back and forth over time. [33] Extreme right parties are clearly anti-democratic. Others, radical but not extreme, claim to be democratic but challenge democracy's liberal components: the constitutional protection of personal and minority rights and often the separation of powers.[34] While not all this illiberalism tends to outright authoritarianism, some populists challenge liberal rights to such an extent that their formal commitment to democracy becomes highly questionable. Milder populist parties espouse illiberal positions on certain policies like immigration without representing a wholesale threat to the systemic, institutional pillars of liberal democracy. Their nativism starts to dilute democracy if it denies migrants and other groups equal rights. The Lega and some parts of the AfD appear to have crossed this line while other populist parties have not.[35]

Value shifts

Numerous surveys in recent years have shown rising support for what pollsters refer to as 'authoritarian values' in many parts of Europe.

---

[33] M. Zulianello, 'Varieties of populist parties and party systems in Europe: From state-of-the-art to the application of a novel classification scheme to 66 parties in 33 countries', *Government and Opposition*, 55/2 (2020), 327–47; D. Albertazzi and S. Mueller, 'Populism and liberal democracy: Populists in government in Austria, Italy, Poland and Switzerland', *Government and Opposition*, 48/3 (2013), 343–71; P. Taggart and C. Kaltwasser, 'Dealing with populists in government: Some comparative conclusions', *Democratization*, 23/2 (2016), 1–21; European Economic and Social Committee, *Societies Outside Metropolises: The Role of Civil Society Organisations in Facing Populism* (Brussels: EESC, 2018); L. Dijkstra, H. Poleman and A. Rodriguez-Pose, *The Geography of EU Discontent* (Brussels: European Commission, 2018).

[34] One amongst many formulations of this distinction between the extreme and radical far-right is C. Mudde, *The Far-Right Today* (Cambridge: Polity Press, 2019). Making a similar point from a different perspective, R. Eatwell and M. Goodwin, *National Populism: The Revolt against Liberal Democracy* (London: Pelican, 2018).

[35] M. Meyer-Rsende, 'Is German democracy back to normal?', Carnegie Europe, 5 June 2019; A. Martinelli, 'Populism and nationalism: The (peculiar) case of Italy', in A. Martinelli (ed.), *When Populism Meets Nationalism: Reflections on Populist Parties in Power* (Milan: ISPI, 2018).

It suffices to mention just a selection of these to illustrate the trend. A World Values Survey in 2016 showed an increase in the number of citizens saying they would favour authoritarian government.[36] An October 2016 YouGov poll found that around half the population across twelve EU states now subscribe to a set of illiberal principles that includes opposition to migration, dislike of human rights laws and support for more nationalist identities.[37] A 2018 Pew survey confirmed that these trends were particularly marked in Eastern Europe over religion, minorities and social issues.[38]

A December 2018 report by the University of Leipzig presented extensive polling showing that 42 per cent of Germans professed authoritarian views.[39] Another 2019 survey of opinion in Germany showed a clear majority believed that democracy was not working and a rising number of citizens were angry and detached from politics, with growing polarization threatening the country's famed consensus-style politics.[40] A University of Cambridge 2020 report suggested that satisfaction with democracy's performance had reached record lows in most, although not all, European countries.[41] Another survey in 2020 found that 'consistent' support for democratic principles reached 50 per cent in only three of thirteen member states polled – Austria, Denmark and Germany.[42]

Reflecting these trends, many writers frame Europe's democratic erosion as one dimension of a broader crumbling of liberal values. They insist that citizens are recoiling from the liberal agenda of progressive individualism in search of a more rooted sense of community and group

[36] R. Foa and Y. Mounck, 'The signs of deconsolidation', *Journal of Democracy*, 28/1 (2017), 5–16.

[37] Five findings from YouGov's mega survey, 28 November 2016.

[38] For example, Pew Research Center, 'Eastern and Western Europeans differ on importance of religion, views of minorities, and key social issues', October 2018.

[39] 'Germans feel like strangers in own land', *The Times*, 8 November 2018.

[40] L. Krause and J. Gagne, *Fault Lines: Germany's Invisible Divides* (Berlin: More in Common, 2019).

[41] R. Foa, A. Klassen, M. Slade, A. Rand and R. Williams, *The Global Satisfaction with Democracy Report 2020* (Cambridge: Centre for the Future of Democracy, 2020).

[42] S. Gaston, 'The divided continent: Understanding Europe's social landscape in 2020 and beyond', European Policy Centre Working Paper, 2020, p. 7.

attachment, bringing apparently latent authoritarian value-sets to the surface.[43] Even some of the most respected liberal writers sense that people seem to place increasing emphasis on local networks and communities rather than values-universalism.[44] After the fall of the Berlin Wall in 1989, in Central and Eastern Europe the recovery of democracy, of sovereignty and of national identity went hand in hand with each other, whereas today there is more tension between them.[45] Even some mainstream liberal-democratic parties in Central and Eastern Europe have increasingly taken on board underlying identities supportive of ethnically based exclusion.[46] Many books and articles assume that European democracy has weakened precisely because it has failed to root itself in a healthy sense of national identity and traditional forms of belonging.[47]

Nevertheless, polling evidence has been varied and disputes have ensued in recent years between experts with differing interpretations of the data.[48] Some extensive academic studies question the notion that there is any decisive trend towards lower levels of satisfaction with democracy.[49] A November 2018 special edition of Eurobarometer

---

[43] I. Butler, *Countering Populist Authoritarians* (Brussels: Civil Liberties Union for Europe, 2018); P. Norris and R. Inglehart, *Cultural Backlash: Trump, Brexit, and the Rise of Authoritarian Populism* (Cambridge: Cambridge University Press, 2018); D. Goodhart, *The Road to Somewhere* (London: Penguin, 2017).

[44] M. Ignatieff, *The Ordinary Virtues: Moral Order in a Divided World* (Cambridge, MA: Harvard University Press, 2017); T. Garton Ash, 'Liberal Europe isn't dead yet. But its defenders face a long, hard struggle', *The Guardian*, 9 July 2018.

[45] J. Rupnik, 'The crisis of liberalism', *Journal of Democracy*, 29/3 (2018), 24–38.

[46] J. Dawson and S. Hanley, 'Foreground liberalism, background nationalism: A discursive institutionalist account of EU leverage and democratic backsliding in East Central Europe', *Journal of Common Market Studies*, 57/4 (2019), 710–28.

[47] 'A manifesto for renewing liberalism', *The Economist*, 13 September 2018; A. Pabst, *The Demons of Liberal Democracy* (Cambridge: Polity); I. Krastev, 'Eastern Europe is a lessons to liberals: Don't be anti-nationalist', *The Guardian*, 11 July 2018; G. Nodia, 'The end of the postnational illusion', *Journal of Democracy*, 28/2 (2017), 5–19; M. Helbing, 'Nationalism and democracy: Competing or complementary logics?', *Living Reviews in Democracy*, 4 (2013).

[48] See submissions to 'Journal of Democracy Online Exchange on Democratic Deconsolidation', April 2017, taking issue with the cited Foa and Mounck article for its methodology and selective use of data, at https://www.journalofdemocracy.org/online-exchange-democratic-deconsolidation/.

[49] C. van Ham, J. Thomassen, K. Aarts and R. Andeweg, *Myth and Reality of the Legitimacy Crisis: Explaining Trends and Cross-National Differences in Established Democracies* (Oxford: Oxford University Press, 2017).

on democracy found that around 65 per cent of the EU population was generally satisfied with the functioning of democracy in Europe, with lower ratings limited to more specific issues such as anti-corruption efforts and political-party performances. Interestingly, this study suggested that younger respondents were more satisfied with democracy than older voters, especially in respect of new opportunities for civic participation.[50]

Other polls have also revealed different nuances. A 2017 Pew survey found that when citizens express deep dissatisfaction with democracy, it is most often partisan rather than deeply structural – that is, people are happier with democracy when their preferred party is in power. The study reported that 70 per cent of EU citizens wanted more direct democracy.[51] An updated Pew survey in late 2019 confirmed high levels of support for democratic values, with only slightly lower scores in Eastern than Western Europe.[52] The 2019 Dalia Democracy Perceptions survey also reported that commanding majorities in all member states thought democracy was important.[53] A Pew survey in 2020 found support was especially high for judicial independence and freedom of speech; it showed wide variation in terms of satisfaction with democracy, with a range from three-quarters being satisfied (Sweden) to three-quarters being dissatisfied (Greece).[54]

Surveys do not always provide clear-cut conclusions. One poll found that strong majorities want *both* core liberal democratic and more

[50] Special Eurobarometer 477, 'Democracy and elections', November 2018, p. 72 and p. 84.
[51] R. Wike, K. Simmons, B. Stokes and J. Fetterolf, 'Globally, broad support for representative and direct democracy', Pew Research Center, 16 October 2017, pp. 22–4.
[52] R. Wike, J. Poushter, L. Silver, K. Devlin, J. Fetterolf, A. Castillo and C. Huang, 'European public opinion three decades after the fall of communism', Pew Research Center, 15 October 2019, p. 34.
[53] 2019 Dalia Democracy Perception survey.
[54] R. Wike and S. Schumacher, 'Democratic rights popular globally but commitment to them not always strong', Pew Research Center, 27 February 2020, pp. 6–8, p. 19 and pp. 23–4.

traditional, often illiberal values.[55] Another found that, despite their support for some of Europe's most prominent populist parties, a firm majority of citizens in the Central and Eastern European member states want fully independent media and civil society organizations and that always-present illiberal outlooks have not necessarily expanded that dramatically in this region.[56] In Britain, a 2019 Hansard Society survey found that 54 per cent of respondents thought the UK needed a strong leader willing to break the rules, but also that a majority wanted to take powers away from government.[57] Surveys have found the relationship between Brexit and value trends to be complex: while support for Brexit has been higher among those more supportive of 'authoritarian values', more generally there has been a steady increase in support for liberal, secular values and different forms of rights-equality among the British population.[58]

Polling questions tend to define 'illiberal' or 'authoritarian values' in social and psychological rather than political terms; those that hold these values do not comprehensively vote for undemocratic political options. Some studies have found an inverse correlation: as EU citizens have become more critical towards how their democracies are working in practice, they have become more strongly attached normatively to the need for better quality democracy.[59] While many analysts and journalists ritually cite these polls as a kind of shorthand confirmation of democracy's crisis, that is not strictly or necessarily what they

---

[55] Results of a project by Open Society European Policy Institute and DPart, summarized in J. Eichhorn et al., *How European Publics and Policy Actors Values an Open Society* (Brussels: Open Society Foundations, 2019).

[56] Globsec Trends 2019, *Central and Eastern Europe 30 Years after the Fall of the Iron Curtain* (Bratislava: Globsec, 2019), pp. 35–7.

[57] Hansard Society, *Audit of Political Engagement: 2019 Report* (London: Hansard, 2019).

[58] J. Curtice, E. Clery, J. Perry, M. Phillips and N. Rahim (eds), *British Social Attitudes Survey 36, 2019 edition*, (London: National Centre for Social Research, 2019), p. 189.

[59] H. Kriesi, 'The implications of the euro crisis for democracy', *Journal of European Public Policy*, 25/1 (2018), 59–82.

measure. Although many polls reveal rising hostility to certain liberal values or particular liberal policies, this does not always denote a loss of support for democracy.

Party systems and voting

One of the most familiar signs of democracy's malaise comes from the figures showing declining trust in political parties and parliaments and falling turn-out for elections. Trends on these questions are not new but have intensified in the last several years in many European countries. Once again, however, the recent data do not point uniformly in a negative direction and can be interpreted in more nuanced ways.

While political scientists have stressed political parties' weakening societal roots for many years,[60] this trend appears to have accelerated in recent years. European citizens' dislike of political parties intensified after 2010, according to large-scale surveys.[61] Eurobarometer surveys show that levels of trust in parties and national parliaments have fallen steadily in the last decade.[62] Yet one survey-based research project found that while young people are less likely than older citizens to vote or join a political party, they have recently become much more likely to become involved in 'non-institutional political participation'.[63]

In parallel with this, election turnout has declined in many EU states, deepening a long-term trend evident in most cases since the 1980s. Turnout in the 2017 French legislative elections was a historical low. In Central and Eastern Europe, voter turnout declined by over 20 per cent between the first free elections at the end of the 1980s and

---

[60] P. Mair, *Ruling the Void: The Hollowing of Western Democracy* (London: Verso Books, 2013).

[61] A. Mungiu-Pippidi et al., 'Public integrity and trust in Europe', European Research Centre for Anti-Corruption and State-Building, Hertie School of Governance, 2015.

[62] For example, European Commission, *Standard Eurobarometer 85* (Brussels: Commission, 2016), p. 14.

[63] European Alternatives, 'Rejuvenating Europe's Democracy', Report of the Euryka project, 2020, p. 19.

2017.[64] Portugal's election in October 2019 saw the lowest turnout since democratic transition in 1974. The trend is not uniform, however. The UK's June 2017 general election saw Britain's highest electoral turnout in twenty years. The turnout for Sweden's September 2018 election was 87 per cent, the highest in three decades. Turnout in the Spanish elections in April 2019 was 75 per cent, the third highest ever. European Parliament (EP) elections in 2019 attracted their highest turnout since the early 1970s.

As voters have drifted away from mainstream parties, concerns have grown over polarization. Polarization is a difficult concept: sharp differences are not intrinsically harmful to democracy and adversarial contestation is in some measure a positive catalyst to necessary reform. Still, some aspects of polarization have begun to undermine the give and take necessary for democratic governance to function, and many European party systems have generated problems of governability. Indeed, European democracies increasingly compare badly on governability with other regions.[65] Declines in the World Bank's measure of government effectiveness were recorded over the 2010s in Austria, Belgium, Denmark, France, Germany, Greece, Hungary, Ireland, Italy, Luxembourg, Netherlands, Spain, Sweden and the UK.[66]

The average amount of time needed to form governments in Europe has increased in the last decade.[67] Several countries have suffered serious problems of coalition formation in recent years – Austria, Belgium, Germany, the Netherlands, Spain, Sweden – leaving them politically adrift for long periods of time. Spain was without a government for 314 days in 2015 and 2016, and elections had to be repeated; two further elections followed in 2019 when another impasse ensued. Finland and Sweden both struggled to form governments in

---

[64] A. Solijonov, *Voter Turnout Trends Around the World* (Stockholm: International IDEA, 2016).

[65] R. Doorenspleet, *Rethinking the Value of Democracy* (London: Routledge, 2018).

[66] The World Bank: Govdata 360.

[67] C. De Vries and S. Hobalt, *Political Entrepreneurs: The Rise of Challenger Parties in Europe* (Princeton, NJ: Princeton University Press, 2020).

2018 and 2019. Belgium spent more than a year without a government in the early 2010s and then nearly two years in a similar impasse from early 2019 to October 2020.

Once again, not all trends point in the same direction. Portugal is a counter example where previously adversarial leftist parties formed a rather unorthodox governing arrangement in 2015; this so-called 'contraption' not only improved governability of the party system but also ensured party debates within the parliament became more meaningful to decision-making.[68] In 2019 and 2020 parties in Austria, Italy and Spain did eventually form coalitions in which fierce adversaries were readier than before to set aside differences in the name of governability. While the unedifying impasse over Brexit put unprecedented strains on British democracy, the UK election in December 2019 seemed to restore a degree of governability. As a rancorous divide over Brexit has at least partially displaced traditional party cleavages, the impact of this shift on the UK's democratic quality remains unclear.

Digital vulnerabilities

Another layer of democratic vulnerability has emerged from the digital sphere. Fears have risen about anti-democratic views spreading on social media, and figures suggest that Europe has been hit especially hard by this trend. In a majority of EU member states, the amount of domestically generated online hate speech and extremist content sits above the global mean.[69] Several EU governments have been amongst the heaviest users of digital surveillance against their own citizens, including France, Italy and Spain.[70] Social media have been especially influential in the far-right's rise in Europe, with radical parties'

---

[68] A. Costa Pinto and C. Pequito Teixeira, *Political Institutions and Democracy in Portugal: Assessing the Impact of the Eurocrisis* (London: Palgrave Macmillan, 2018).

[69] S. Feldstein, *How to Tackle Europe's Digital Democracy Challenges* (Brussels: Carnegie Europe, 2020).

[70] S. Feldstein, *The Global Expansion of AI Surveillance* (Washington, DC: Carnegie Endowment for International Peace, 2019).

presence online exceeding their vote shares.[71] Some tech analysts refute such critical assumptions and offer data showing that social media has actually increased individuals' exposure to different points of view.[72] Yet a growing litany of concern about the harmful impact on democracy of social media has become a staple part of European political debate.

Covid-19 intensified many digital distortions and deepened privacy concerns as European governments rolled out tracing apps to help contain the pandemic. Europe saw the most pronounced increases across regions in disinformation flows linked to Covid-19.[73] Moreover, worries have sharpened over the power wielded by technology companies over EU politics. Some writers argue that a whole new economic system has taken shape in which personal data is used for profit in a way that emasculates the self-determining individual agency upon which democracy depends – and insist that data-driven techno-consumerism is the prime cause of Europe's recent democratic regression.[74] The European Commission has warned of the mounting political pathologies that flow from this 'attention economy'.[75]

More directly, European states have faced threats from so-called influence operations. By the late 2010s, over three-quarters of organizations in the EU had suffered cyberattacks; nearly half of such attacks globally have been aimed at EU member states.[76] Most attacks have come from Russia and China, although from thirty other countries

---

[71] B. Ganesh and C. Froio, 'A "Europe des Nations": Far right imaginative geographies and the politicization of cultural crisis on Twitter in Western Europe', *Journal of European Integration*, published online 19 August 2020; Avaaz *Far Right Networks of Deception* (London: Avaaz, 2019).

[72] G. Blank and E. Dubois, 'The myth of the echo chamber', Oxford Internet Institute, 9 March 2018.

[73] 'In Europe, COVID-19 misinformation runs rife on Facebook', *Politico*, 5 May 2020.

[74] S. Zuboff, *The Age of Surveillance Capitalism* (London: Profile Books, 2019); M. Moore *Democracy Hacked* (London: Oneworld, 2018); E. Morozov, 'Techno-populism', *The Guardian*, 27 November 2018. See also J. Anderson and L. Rainie, 'Many tech experts say digital disruption will hurt democracy', Pew Research Centre, 21 February 2020.

[75] European Commission, 'Technology and democracy: Understanding the influence of online technologies on political behaviour and decision-making', Joint Research Centre, 2020.

[76] European Court of Auditors, 'Challenges to effective EU cybersecurity policy', ECA briefing paper, 2019.

too.[77] These attacks have increasingly targeted elections, very directly threatening the integrity of European democratic processes. By 2019, seventeen EU states had experienced digital attacks against elections. Russian operations in UK elections and the 2016 Brexit referendum engendered especially high-level political tensions.[78] The strategic misuse of embryonic artificial intelligence has raised the prospect of further intimidation against democratic institutions.[79] While European elections still show a high degree of democratic integrity, digital vulnerabilities represent additional problems to those that show up in democracy indices.

Assessment: Multiple democratic trends

The multiple measurements, trends and surveys summarized above provide a general idea of the state of play in European democracy. The data offered here is far from being exhaustive; debates related to the Eurozone economic crisis and EU-level political developments are addressed later in the book. There are contrasting views on what good quality democracy should look like and how to measure this. All indicators and surveys carry their own inbuilt biases and assumptions on this question and can be read in different ways depending on one's understanding of what democratic quality rightfully requires. Indeed, a theme running through the chapters that follow is that democratic rebuilding needs to be advanced in ways that call for broader assessments of democratic quality than those contained in many indices and surveys. Still, the information above broadly illustrates the

---

[77] S. Shackelford, 'The battle against disinformation is global', *The Conversation*, 20 March 2020.

[78] Flowing from assessments presented in a high-profile parliamentary report in mid-2020: UK Parliament Intelligence and Security Committee, *Russia* (London: House of Commons, 2020).

[79] European Political Strategy Centre, 'Rethinking strategic autonomy for the digital age', European Commission, EPSC Strategic Note, 2019; Centre for European Policy Studies, 'Rethinking the EU's cyber defence capabilities, Report of CEPS Task Force, 2018.

standard range of indicators routinely cited in recent years to reflect Europe's democracy problems.

These overarching trends in European democracy show many negative trends and reasons for concern. Most EU states have suffered declines in democratic quality in the last decade, a small number of them to a dramatic extent. While European countries have remained highly placed in global democracy indices, Europe has also become one of the key global sites of democratic erosion. Nevertheless, democratic declines in most countries have been relatively contained, and democratic advances have not been entirely absent from the picture. There has been variation across EU states, rather than a wholesale or dramatic collapse of democracy. While the populist wave has led to an assault on some liberal rights, democracy in Europe is still largely liberal democracy.

The challenges to European democracy have come from a range of sources and actors – governments, parties, citizens' value-shifts and external bodies – an eclecticism that underpins and feeds into this book's multi-actor framework. One dynamic has been a pattern of gradual democratic erosion through executive aggrandisement.[80] Such autocratic dynamics have become more clandestine and often better able to proceed because they are surreptitious.[81] Government-led restrictions have become an even more pressing concern in the wake of the Covid-19 pandemic. Another dynamic has come from opposition parties adopting illiberal agendas, which has fed into problems of governability within many European democracies. Another, conceptually distinct and underlying concern has come from broader public doubts over democratic norms and the rise of apparently less liberal identities.[82]

---

[80] N. Bermeo, 'On democratic backsliding', *Journal of Democracy*, 27/1 (2016), 5–19.
[81] A. Luhrman and S. Lindberg, 'A third wave of autocratization is here: What is new about it?', *Democratization*, 26/7 (2019), 1095–113.
[82] T. Daly, 'Democratic decay: Conceptualising an emerging research field', *Hague Journal on the Rule of Law*, 11 (2019), 9–36.

The relentless focus on populism in recent years has arguably taken attention away from the wider span of democratic problems. Populism has been a major challenge, but so have the somewhat illiberal actions of mainstream governments and parties. Serious rule of law and civic-space problems predated the late-2010s populist surge.[83] Populist parties have not become the dominant political force in a general sense across Europe, even as they have wielded undoubted influence over identity debates.[84] Many accounts tend to the dramatic assumption that populism has already battered down the main pillars of European democracy; others have been perhaps too sanguine in believing that the populist surge has already peaked. While some populist parties undoubtedly threaten democratic quality, a subtler question is whether the grievances that populists express can be made compatible with reworked forms of democracy.[85] On this most vital question, European trends have been inconclusive.

The detailed data casts doubt on one argument that has become widespread in recent years, namely that Europe is in the throes of a struggle between democratic illiberalism and undemocratic liberalism. This follows from the general assumption that populists seek majoritarian democracy without liberal rights protection, while governments and EU institutions have advanced liberal social and economic policies without much democratic consent or legitimacy.[86] In truth, the picture has been more complex and does not reveal a sharp or mutually exclusive binary between democracy and liberalism

---

[83] N. Lacey, 'Populism and the Rule of Law?', LSE International Inequalities Institute working paper 28 (2019), p. 19.

[84] K. Simmons, L. Silver, C. Johnson and R. Wike, 'In Western Europe, populist parties tap anti-establishment frustration but have little appeal across ideological divides', Pew Research Centre, 12 July 2018.

[85] F. Fukuyama, *Identity: The Demand for Dignity and the Politics of Resentment* (London: Macmillan, 2018); P. Deneen, *Why Liberalism Failed* (London: Yale University Press, 2018).

[86] C. Mudde and C. Rovira Kaltwasser, *Populism: A Very Short Introduction* (New York: Oxford University Press, 2017). On the concept of 'neo-illiberal democracy', see A. Tucker, *Democracy Against Liberalism* (Cambridge: Polity Press, 2020).

in Europe. The governments that have done most to challenge liberal rights are also those that have gone furthest in undermining democracy. Rather than Europe housing two separate camps of the non-democratic liberals and the non-liberal democrats, the reality has been a messier one of challenges arising simultaneously to some areas of liberal rights and some areas of democratic quality.

The overall picture painted by the aggregate information included in this chapter is a nuanced one. In many countries, democratic institutions appear to be stagnating, gradually losing their appeal and vitality, holding on but with less enthusiastic buy-in from citizens. European democracy weathered the Eurozone crisis and other dramatic challenges of the 2010s, and for the moment at least has belied the many dramatic prognoses of collapse. While Covid-19 has placed additional stresses on democracy, it has not (yet) left a major dent in democratic quality and has in some ways awoken stronger critical scrutiny of government actions. One noted expert sees the danger to lie in democracy's 'drift into cranky obsolescence'.[87] The many reasons to be worried are fairly self-evident; yet in the rush to highlight emerging risks to democracy, analysts have perhaps underplayed the factors pointing to democracy's resilience.[88]

This chapter has offered a summary of the main themes or substantive arenas across which European democracy has been challenged and, conversely, the vectors on which it has shown such resilience. Flowing out of these main themes, the following chapters look at each of the actors that have developed strategies of democratic resistance and renewal, starting from citizens, through CSOs, national governments, political parties, digital organizations and the EU. The trends and measurements summarized above set an explanatory backdrop for the book's main argument. Actors' different strategies of resistance and renewal have gathered significant momentum and help

---

[87] D. Runciman, *How Democracy Ends* (London: Profile, 2019), p. 71 and p. 80.
[88] J. Moller, 'Reslient democracies', *American Interest*, November 2018.

explain why the fall in democratic quality has not been more dramatic across Europe. Yet the empirical measurements also suggest the need for more ambitious democratic rebuilding. With threats coming from sources within and beyond governments and from multiple parts of the political sphere, the trends powerfully reinforce the case for more contentious and probing forms of citizen-oriented politics.

3

Citizen responses: The people mobilize

A first strand of democratic renovation in Europe has emerged bottom-up from citizens. Citizens have increasingly mobilized where democracy is at risk, while also engaging in civic programmes to rethink the way democracy works. These bottom-up dynamics entail both democratic resistance and renewal. In many places, civil society was initially slow to react to the threat of democratic erosion in the early 2010s. Yet, citizens have gradually begun to react and fashion different kinds of bottom-up strategies to rebuild democracy. While the Covid-19 pandemic created difficulties for citizen mobilization, it has also further galvanized many types of civic initiatives. A European civic awakening has continued to gather momentum.

There are two dynamics in this awakening. One is the spread of mass protests, the other is a growth in the more structured efforts of civil society organizations (CSOs). The gathering intensity of protests is the most disruptive and tumultuous facet of Europe's incipient democratic regeneration. Alongside protests, a wide range of organized civil society initiatives has formed aimed specifically at protecting and advancing democratic values. While these trends are significant, shortcomings and downsides have also surfaced to such civic activism. The chapter argues that these bottom-up civic politics based around open-ended contestation represent one of the most vital areas of reform and still need to be strengthened as an essential, constructive strand of European democratic resistance and renewal.

Civilian Anti-Government Protests in Europe

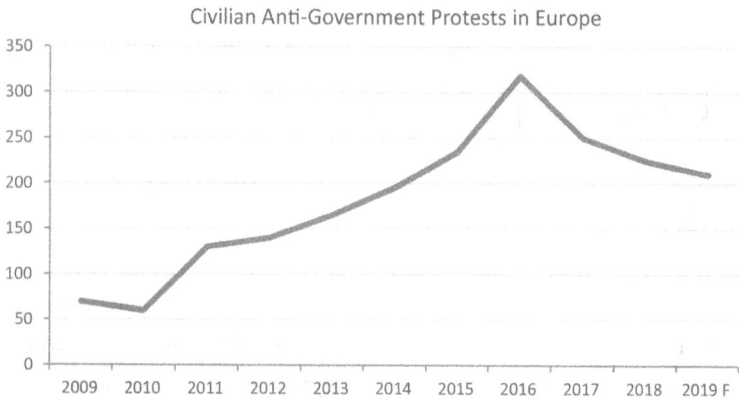

Figure 3.1 Civilian anti-government protests in Europe
Source: G-DELT database – reproduced in S. Brannen, C. Haig and K. Schmidt *The Age of Mass Protests* (Washington, DC: CSIS, 2020).

Democracy by protest

Citizens have in recent years mobilized with unprecedented intensity to defend democratic principles in Europe. Many observers have noted a rise in disruptive activism across Europe in the last decade.[1] Data shows that 'civil resistance' has become arguably the most widespread response to democratic erosion.[2] One database shows a rise in protest events in Europe from just over fifty in 2009 to over two hundred in 2019 with a peak of over three hundred in 2016 (shown in Figure 3.1).[3] Recent Eurobarometer surveys show that EU citizens have moved their political engagement outside of established political structures towards forms of direct action. The Varieties of Democracy data set shows that European protests have been part of a global rise in mass mobilization

---

[1] S. Hessel, *Indignez-Vous* (Montpelier: LP, 2010); Economist Intelligence Unit, *Rebels without a Cause: What the Upsurge in Protest Movements Means for Global Politics* (London: EIU, 2013); M. Kaldor and S. Selchow, *The Bubbling Up of Subterranean Politics in Europe* (London: LSE, 2012).

[2] E. Chenoweth, 'The future of nonviolent resistance', *Journal of Democracy*, 31/3 (2020), 69–84.

[3] S. Brannen, C. Haig and K. Schmidt, *The Age of Mass Protests* (Washington, DC: CSIS, 2020), p. 6, using the GDELT database.

Mass Mobilization

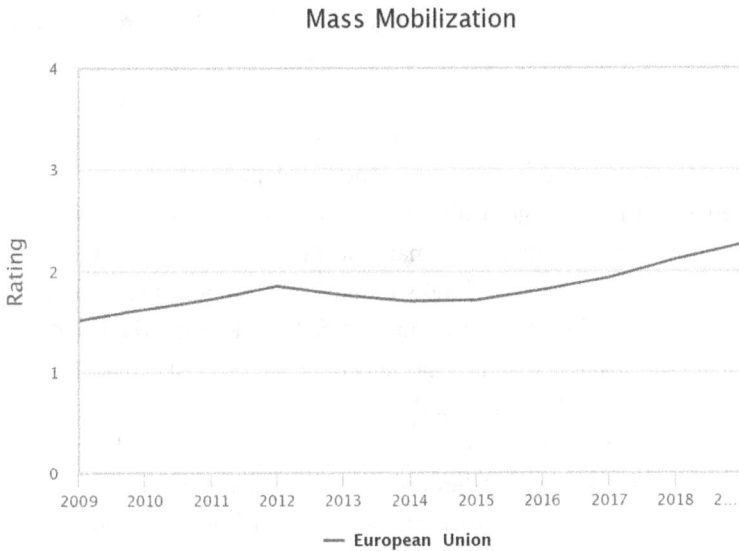

Figure 3.2 Mass mobilization
Source: V-Dem dataset.

(see Figure 3.2). The size, geographical spread and regularity of protests suggest that many citizens have been far from apathetic or relaxed about the state of European democracy – and have committed themselves to resisting democratic erosion through direct street action.

In the early 2010s, a wave of protests swept Europe that was mainly aimed against austerity cuts. Occupy-style protests took place in a large number of EU member states. The Indignados Movement in Spain mixed anti-austerity demands, a revolt against political corruption and a very specific demand for open party lists (due to the country's closed list system facilitating a lack of accountability over corruption). In Portugal the so-called 12 March Movement organized the biggest protests since the county's 1974 transition to democracy. Protests in Greece were also large and insistent as the country took the hardest economic hit of all during the economic crisis. The Aganaktismeni (Indignant Citizens) movement and 'I Won't Pay' campaigns staged multiple protest activities and public assemblies to debate responses to the crisis.

As the 2010s proceeded and the economic crisis subsided, the focus of European protests changed. In many cases, protests took on a more overtly political tone and were aimed at democratic resistance and renewal. This is categorically not to suggest that all protests have been pro-democratic, simply that many of them have been and these are the ones relevant to this book's remit. Several types of such protests can be identified; the selection that follows is not exhaustive but highlights just some of the especially notable events. It can be difficult to define precisely what is and what is not a pro-democracy protest; many protests led by hard-right groups claim to mobilize in the name of democracy, but they are not highlighted in the cases covered below as these groups clearly menace the core liberal components of democratic principles. Still, examples are given of instances where there has been sharp contestation over the democratic credentials of some protests.

Protests against political illiberalism. A first type of protest has been directly against grave democratic erosion. Some of the most explicitly pro-democratic protests took place in Poland. Here, protests erupted against the Law and Justice (PiS) government's assault on democratic checks and balances. Many of these events were spontaneous and run by relatively informal social organizations. One more structured civic organization that helped mobilize citizens was the Committee for the Defence of Democracy (KOD).[4] This started as a Facebook group before becoming one of the several forces behind regular street demonstrations; its members were generally older than those involved in pre-existing social movements.[5] Each time the government tightened its control over the judiciary, large protests took place in cities across Poland. This happened in July 2018 after the government assumed

---

[4] J. Formina and J. Kucharczyk, 'Populism and protest in Poland', *Journal of Democracy*, 27/4 (2016), 58–68.

[5] Committee for the Defense of Democracy in Poland, 'Rebellion of the "Beneficiaries of the Transformation?", Institute for Humans Sciences, 26 February 2016.

more powers over court appointments, and again in 2019 in Krakow after the government sacked a much-respected public prosecutor.

Polish women's rights activists have protested on a rolling basis since 2016 and have increasingly focused on the country's democratic decay. In 2016 they mobilized several times against the government's proposal to ban abortion, attracting young demonstrators also focused on general political grievances.[6] These protests succeeded in getting the PiS to back away from the abortion proposal. As the government then made fresh attempts to restrict abortion in the years that followed, so the protests regularly reconvened. Through an increasingly localized set of groups, the women's rights movement gradually widened its focus to the government's assault on Polish democracy, and it assumed a vanguard role in this political struggle.[7] Protests reached a new level of intensity over many weeks in late 2020 after the constitutional tribunal ruled against abortion of a foetus with serious defects. While this 'Women's Strike' centred on abortion, it was also framed as a democracy issue to the extent that the government used its effective control over the tribunal to push through the restrictions. The strike attracted participants from multiple political profiles beyond the women's movement. When the government moved ahead with the restrictive law in February 2021, a new round of broadly framed pro-democracy protests erupted.

Protests also occurred in Hungary targeting various infringements of democratic freedom. Pro-democracy revolts gained traction in 2014, gathering close to 100,000 people on several occasions that autumn.[8] In April 2017, around 70,000 Hungarians protested in Budapest against a bill that imposed stringent conditions on the Central European University, a school founded by Hungarian-born billionaire George Soros. They failed to halt the bill, and in 2019 the university was forced to move to Vienna. In early 2019, protests took place against a so-called 'slave law' that allowed companies to demand that staff work

---

[6] 'Poland's abortion ban proposal near collapse after mass protests', *The Guardian*, 5 October 2016.
[7] 'Polish women march in annual Manifa demonstration', *Poland In*, 3 March 2019.
[8] 'Thousands attend Hungary "public outrage day" protest', *BBC News*, 17 September 2014.

up to four hundred hours overtime a year. These protests expanded and became a platform for the public to air other grievances against the government, including new controls over the courts and erosion of media independence. In June 2019 protestors mobilized against the government's plans to tighten its control over the Hungarian Academy of Sciences. In summer 2020 protests took place against the government's takeover of an independent media outlet and then its political appointments to the board of the University of Theatre and Film Arts.

Protest activity has also been intense outside these two most serious cases of democratic regression. In late 2019, the Sardines movement brought a powerful wave of protest activity to Italy. The movement started by mobilizing against a Lega party rally for regional elections in Emilia-Romagna. Four friends organized this first flash mob from scratch in six days via Facebook. Over ten thousand people filled the main square in Bologna. The objective was to have people tightly packed close to each other in the square – hence the name Sardines. The organizers asked participants not to bring flags or political slogans. Left-leaning parties came out in support of the Sardines, but the movement declined any political alliances. The movement declared itself against Italy's tide of political illiberalism and issued a manifesto calling for democratic reform. The coordinators of protests that took place in 113 Italian cities wrote the manifesto together. The biggest event gathered 120,000 people in Rome in December 2019. The Sardines helped galvanize public opinion sufficiently to prevent the Lega from winning the Emilia-Romagna elections in January 2020, although their activities tailed off somewhat after this.

Protests against corruption. A second type of protest has spread against government corruption linked indirectly to a decline in democratic standards. Political corruption has become an issue capable of bringing large numbers of people out onto the streets, often in sufficient force to secure important policy changes. Anti-corruption protests have increasingly morphed into a wider set of popular grievances about the general state of democracy. One case where they had notable impact was in Slovakia, where ten thousand-strong anti-corruption protests in 2017 and 2018 after the murder of an investigative journalist forced Prime Minister Robert Fico to resign. Similarly, protests in Malta forced Prime Minister Joseph Muscat to resign in early 2020. Protestors' main focus here was suspected government involvement in the murder of investigative journalist Daphne Caruana Galizia and also the wider political corruption that she helped uncover. The protests adopted a narrative of defending democracy as they linked government corruption to manipulation of the judiciary. Several civil society groups helped organize the protests, but previously unengaged and unorganized citizens were equally in the vanguard. In months of sustained pressure, nearly twenty rounds of protests took place over the latter part of 2019. These were strong enough to push Muscat from power, although smaller scale protests then continued under a 'Nothing has changed' motif, as a familiar Labour Party elite retained power. [9]

The Czech Republic provides another dramatic example of corruption related protest. Protests gathered momentum though 2017 and 2018 after Prime Minister Andrej Babiš was implicated first in a tax evasion scheme and then accused of benefitting illegally from EU subsides.[10] In 2019 protests grew even larger with 50,000 people filling Wenceslas Square in Prague. The Million Moments for Democracy (Milion Chvilek) movement defined the protests as a pushback against the 'serious assault on democracy'.[11] In June, protests grew to record levels, first with a mobilization of around 100,000 people, then another with 250,000 people, the country's biggest anti-government protest since the communist era. Protestors coordinated with political parties to push for an anti-corruption judicial case against Babiš and were backed by a 2019 EU auditors report detailing charges against the prime minister. With protests reaching a new crescendo in December

---

[9] 'Protesters say "nothing has changed"', *NBC News*, 5 June 2020.
[10] 'Czech Republic: Thousands protest replacement of justice minister', *DW*, 30 April 2019.
[11] 'Protests grow against authoritarian slide in Czech Republic', *Aljazeera*, 21 May 2019.

2019, prosecutors reopened legal proceedings against Babiš. Without the protests, more pronounced authoritarian dynamics could easily have taken root in the Czech Republic.

Anti-corruption protests took place in Bulgaria frequently during the 2010s, before reaching a crescendo in 2020. Protests drove Prime Minister Boyko Borissov out of power in 2013; these fused a pushback against electricity price hikes, anger at corruption and Russian-linked anti-fracking groups. Even larger protests then ran for months against the follow-on Socialist-led government, mainly around political nepotism, and eventually forced this administration to step down. After Borissov's return to office, corruption became more systemic and after several dramatic episodes involving oligarchs and illegal tape recordings, protests moved up a gear from July 2020. Protestors rallied every day for several months, often with more than ten thousand people in the streets.

The protests involved rights-oriented CSOs, looser social movements and unaffiliated citizens and were also backed by opposition parties and the president. Protestors widened their range of tactics to include creative forms of civil disobedience. The government offered concessions in the form of subsidies and ministerial sackings, but the protestors raised their demands to insist on Borissov's resignation and political reform. Borissov touted constitutional changes, yet some of these seemed to undermine democracy even further. During the Covid-19 pandemic, protestors focused increasingly on wider rule of law concerns too. The protests prompted one party in the ruling coalition to move into opposition, leaving the government without a majority; after losing support in elections in April 2021 and struggling to construct a new government, Borissov announced he would step down.

Protests on indirectly related policy issues. A third type of protest has been organized around more specific policy issues that are not strictly about democracy but overlap with politically systemic concerns. Many of these seek to give democratic rights more concrete value through a focus on social, economic and environmental rights. Occasional protests have continued on a sporadic basis against cuts to social services, pension reforms and labour market liberalization, often raising broader concerns about democracy. For example, the 2016 Nuit Debout protests in France against labour law reforms developed a secondary concern with participative assemblies.

Perhaps the most notable illustration of issue-specific protests is seen in the spread of protests about climate change. The protests led by Extinction Rebellion (XR) have become especially powerful and large-scale. These protests started in London in late 2018 and then spread across Europe and beyond. During 2019, regular protests attracted tens of thousands of citizens. While climate protests have occurred on and off over many years, XR's approach was distinctive in its push for a climate assembly in Britain. XR claimed to be less interested in standard climate advocacy than in fostering citizen participation as the key to achieving a breakthrough on tackling climate change. One of the group's founders stood in European elections on an agenda of democratic renewal, and in 2020 XR pushed for an EU-level climate assembly, hoping to repeat its success in Britain. This confluence of climate and democracy activism was an innovation in European protests.

Some of the group's protests have become more disruptive. In October 2019, the British police sought to restrict their scope in central London, and this reinforced the movement's attempt to link climate issues with the defence of civil liberties. The group advocates so-called holocracy, the idea that participants should enjoy autonomy and not be bound by a search for complete consensus on every detail of each issue. Internal debates have taken place on the climate-democracy link: some activists have argued that climate change needs to be addressed even if this requires going against popular preferences, while some democracy-oriented CSOs have criticized XR for being doctrinaire and impatient with the checks and balances of liberal democracy.[12] In September 2020, these criticisms grew after XR protests in London stopped the publication of newspapers deemed as unfavourable to the group; the

---

[12] 'Now we know: Conventional campaigning won't prevent our extinction', *The Guardian*, 1 May 2019.

UK government announced restrictions against the group's future protests.

Protests with highly contested meanings. Some protests have attracted even more sharply differing readings, with their participants claiming to be advancing democracy but detractors seeing them as a danger to democratic tolerance. In some cases, the very meaning of contentious politics has itself been unclear. Two examples stand out: the Gilets Jaunes protests in France and some of the independence protests that have taken place in Catalonia.

The Gilets Jaunes protests erupted at the end of 2018 most directly against President Macron's tax hike on fuel but also demanding direct democracy in the form of citizen-triggered referendums.[13] Critics lamented that right- and left-wing radicals increasingly took over the protests as they continued through 2019. The protests included many so-called *casseurs*, intent on violence and the destruction of property. Some protestors pushed anti-immigration and anti-Semitic positions. Many other participants have tried to push aside all these more extreme elements. The movement put up candidates for the EU elections but did not succeed in these. Into 2020 the protests continued but on a small scale. Their initial ethos of non-aligned, local citizen protests focused on community democracy was at this stage superseded by a more traditional trade union-led protest against pension reforms. While the Gilets Jaunes were one factor that pushed Macron to launch his so-called Grand Débat (covered in the next chapter), many questioned their liberal-democratic identity.

Catalonia is another case where the democratic implications of protests have been highly contentious. There have been large-scale and frequent demonstrations in favour of Catalan independence for over a decade. The intensity of these mobilizations increased during the 2010s and reached a crescendo around the 2017 referendum called by the Catalan regional government. Protests have involved a number of CSOs

---

[13] S. Hayat, 'The Gilets Jaunes and the democratic question', *Viewpoint Magazine*, 13 February 2019.

and have become closely aligned with Catalan regional authorities and pro-independence political parties. Catalonia's national day march in 2014 mobilised two million people out of a population of just over seven million. Pro-independence groups attached a democracy narrative to such events, framing their struggle for statehood as a question of democratic self-determination. Counter-protests against secession have taken place in Catalonia and elsewhere in Spain, with their leaders claiming it is they who are defending democracy against the separatists.

In October 2019, protests took a dramatic turn. After the Spanish constitutional court handed down harsh jail sentences to separatist leaders, revolts erupted across Catalonia. Protestors insisted this was a tide of democratic resistance. Spanish authorities and political parties pressed for a hard-line response, insisting that the protests were a threat to rather than expression of democracy. They closed down an influential online app used by protestors (a controversy covered in Chapter 6). Increasingly the two narratives have clashed in uncompromising terms, one painting the protests as healthy local democratic expression, the other discrediting them as inimical to constitutional politics.

Protest in the Covid-19 era. In 2020, the Covid-19 virus temporarily curtailed protest activity, as social distancing rules militated against mass gathering. However, the virus then unleashed a new round of protest activity adapted to the altered circumstances. Innovative actions targeted governments' restrictive pandemic measures. Polish civic groups ran a car-based 'Alarm Signal to the Government' protest. The Sardines resumed low-key protests and branched out into fundraising for local communities in Italy. Revolts erupted in Paris and several other French cities against heavy-handed police enforcement of the country's lockdown and in particular police actions that led to serious injuries to people from minority backgrounds. In the UK, protestors mobilized in front of the parliament to push for a citizen assembly on Covid-19 recovery plans.

Protests against social distancing, rules on mask-wearing and other Covid restrictions became increasingly large and frequent in the latter months of 2020 and into 2021 – especially in France, Germany, Italy, the Netherlands and Spain. The demonstrations mostly reflected a general desire to get back to normal and concerns about the pandemic's economic impact, yet they also deployed a democracy narrative and criticized Covid-related executive overreach. While they attracted movements from across the political spectrum, far-right and ultra-libertarian groups were prominent participants. This presented a puzzle for democracy concerns, as some of the continent's most illiberal-authoritarian parties somewhat opportunistically led calls for democratic rights to be restored. Stressing the involvement of far-right groups, governments painted the protests as a threat to democracy. In many cases, far-right groups piggy-backed on revolts organized by moderate CSOs who were left frustrated that the presence of radical elements allowed governments to divert attention away from their own crisis mismanagement.

In parallel to Covid-19, in June 2020 protests erupted across Europe after US police were filmed killing Afro-American citizen George Floyd. Several thousand protested in Berlin, London, Paris and other European cities. These highlighted European police brutality and wider racial discrimination across Europe. Protestors in France drew parallels to several high-profile killings by the French police; in November 2020, over a hundred thousand protestors in Paris got the French government to backtrack on a new security law that promised the police various forms of protection. In early 2021, protests in Spain against the detention of a rapper pressed the government to loosen security-law restrictions on the freedom of expression, while in the UK thousands mobilized against a proposed law that would impose additional limitations on marches. In many countries these kinds of events became protests concerned with the core equality of democratic rights, and they won concessions from governments in many countries where they occurred. Taken together, these diverse revolts showed that the pandemic era was far from being one in which citizen action was quelled.

Civil society and democratic renewal

Bottom-up efforts to defend and rethink European democracy have not only taken the form of protests. In addition to the revolts of recent years, more organized civil society has also continued to develop and thicken its networks and political activity across Europe. As with protests, different types of civil society activity have taken shape related to European democracy.

Resisting government restrictions. One strand of emerging civic activity comes from numerous efforts to push back against restrictions on civil liberties. This area of civic activism is significant because, as Chapter 2 outlined, the restriction of civic freedoms and civil society space has been one of the main sources of European democratic regression in recent years. CSOs have developed strategies to fight back against these restrictions. They have begun cooperating with each other more systematically to defend democratic freedoms. A number of prominent rights organizations banded together to form a Front Line Defenders consortium dedicated to protecting democracy activists from state repression within Europe and beyond. Various initiatives have begun to raise the profile of government attacks on civic groups, with organizations like Civicus and the European Civic Forum monitoring these abuses and creating broad civil society alliances to pressure against those governments.

Many initiatives have sprung from gathering risks to democracy. In Latvia, CSOs combined to mount a campaign that got the government to reverse unfavourable changes to civil-society financing rules and to create a post for cooperation with CSOs in the cabinet. In Lithuania, CSOs cooperated in a similar vein to get political parties to sign a memorandum before the elections committing to respecting civil liberties and advancing active citizenship. In Slovenia, a 2019 campaign resulted in the government setting up a new council in cooperation with CSOs and promising to protect democratic rights. In Slovakia, the Voice of Civic Organizations consortium launched a high-profile initiative to preserve civic freedoms after elections in 2019.

Other initiatives focused on specific attacks against civil society. A civic organization called Citizens for Poland campaigned against government attacks on civil society and succeeded in limiting legal sanctions on protestors. An alliance of Irish CSOs formed in 2019 to pushback against government moves to narrow civil society's 'political' actions. In Italy, activists from several CSOs launched Mediterranea as a loose 'action movement' against government moves to criminalize refugee rescue operations. At a pan-European level, sixteen foundations formed a new consortium, Civitates, to support initiatives aimed at combatting democratic regression and civic restrictions. The European Foundation Centre and Daphne networks launched an initiative to work with CSOs on using EU laws against government restrictions. [14]

CSOs across Europe have also rethought many of their tactics in order to protect themselves from state restrictions. In some of the more difficult environments, they have taken on flexible organizational structures and sometimes do not register as formal entities anymore. Some now present themselves as cultural entities or social enterprises to mask their sensitive political agendas. Most CSOs have also moved to invest heavily in digital security, and a cluster of new civic initiatives have sprung up providing cyber security services to civil society groups – initiatives like the Freedom Online Coalition, The Engine Room, Access Now, the Electronic Frontier Alliance and Security-in-a-Box. Some democratic activism is returning to covert, offline tactics in an attempt to evade state surveillance (Chapter 6 covers digital initiatives in more detail).

Many CSOs have also begun to shore up their own credibility among society at large. One challenge is that in many EU states the CSOs targeted by governments have often won limited support from the wider population. This has prompted some CSOs to devise new strategies for

---

[14] For more on the examples in these two paragraphs, see European Civic Forum, *Civic Space Watch Report 2019* (Brussels: ECF, 2019).

embedding themselves more strongly within local societies as a means of being more effective in defending democracy. As governments stir up hostility towards the external funders of civil society projects, CSOs have looked increasingly to obtain their own resources locally.

Building grassroots democracy. There has been an equally notable expansion in practical, community-level civic activism. Experts define this as a wave of 'activist citizenship'. This entails very informal, structure-lite civic activism built around everyday issues like local employment opportunities and service provision. Cooperative sharing and mutualism have made a comeback, in large measure as a legacy of Europe's economic crisis. Much of this new activism has been focused around creating and protecting urban spaces designed to facilitate democratic engagement – what has come to be called the 'social infrastructure' of communal places where civic and political action can more easily take place.[15]

Another trend has emerged of grassroots monitoring or 'citizen reporting' exposing political corruption and bad governance practices. In some ways, this has all led to a greater density of civil society organizing than the traditional, formal NGOs that tend to involve a relatively limited number of fully professional activists. These groups offer a kind of democracy-by-doing, rather than allegiance to any particular political party or platform.[16] Even those leading overtly political protests in countries like Poland have come to recognize the need to focus more on this kind of very local civic politics to involve a larger number of ordinary citizens.[17]

Self-help participative groups have been active in Greece and Spain and have more recently spread to all corners of the continent.

---

[15] E. Klineberg, *Palaces for the People* (London: Penguin Random House, 2018).

[16] CitizensLab, *Mapping New Forms of Civic Engagement in Europe* (Berlin: CitizensLab, 2017); G. Monbiot, *Out of the Wreckage: A New Politics for an Age of Crisis* (London: Verso, 2017); International Civil Society Centre, *Riding the Wave* (Berlin: International Civil Society Centre, 2013); Civicus, *State of Civil Society Report 2015* (Johannesburg: Civicus, 2015); F. Polletta, 'Social movements in an age of participation', *Mobilisation*, 21/4 (2016), 485–97.

[17] K. Wigura and J. Kuisz, 'Want to save Europe? Learn from Poland', *New York Times*, 23 May 2019.

The Associazione Ricreativa e Culturale Italiane, Italy's biggest civil society network not linked to the Catholic church, has run a significant increase in initiatives using cultural cooperation to rebuild support for democratic engagement against the national-populist right. The economic crisis gave rise to a wave of new-style social enterprise initiatives working on supporting a locally rooted social economy, representing hybrids of civil society and private sector actors.[18]

An increasing number of grassroots initiatives has formed to design tactics for pushing back against illiberal groups: examples include Arguments Against Aggression, React and More in Common.[19] Strikingly creative and original initiatives have formed. Democracy Fitness formed in 2017 offering pop-up training sessions where participants exercise their 'democratic muscles' like empathy, active listening, compromise and activism.[20] Escape Fake creates virtual escape rooms as a way for young people to learn about fake news through checking facts and solving riddles to escape from locked rooms.[21]

Even in the most challenging contexts of Central and Eastern Europe, civil societies have continued to grow, in terms of members, financial scale and numbers of citizens volunteering. In each state, tens of thousands of CSOs are now active, and in several of them, more than half the population is involved in some way with civil society activity especially at a very grassroots level.[22] In the Czech Republic several civic groups joined forces to launch NeoN, a programme to uphold democratic principles.[23] After the far-right EKRE party entered government in Estonia, activists formed a loose movement called Koigi Eesti (My Estonia Too) designed to restore support for core liberal-democratic

---

[18] Economic and Social Committee, *The Future Evolution of Civil Society in the European Union by 2030* (Brussels: ECSC, 2017), p. 17.

[19] Their respective websites are www.contra-aggression.eu, www.reactnohate.eu and www.moreincommon.com.

[20] https://citiesforeurope.eu/en/democracy-fitness.

[21] www.escapefake.org.

[22] P. Vandor, N. Traxler, R. Millner and M. Meyer, *Civil Society in Central and Eastern Europe: Challengers and Opportunities* (Vienna: ERSTE Stiftung Studies, 2017), pp. 20–3 and p. 33.

[23] Information at www.glopolis.org.

values. This began as a social-media campaign, growing quickly to have more followers than any other political movement online, and then moved to offline meetings at a local, community level.

Running participation. A further cluster of civic activity relates to an increasing number of organizations set up specifically to organize deliberative citizen initiatives. The following chapter examines the trend in participative assemblies launched by governmental authorities. In parallel to these government run initiatives, CSOs have increasingly run their own democratic participation. While many civic bodies sign up to government-led consultations and work with authorities to make them a success, other CSOs fear these entail too much co-option and have rather focused on informal, civic consultations kept separate from official initiatives.

The Participedia initiative registers a mushrooming of such civic initiatives across Europe and has played a role in generating additional momentum behind this kind of civil society engagement in democracy.[24] One anthology records scores of new civil society initiatives working on democracy-related innovations like the design of different means of voting, the generation of collective intelligence for democracy, political communication, participative socially owned enterprises, democracy labs, factories, think-ins and other get-togethers of self-defined innovators. This type of organization normally comprises a mix of professional facilitators, software developers, design experts, psychologists and civic activists.[25]

Perhaps the densest concentration of civil-society democratic innovation groups has grown in the UK. The Brexit impasse has acted as catalyst for a plethora of civic initiatives aimed at reshaping British democracy. Involve UK has run an increasing number of deliberative processes across the country, some with government bodies, others with civil society groups. The New Citizenship Project works with

[24] See www.participedia.net.
[25] For overview of this growth, see Das Progressive Zentrum Democracy Lab, *Anthology on Democratic Innovation* (Berlin, 2017).

a range of organizations to help them involve citizens in a more participative fashion and move from treating them as 'consumers' to 'co-creating agents'. The Participatory City Foundation has created citizen forums in places like Dagenham, east of London. In 2018, civil society groups set up their own citizen assembly in Northern Ireland to discuss social care for elderly people.[26] Flatpack Democracy promotes self-organizing in local politics, while Its Our Time runs crowdsourcing for pro-democracy campaigns. In 2020, the Ada Lovelace Institute ran deliberative forums on the government's Covid-19 track-and-trace app.

In Belgian the vanguard G1000 organization ran a citizens' summit comprising seven hundred participants as a response to the year-long failure of political parties to form a government in 2011. Democratie Ouverte is a prominent example in France that has developed tools for citizen engagement and the collaborative drafting of legislative proposals.[27] In Germany, where state authorities have not yet embraced citizen participation, a civil society group held an assembly in Frankfurt in 2019 to press for permanent citizen input into municipal decision-making.[28] The CSO MehrDemokratie ran an assembly for the entirety of Germany in autumn 2019; its participants recommended more far-reaching measures of citizen participation and direct democracy. In Denmark, the We Do Democracy civic initiative has run citizen assemblies in Copenhagen. In a particularly challenging context, the Sortition Foundation ran a climate assembly in Budapest in 2020. The Innovation in Politics Institute has created an annual awards programme for these kinds of initiatives across Europe.[29] These are only a few illustrative examples; many more could be cited from a burgeoning world of very practical democracy-implementers civil society.

Pushing for EU democracy. A different area is the development of a denser network of CSOs working on democracy within debates

---

[26] T. Hughes, 'Citizens' Assembly for Northern Ireland Meets for the First Time to Discuss Social Care for Older People', *Involve*, 29 October 2018.

[27] www.democracieouverte.org.

[28] V. Friederike Hasel, 'Germany's democracy problem', *Politico*, 16 May 2019.

[29] https://innovationinpolitics.eu/en/our-work/.

about the EU. Civil society at the EU level has traditionally been a somewhat circumspect collection of 'insider' groups cooperating with the European Commission on fairly technical issues for mutually beneficial gain. Yet, a more contentious and political layer of European civil society has taken shape in recent years. One EU study found that CSOs at the European level have in recent years shifted their focus to reach downwards to engage citizens and move beyond their traditional lobbying within the Union's formal institutional processes.[30]

Again, many examples could be given. WeMove.eu has galvanized direct citizen engagement and participatory offline and online tools specifically around new EU reform ideas. The Citizens Assembly for Europe project ran mini-publics across a number of member states and found some support for the idea of an EU-level citizens assembly. European Alternatives works as a pan-European group, mobilizing citizens around innovative proposals for a more democratic and just process of European integration. Democracy International managed an initiative for a citizen assembly to feed into a new EU treaty. The Austrian Election-Watch.eu conducted the first citizen-based election monitoring across member states. Alliance4Europe.eu started to build networks and cooperation between CSOs in different member states working on democratic rights, aimed especially at connecting young people. The Citizens for Europe organization launched a Democracy Network initiative with similar aims. In 2019, the European Citizen Action Service expanded by 50 per cent its activities aimed at helping citizens use EU laws to protect their democratic citizenship rights. These kinds of initiatives show that civil society's focus on the limits to EU-level democratic accountability has intensified notably.

Covid-19 initiatives. Within each of these categories of activism, many more initiatives emerged specifically in response to the Covid-19 pandemic. Indeed, the virus emergency served dramatically to catalyse civic engagement. This was seen both through new groups forming

---

[30] European Economic and Social Committee, *Societies Outside Metropolises: The Role of Civil Society Organisations in Facing Populism* (Brussels: EESC, 2018), p. 150.

and established CSOs creating coalitions for work on the pandemic. There was a striking increase in volunteerism in the pandemic. The thousands of 'mutual aid' groups that emerged were generally not political but about very practical issues like organizing food supplies or online classes and advice. A Madrid neighbourhood self-help group, Somos Tribu, won the European Parliament's European citizen award for 2020. In the UK, Covid Mutual Aid was formed to offer support to local communities by running errands and providing emotional support; it mapped thousands of such new initiatives even down to street level.[31] In the London borough of Camden, the Full Fact initiative delivered food to vulnerable people along with factsheets on Covid-19 as an antidote to fake news.

Many civic organizations turned to making masks and supporting medical staff, including FabLab and En Premiere Ligne in France. French CSOs created an initiative to spur local-level consultations on post-virus rebuilding. Across Central and Eastern Europe, local groups organized service delivery functions in frustration at governments' underwhelming responses to the pandemic. In Estonia, a network of movements ran a hackathon that generated nearly a hundred ideas on how social cooperation could help combat the virus.[32] Some new CSO initiatives contested the democratic narrowing involved in governments' emergency pandemic responses and especially the use of intrusive tracing apps: watchdog organizations were especially high profile and powerful on this issue in Germany.[33] Especially notable CSO initiatives monitored police abuses under emergency laws in France, Hungary and Spain.[34] A powerful grassroots organization formed in Spain to strike against rent demands during the pandemic.[35] At the EU level new initiatives like Citizens Takeover Europe and EUmans

---

[31] See www.covidmutualaid.org.

[32] At www.accelerateestonia.ee.

[33] J. Delcker, 'Coronavirus triggers soul searching on privacy in Germany', *Politico*, 9 April 2020.

[34] G. Negri, 'Civic space under Lockdown', in *European Civic Space Watch 2020: Stories from the Lockdown* (Brussels: European Civic Forum, 2020), pp. 44–7.

[35] See www.suspensionalquileres.org.

formed to push for deeper EU cooperation in response to the virus. The overarching Build Back Better civic movement took shape to coordinate pressure for reforms in Covid-19's wake.

Profile: Romania

It is instructive to look at one case in greater detail to examine the dynamics of protest and civil society activism and how these relate to issues of European democracy. Romania provides an example of how protest has become a pivotal and quasi-permanent feature of democratic resistance and renewal and has fed into more permanent civic organization. It shows how the nature of protest and civil society activity has changed over time and demonstrates the challenges of harnessing this bottom-up potential for rebuilding democracy.

Romanian protests began in winter 2012 most proximately against the privatization of health services, but also indirectly embodying a frustration that democratic reforms seemed to have stalled. In 2013 and 2014 mobilizations intensified, especially on more specific matters like companies' illegal exploitation of forestry resources and the government's decision to allow a mining company to open Europe's largest open-cast gold mine in a small village. In 2015, more protests erupted after a nightclub fire left many dead and was widely seen as the result of corruption. The 2015 protests forced the centre-left PSD government out of office, although the party won power again in elections at the end of 2016.

By 2017, the protests had a narrower agenda against PSD corruption. Their main focus changed from issues related to economic and anti-austerity policies to more political concerns over corruption and politicians' apparent impunity for their misdemeanours in office, with many now seeing PSD actions as a kind of unresolved hangover from the communist regime.[36] Protests peaked in early 2017 with 600,000

---

[36] V. Stoiciu, 'Romanian social movements – between repoliticization and reinforcement of the status quo, 2012-1017', Studia Universitatis Babes-Bolyai, 2017.

people taking to the streets after the government introduced laws to decriminalize low-level corruption in order to get its members out of court cases. The protests were the largest Romania had seen since the fall of communism. The government removed the law, but protests continued.

After the protests eventually dispersed, the government moved once again to frustrate anti-corruption moves. Another round of mass protests took place in early 2018, aimed against further government attempts to change several justice and penal provisions. Smaller protests rumbled on, and then another mass mobilization took place in August 2018 after the government sacked the head of the National Anticorruption Directorate, Laura Kovesi. Over these tumultuous months, protests led to two government teams resigning and several laws being retracted; yet the PSD administration continued its assault on judicial independence as it sought to dilute anti-corruption measures.

Protestors increasingly targeted more general democratic deficiencies beyond the issue of corruption. While the largest protests took place in Bucharest, smaller protests were also held in a dozen other cities across the country. A social-media rally called Diaspora at Home called on Romanians living abroad to return home and demand the government's resignation. Thousands of Romanian expatriates duly joined their compatriots in Bucharest for a march in August 2018, calling on the country's leaders to resign and hold early elections. Police broke this protest up with water cannons and tear gas.[37] Expatriates also organized protests in Ireland, Italy, Germany, the UK and Belgium. 'No amnesty! We want democracy!' become one of the protestors' defining slogans.[38] While the main group of protestors were young and urban, they also reached out to the rural population.

Prior to the May 2019 EU elections, protestors' focus on the state of democracy in Romania became entwined with concerns over the

---

[37] 'Romanian expats return home for major anti-government protest, clash with the police', *DW*, 10 August 2018.
[38] 'Hundreds of Romanians also protested in the diaspora', *Digi 24*, 12 August 2018.

government's apparent drift towards Euroscepticism. Many saw the PSD becoming more inward looking and nationalistic.[39] Pro-European banners began appearing in the regular protests that continued against the government. Huge protests on the apparently separate issue of the police's failure to respond to the kidnapping of a 15-year-old female hitch-hiker fed into the wider political tumult. In August, on the one-year anniversary of the violent police crackdown against protestors in 2018, thousands of Romanians took to the streets of Bucharest again for an anti-corruption protest.[40]

Civil society networks and communities have also formed in parallel to the revolts. Several civic organizations such as Coruptia Ucide (Corruption Kills), Rezist (Resistance) and Initiativa România (Initiative Romania) emerged out of the protests. The founder of the Corruption Kills Facebook page was awarded the Personality of the Year prize at the 2018 European Leadership Awards for his work on fighting disinformation. Initiativa România promotes 'freedom, rule of law, integrity, competence, solidarity, responsibility and transparency' and supports 'individuals and communities that act for change'. The movement's mission is to support citizens in building strong civic communities and to promote the ethical exercise of power.[41] A civic entrepreneurship hub called Civic Starter formed, along with Activists House, to bring together different activists.

Va Vedem din Sibiu (We Are Watching You from Sibiu) began silent flash mobs in the streets of Sibiu calling for democratic reforms. In 2019, a coalition of CSOs got the government to remove a draft law introducing onerous financial reporting burdens on civil society. In addition to these social movements, several new political parties emerged from activists involved in the protests, as Chapter 5 will explain. Not all new initiatives were liberal. The powerful Coalition

[39] A. Rettman, 'Romania heaps scorn on "revolting" EU criticism', *EUobserver*, 15 November 2018.
[40] 'Romania: Tens of thousands rally against Governement in Bucharest', *DW*, 11 August 2018.
[41] www.initiativaromania.ro.

for the Family rose to prominence as an alliance of conservative civic organizations; its members participated in the protests and deployed a democratic narrative but with a conservative values agenda that aimed to narrow the rights of sexual-minority citizens. In 2017, this movement gathered three million petition signatories to secure a referendum in effect on same-sex marriage. When this failed due to low turnout, the group disbanded and reformed itself as a new Civic Platform Together that included over five hundred conservative CSOs.[42]

Taken together, the on-off protests and civic initiatives represented an awakening of Romanian citizenship. Their impact became apparent in 2019. In May 2019, President Klaus Iohannis called a referendum, in which over 80 per cent of voters supported a ban on pardons for corruption offenses and on emergency judicial decrees. PSD leader Liviu Dragnea was convicted and sent to prison. In the autumn of 2019, the PSD government was forced out of office and a coalition led by the centre-right National Liberal Party took power. The protests were not without their doubters, as sceptics felt they morphed into a general right-of-centre agenda against the PSD and included many elements that were not particularly liberal.[43] Yet, the new government's commitment to strengthen anti-corruption measures and democratic reforms when it took office in November 2019 certainly owed much to the sustained citizen pressure on these issues. Romania was a case where bottom-up civic momentum interlaced with EU pressure too (as examined in Chapter 7). While much remained to be done to shore up democratic norms even as the nominally reformist coalition regained power in December 2020, protests had at least opened the possibility of change.

---

[42] D. Margarit, *Insurgent Conservatism in Romania* (Bucharest: Friedrich Ebert Stiftung, 2020).

[43] 'Romania's protests: From social justice to class politics', *Critic Attack*, 27 February 2017.

Assessment: Civic awakening?

In the last several years, Europe has experienced a surge in citizen-led engagement containing elements of both democratic resistance and renewal. Protests and civic campaigns have emerged with force to resist and push back against governments' assaults on democratic liberties. At the same time, many of these activities have fashioned new forms of political practices in pursuit of qualitative democratic renewal. Their growth has bred talk of a new 'post-representative politics' across Europe.[44] These citizen-led efforts have proven more dynamic and energetic than other areas of democratic rebuilding covered in this book, helping to push forward more open and spontaneous forms of democratic participation. As we will see later in the book, their ethos contrasts with the more cautious strategies that governments, local authorities and EU institutions have pursued.

Protests' rising potential. European protests have increased in number and size, and protestors' tactics have also become more agile and creative. The examples above show a typology of multiple forms of protest spreading to most European countries in recent years. In each country, protests have typically occurred over several repeat cycles, persisting for sustained periods of time. They have become a mainstream, regularized feature of European democratic politics. Their concerns with democracy-related issues have extended across the ideological spectrum and not been limited to any single political family. Despite initial fears that Covid-19 would militate against democratic dissent, citizen mobilization in 2020 and 2021 has in many instances even been stronger and more contentious than might have been optimal for health-crisis imperatives. While protests have certainly not conclusively turned back the tide of democratic erosion, they have commonly scored some success. In many of the cases outlined above, they have made a difference in limiting anti-democratic politics, pushing out illiberal leaders or in forcing governments to bring forward

---

[44] S. Tormey, *The End of Representative Politics* (Cambridge: Polity Press, 2015).

at least partial democratic reforms. European governments have most commonly responded to civic pressure by agreeing reforms that are meaningful but forestall far-reaching democratic renewal.[45]

Still, many writers view the rise in protests in strikingly negative terms. Sceptics have ritually warned that the rise in protests risks a descent into mere 'mob rule'. Many have berated protestors for simply attacking existing democratic processes without proposing constructive alternatives.[46] Politically illiberal forces have been prominent in some protests in recent years, especially during the Covid-19 pandemic. Some protests have been about specific sectors of the population seeking to preserve group benefits more than universally beneficially aspects of democratic improvement. Analysts argue that as citizen revolts mobilize around these inward-looking goals, they have done little to help regenerate democracy.[47] Protests have often struggled to have an impact in the headwinds of democratic erosion and have not been potent or cohesive enough to override elites' resistance to deep reform.

Notwithstanding such sobering realities, the criticisms of Europe's protest surge look unduly harsh. Protests have evolved over time and rarely seek a purely destructive disruption of mainstream politics as they might have done a decade ago. While populists have indeed taken advantage of revolts, it is simplistic to conclude that these forms of deeper popular engagement are inimical to democratic renovation. Even if some have included anti-democratic elements, most have been organized around liberal agendas.[48] After anti-austerity protests in the early 2010s met with relatively limited success, protestors have often focused on more flexible, targeted and attainable goals. They have also increasingly explored ways of feeding their activism more

[45] C. Bedock, *Reforming Democracy: Institutional Engineering in Western Europe* (Oxford: Oxford University Press, 2017).

[46] Such negative views are, for example, apparent in I. Krastev, S. Dennison and M. Leonard, *What Europeans Really Wanted: Five Myths Debunked* (London: ECFR, 2019).

[47] P. Rosanvallon, *Counter-Democracy: Politics in an Age of Distrust* (Cambridge: Cambridge University Press, 2008).

[48] M. Hume, *Revolting!* (London: William Collins, 2017).

constructively into party politics – a theme explored in subsequent chapters. And their links to organized civil society have also improved; in one example, over sixty Polish CSOs mobilized to help the autumn 2020 protests have more of an impact in international institutions. Even when protests have fallen short of their stated aims, the very fact that large groups of citizens have increasingly registered discontent has established a platform for more public influence over European democracy. They may not have succeeded in pushing governments to implement wholesale democratic reforms, but they have signalled the importance of these issues and helped build a more solid civic spirit that can be mobilized at points of reform opportunity. They represent a genuine and meaningful civic awakening, one area of bottom-up reaction to both populist-illiberalism and executive aggrandizement.[49] Protests are one among many factors that help explain why Europe states' overall democracy scores have held up reasonably well, even if they have not been effective enough to improve those scores.

CSOs' innovative change. In parallel to Europe's protests, other kinds of civil society initiatives have also moved up a gear in recent years. Of course, CSOs have been active and central to democratic reforms across many EU states for a long time, and analysts have long emphasized their importance to democracy's health and evolution. Yet, interesting and innovative kinds of CSO initiatives have emerged over the late 2010s that reflect the different ways in which European democracy has been under attack. Crucially, the Covid-19 crisis has reinforced this trend and acted as catalyst for another layer of democracy-focused civil society.

European civil society has changed in both quantitative and qualitative terms. The number and density have increased of organized civil society initiatives related in some manner to democracy. These initiatives include CSOs directly defending civic space, those

---

[49] For a more extensive and analytical study of these features of contemporary protest movements, see R. Youngs, *Civic Activism Unleashed: New Hope or False Dawn for Democracy?* (Oxford: Oxford University Press, 2019).

constructing a more robust community-level democratic politics, those pioneering citizen-owned participation and campaigns addressing the overarching challenge of making the EU more democratic. This growth of grassroot civics has helped connect larger numbers of citizens on a daily basis around concrete areas of 'democratic repair' in a way that structures like citizen assemblies or political parties struggle to do.[50]

This expansion of civic initiatives has laid down a thicker foundation of democratic capacity at a deep societal level. This development easily gets overlooked when the gaze of political scrutiny falls more readily on government actions, summits and idiosyncratic populist leaders. The thickening of democracy-oriented civic initiatives is not fully apparent in the overarching data outlined in Chapter 2, and yet it reflects a pluralist vibrancy that has increased the pressure against governments' moves to undermine democratic quality. This dimension of civic awakening does not guarantee immediate democratic regeneration but makes it more possible in the future.

Nevertheless, civil society regeneration needs to extend further if it is to play a primary role in turning back government assaults on civic freedoms and in this way improve Europe's overall democracy indicators. In many European countries, civil society is still on the defensive, and the economic and political constraints of the Covid-19 pandemic have added to its difficulties. A huge number of small-scale civic initiatives emerged in 2020 but with little overarching coordination sufficient to give them high-level political influence in the pandemic. Many CSO projects are successful as individual initiatives, but the challenge remains of fusing these into coherent civic-led democratic renewal. Many new civil society initiatives have remained exploratory, often comprising a few experts and specialists putting forward novel ideas for 'future politics'. Many revolve around digital issues that we will pick up in Chapter 6. These are promising and impressive in

---

[50] C. Hendricks, S. Ercan and J. Boswell, *Mending Democracy: Democratic Repair in Disconnected Times* (Oxford: Oxford University Press, 2020).

their intellectual freshness, but they are yet to attract wide popular mobilization behind them.

Taken together, protests and CSO initiatives represent a vitally important element of European democratic resistance and renewal – and most recently, the avenues through which Covid-19 may have planted the seeds for democracy's 'reimagining'.[51] There are certainly legitimate concerns about their potential to be too disruptive and menace core tenets of liberal-representative democracy. Yet, mass-based citizen engagement and critically assertive CSOs have evolved and increasingly play a largely positive role in helping to push a necessary mobilization and contestation over democracy's failings. Democracy indices still struggle to capture the growth in these kinds of democratic rebuilding; their significance and reach extends beyond the kind of democracy scoring outlined in Chapter 2. They usefully embody an action-based form of democratic participation quite different from initiatives aimed at more restrained or consensus-building deliberation, that are discussed in this book's subsequent chapters.[52] While the civic sphere has suffered the brunt of democratic narrowing across Europe, it has also generated some of the most promising pro-democratic dynamics of recent years. These innovative forms of civic politics need to be developed further and their current shortcomings corrected if they are to fulfil their potential in improving European democracy. The concluding chapter returns to the question of what this would imply for the continent's overarching template of democratic politics.

---

[51] K. Nicolaidis, 'Reimagined Democracy in Times of Pandemic', in M. Maduro and P. Kahn (eds), *Democracy in Times of Pandemic* (Cambridge: Cambridge University Press, 2020).

[52] F. Hendriks, 'Democratic innovation beyond deliberative reflection: The plebiscitary rebound and the advent of action-oriented democracy', *Democratization*, 26/3 (2019), 444–64.

4

Government responses: Democratic consultation on the rise

In parallel with bottom-up mobilization, a more top-down and formal element of democratic innovation has come from governments and public authorities introducing new initiatives that engage citizens directly in political decisions. Two broad types of such democratic consultation have become more extensive across Europe in recent years. One type is the deliberative mini-public that in several different formats has spread across most European countries. The other track is that of direct-democratic referendums that have also become more frequent, especially at the local level.

This chapter charts how European governments and public authorities have shown greater interest in exploring these forms of citizen consultation. It shows that the use of these very different types of democratic engagement has expanded but also that authorities have in most cases constricted their scope and impact. National and local governments have seen the need to widen participation to temper popular discontent yet have so far kept this within relatively tight and controllable boundaries. Unpacking how these trends in deliberative and direct democracy represent a promising yet relatively contained approach to democratic renewal, the chapter concludes by suggesting ways in which these contrasting forms of citizen consultation need to be deepened and connected to other types of political change.

Deliberative participation

Deliberative mini-publics offer a particularly structured form of citizen participation that bring together small numbers of preselected participant to debate very specific issues. This type of democratic participation has experienced a notable growth in recent years. Data is patchy, but very roughly by 2020 there were four or five times more public deliberative exercises being held each year than in the early 2000s. Such initiatives come in different variations – citizen assemblies, panels, juries and others – in line with their duration and size and whether their aim is to provide precise recommendations or simply canvass opinions. Over 80 per cent of them have taken place at a subnational level around local issues of urban planning, health, environment and municipal infrastructure projects.[1] The general measurements of European democracy outlined in Chapter 2 do not fully incorporate the spread of these initiatives. Curiously, the same governments that have been guilty of abridging some democratic rights have simultaneously overseen new initiatives for deliberative participation; and this is true for right-wing, centrist and left-wing administrations. Many examples could be given, but a selection suffices here to demonstrate the general trend.

Ireland. Ireland probably did more than any other country to kick-start the wave of citizen assemblies across Europe in the 2010s. In 2012, the Irish parliament established a constitutional convention that ran through to 2014 and involved sixty-six randomly selected citizens tasked with recommending constitutional amendments.[2] From this, the issues of same-sex marriage and the minimum age to stand for president were put to referendum in 2015. In 2016, the Irish government transformed the convention into a ninety-nine-person Citizen Assembly that ran through 2018. Its participants considered five topics: abortion, aging, climate change, fixed-term parliaments and the use of referendums.

---

[1] OECD, *Innovative Citizen Participation and New Democratic Institutions: Catching the Deliberative Wave* (Paris: OECD, 2020), p. 20 and p. 23.
[2] Bertelsmann Stiftung, *Citizens' Participation Using Sortition* (Gutersloh: Bertelsmann Stiftung, 2018).

This led to referendums in May and October 2018, legalizing abortion and removing the offence of blasphemy from the constitution, respectively. In June 2019, the centre-right government approved two new citizen assemblies on gender equality and the structure of Dublin's local government.[3]

Belgium. Belgium has also launched several significant experiments in citizen participation.[4] In 2019, the German-speaking community in East Belgium launched what is probably Europe's most elaborately structured sortition-based decision-making process.[5] This East Belgian model involves several layers of deliberation, with short-term Citizen Assemblies meeting to debate different issues up to three times a year and the local parliament then discussing their recommendations. This model is notable for allowing citizens to shape the policy agenda not merely address questions decided by the authorities.[6] Belgium's French-speaking parliament has moved to create its own, similar assemblies, potentially linking deliberative and representative dynamics. In addition, the ecologist party Ecolo has used its mandate in fourteen Brussels municipalities to involve citizens in regular deliberations, and in early 2020 succeeded in pushing forward a scheme for mixed municipal forums combining elected officials with citizens to meet once a year.[7]

Spain. Spain has hosted some of the world's most developed participative schemes at city level. One example among many was in Madrid. The leftist Ahora Madrid coalition that won the city's municipal elections in 2015 opened a dedicated policy for citizen participation. It created an online portal – which is examined in Chapter 7 – alongside a range of other participation schemes. It

[3] 'Cabinet approves citizens' assemblies on gender equality and Dublin's local government', *Journal*, 11 June 2019.
[4] Bertelsmann Stiftung, *Citizens' Participation Using Sortition* (Gütersloh: Bertelsmann Stiftung, 2018).
[5] 'German-speaking community of Belgium becomes world's first region with permanent citizen participation drafted by lot', *Foundation for Future Generations*, 26 February 2019.
[6] D. van Reybrouck, 'Belgium's democratic experiment', *Politico*, 25 April 2019.
[7] 'Less fear more participation', *Green European Journal*, 19 June 2019.

provided a hundred million euros of the municipal budget to be decided by citizens voting for projects in order of preference, one of the largest participatory budgets in the world. Over the government's mandate, 844 public funding projects were chosen through this method. A rich network of local neighbourhood and district forums gathered momentum around specific issues. In addition, the administration ran a programme of so-called Citizen Laboratories to generate policy ideas from neighbourhoods around the city. In one suburb, Alcobendas, the council created a School of Citizen Participation and Innovation.

In 2019, the municipal government converted a long-existing body called the City Observatory – made up of former councillors – into a permanent body of forty-nine randomly selected citizens. This body began work in March 2019 and was scheduled to meet eight days a year to debate how to take forward the ideas that received the most votes on the city's online petitioning platform. Soon after, a new right-wing administration took office and discontinued the observatory; the body's citizen members pointedly continued to meet of their own accord in the street.[8]

Poland. Poland's rich experience in deliberative participation has occurred despite the country's democratic regression. A notable network of citizen assemblies operates in Gdansk, where the former mayor, Pawel Adamowicz, fostered numerable civic innovations before his assassination in 2019. He created the first Citizen Assembly in Poland, a panel of sixty-three randomly selected citizens that focused on issues of pollution, flooding, democratic engagement and LGBT rights. Gdansk residents can request a citizen assembly with a thousand signatures; the mayor implements decisions that get an 80 per cent level of support in the assembly and has discretion on whether or not to do so if the level of support is 50–80 per cent. Other cities have increasingly replicated the Gdansk model; Lublin has used it for tackling poor air

---

8   For an extensive account of the whole 2014–19 experience of citizen participation in Madrid, see MediaLab, *Future Democracies: Laboratory of Collective Intelligence for Participatory Democracy* (Madrid: MediaLab, 2019).

quality.[9] Poland now has the largest number of participatory budgeting experiments in Europe.[10] In 2020, the Polish opposition pushed to get citizen participation integrated into the upper house of the parliament – after elections gave them control of that chamber – as a means of taking on the government and undercutting the PiS's own rhetorical support for direct citizen participation.

Estonia. In Estonia, the centre-right, coalition government set up a people's assembly in 2013 after citizen pressure sparked by a political party corruption scandal. This led to reforms on party financing and new provisions for e-petitions, although the parliament stalled on most of the recommendations. Further assemblies were held on ageing in 2017, climate issues in 2018 and forestry management in 2019. In 2018 and 2019, the government oversaw thirty-four community discussions across Estonia; over 350 people participated in the drafting of ninety policy proposals that were fed into parliamentary debates.[11]

United Kingdom. There has also been a notable expansion of initiatives in the UK under both Labour and Conservative administrations, linked to an ongoing process of democratic decentralization of the British state over the last decade.[12] The British parliament commissioned and funded a citizen assembly on health and social care in 2018. In 2019, the government's Innovation in Democracy Programme supported citizen assemblies in three local authorities (after an initial commitment to run eight such initiatives). Six parliamentary select committees opened a 110-member national citizen assembly on climate change that published its recommendations in September 2020. A number of local authorities – such as Lambeth, Frome, Glasgow and Camden councils – launched assemblies on local planning issues and climate

---

[9] M. Gerwin, *Citizens' Assemblies: Guide to Democracy That Works* (Krakow: Otwarty Plan, 2018).

[10] G. Sgueo, 'Participatory budgeting: An innovative approach', European Parliament Research Service, 2016.

[11] 'Deliberative democracy attempts in Estonia', rahvakogu.ee, Spring 2019.

[12] P. Dunleavy, A. Park and R. Taylor (eds), *UK Democratic Audit 2018* (London: LSE Press, 2018), p. 41.

change. Municipal authorities have increasingly used so-called citizen panels regularly to inform decision-making on local issues.

In April 2019, the Scottish Government announced that it would convene a citizen assembly on the country's future. This came after such assemblies had already been set up to deliberate on social care and the welfare state. Several British politicians from across the political spectrum teamed up to campaign for a Citizens' Convention on UK Democracy, and in the 2019 election both the Labour and Liberal Democrat manifestos supported the idea. While the incoming Conservative government instead convened a more traditional commission on British democracy made up of elite figures and experts, leaders of the Citizens' Convention campaign pushed to have a citizen assembly feed into this. In total, as of summer 2020, there were fifteen public-authority assemblies either running or being set up in the UK, up from ten at the end of 2019; two of these were at the national level (on climate change and food policy), the rest at local level; thematically, ten were on climate change.[13]

Germany. While the federal German government has largely stood aside from the wave of participation, since 2015 it has funded local-level participative forums through an Actively Engaged City programme, a Live Democracy scheme and a series of Local Partnerships for Democracy.[14] The state of Baden-Württemberg set up randomly selected citizen assemblies on several issues, including one in 2018 on the future of the European Union.[15] Nearly a hundred German local authorities have implemented participatory budgeting.[16] The German federal parliament convened a citizen assembly to propose ideas for improving German democracy nationally; this Bürgerrat Demokratie consisted of 160 randomly selected participants and presented its

---

[13] For details on these UK examples, see Involve, 'Citizens' assembly tracker', with running updates.

[14] 'Federal Ministry for Family Affairs, Senior Citizens, Women and Youth', Civic engagement policy, 14 May 2020.

[15] Baden-Württemberg European dialogue, 'We'll go ahead!' Ministry of Justice and for Europe, 2018.

[16] Participatory budgeting in Germany, www.buergerhaushalt.org.

reform suggestions to the Bundestag in November 2019.[17] In 2020, two German Länder – Saarland and Thüringen – launched citizen assemblies on regional policy, while the Bundestag called one on Germany's role in the world.

These select examples give just a taste of the kinds of initiatives that have become widespread in recent years. On the back of this expansion, the International Observatory on Participatory Democracy, based within the Barcelona municipal government, has worked to coordinate and link together innovations in city-level participation.[18] In 2020, the Covid-19 emergency presented obvious logistical challenges to these forums, but it did not derail the momentum behind participative deliberation. Indeed, several cities and regions opened citizen assemblies specifically on the pandemic: such forums ran in Bordeaux, Marseilles, Nancy, Nantes and Poitiers in France; in Chemnitz in Germany; in Murcia in Spain; and in the West Midlands and Bristol in the UK. [19] While governments' immediate priorities understandably lay elsewhere in 2020, the uncertainties of the post-pandemic world look set to generate more demand for deliberative democratic renewal.

Referendums

While deliberative assemblies have multiplied, there has not been an equally dramatic increase in the use of referendums across Europe in recent years. The controversies surrounding a number of high-profile referendums have made many governments more hesitant about this form of direct democracy. Yet, local-level authorities in many EU states have become more receptive to direct democracy and have facilitated an increasing number of referendums. While this trend may not be of

---

[17] Germany's citizens' assembly on democracy; www.participedia.net.
[18] See www.oidp.net.
[19] See Eurocities' running updates of such Covid-19 initiatives, at https://covidnews. eurocities.eu/category/covidnews/governance/.

macro-level political significance and has generally gone unnoticed within debates about the state of European democracy, it has given citizens some influence over second-order decisions in their immediate localities.

A number of EU-related referendums took place across Europe in the 2010s. In December 2015, Danish voters rejected the government's proposal to soften the country's opt out from EU cooperation on Justice and Home affairs. In July 2015, Greek citizens rejected EU bailout conditions, although Prime Minister Alexis Tsipras ended up accepting these anyway. In October 2016, Hungarians rejected EU migrant quotas, albeit with a turnout short of the 50 per cent threshold required for the referendum to be valid. In April 2016, Dutch citizens voted against an association agreement between the EU and Ukraine, although this was passed anyway after a few minor tweaks. Most dramatically, of course, British voters chose to leave the EU and plunged the country into a protracted political deadlock that was not merely about the country's relation with Europe but also the legitimacy of direct democracy relative to parliamentary sovereignty.

In a very different but equally momentous case, the Catalan regional administration held a referendum on independence in October 2017 without approval from the Spanish government. The illegal vote was strongly in favour of independence and dramatically deepened long simmering tensions between Catalonia and the Spanish government. The referendum unleashed polarization and political radicalization on both sides of the conflict and tensions over democracy itself. Catalan secessionists argued that only a legal, state-backed referendum could resolve this crisis. The Spanish state and political parties criticized the concept of popular direct democracy with increasing vehemence, insisting that defending democracy was about upholding formal constitutional provisions prohibiting secession. Of the national-level parties, only the leftist Unidas Podemos suggested that a legal referendum might be the best democratic way to solve the crisis but made little headway with the argument as positions hardened on both sides.

More generic doubts have intensified about referendums because populist parties have been strong advocates of direct democracy, and this has increased fears that this form of democracy is sharply at odds with the liberal component of European democracy – that is, the protection of certain rights if necessary against majority positions. Empirical research has shown that citizens drawn to populist parties are generally more supportive of direct democracy.[20] Italy's Five Star Movement, the Danish People's Party, the AfD in Germany, the Forum for Democracy in the Netherlands, the Freedom Party in Austria, the PiS in Poland and the Freedom and Direct Democracy Party in the Czech Republic have all pushed for a more regular and systematic use of referendums.

There have been several examples of populist parties advancing direct-democracy measures. In June 2018, the new Italian coalition government came to power promising more direct democratic voting. In 2019, the Five Star's minister for direct democracy introduced a proposal to allow citizens to suggest new laws to the parliament and get a direct vote on them if they attracted a certain level of support. In September 2020, the Five Star-led government held and won a national referendum on its proposal to cut the number of Italian parliamentarians. The somewhat Eurosceptic and populist Czech government made it easier for citizens to trigger a national referendum. Coming to power in 2017, Austria's coalition government that included the far-right Freedom Party called for more direct democracy, although it stirred controversy when it actually reversed a citizen initiative to ban smoking in bars and restaurants.

Against this backdrop, several mainstream governments have sought to curtail the use of referendums for highly sensitive, and especially EU-linked, questions.[21] In 2018 the Dutch government repealed the law that had been introduced in 2015 providing for citizen-led

[20] S. Mohrenberg, R. Hubert and T. Freyburg, Love at First Sight? Populist Attitudes and Support for Direct Democracy, *Party Politics* (2019).
[21] I. Krastev *After Europe* (Pennsylvania: University of Pennsylvania Press, 2017).

referendums. Surveys find a clear disjuncture: while citizens express strong support for more direct democracy (including those voters that are not supportive of populist parties), parliamentarians, state and EU officials have in recent years become more hostile.[22] While the number of referendums has increased since the early 1990s, in general they are subject to restrictive conditions in EU states. Most national referendums are called because they are constitutionally required. Citizen-led referendums have remained infrequent, and even when they are held most fail to meet minimum turnout levels.[23] Romanian and Croatian referendums against same-sex marriage did not carry due to low turnouts, although a 2019 non-binding vote in Romania more usefully helped the push for stronger anti-corruption measures.[24]

However, while the spotlight has often fallen on high-profile national referendums especially over EU questions, a less divisive layer of local-level direct democracy has quietly put down roots across Europe. The growth in local referendums is a long-term trend that started in the 1990s and accelerated in the 2010s, and was not driven primarily by populist administrations. This trend has helped push EU states' overall use of referendums to a higher level than other regions of the world.[25] Denmark, the Czech Republic, Italy, Lithuania, Poland and Slovenia have been high users of such direct votes, while France has remained one of the states using them least frequently. The increased use of local referendums includes both those called by authorities and instances where these authorities have allowed citizen initiatives to force referendums. Despite their misgivings about referendums, European governments have in some instances facilitated and supported their

[22] European Economic and Social Committee, *Societies Outside Metropolises: The Role of Civil Society Organisations in Facing Populism* (Brussels: EESC, 2018), pp. 147–8.
[23] M. Qvortrup, 'Demystifying direct democracy?', *Journal of Democracy*, 28/3 (2017), 141–52.
[24] A. Slavov, 'National referendums: Between legitimate popular decision-making and populist take-over', in S. Blockmans and S. Russack (eds), *Deliberative Democracy in the EU: Countering Populism with Participation and Debate* (London: Rowman and Littlefield, 2020), pp. 261–2.
[25] B. Griessel, 'Democratic innovations in Europe', in S. Elstub and O. Escobar (eds), *Handbook on Democratic Innovation and Governance* (London: Elgar, 2019), p. 406.

increased use on local issues. Officials have in many places become more positive towards a local-level 'direct democracy of proximity'.[26] Many examples could be cited; again, a small selection suffices to demonstrate the trend. Between 2006 and 2017, 259 local referendums were held in Czech municipalities, generally on infrastructure projects or environmental issues.[27] In June 2017, a referendum in the Bulgarian city of Tran forestalled gold mining in the region. In Greece, referendums in Thessaloniki and the Ionian Islands stopped the privatization of water supplies and airports, respectively. A 2018 decentralization reform in Greece opened the possibility for local referendums to be held on a widened scope of policy issues. In Budapest the level of support for a referendum on Hungary's bid to host the 2024 Olympic Games was so great that the government withdrew from the competition even without a vote actually taking place.[28] In Romania, several local-level votes have been held on fracking for shale gas and gold mining.[29] In local referendums in 2017, the two northern Italian regions of Lombardy and Veneto voted in favour of greater autonomy in areas such as fiscal, security, immigration and education policies. An extensive databank has been built up showing the increased use of local direct democracy across Germany in recent years.[30] In 2020, authorities promised referendums in Paris and Amsterdam on restricting visitor numbers.

While Poland's overall democracy scores have worsened, an increasing number of local referendums have been held and wielded significant influence. In the 2010s, between thirty and forty local referendums were held each year in Poland. The largest number of these have been to remove elected officials from office – mayors in a

---

[26] European Economic and Social Committee, *Societies Outside Metropolises: The Role of Civil Society Organisations in Facing Populism* (Brussels: EESC, 2018), p. 148.

[27] 'Local referendums often held in Czech Republic', *Prague Daily Monitor*, 29 September 2017.

[28] M. Dunai, 'Hungary to withdraw Budapest's 2024 Olympic bid: Government', *Reuters*, 22 February 2017.

[29] 'Lower than needed turnout for local referendums on environmental impact of projects in Romania', *Romania Insider*, 11 December 2012.

[30] See online database at http://www.datenbank-buergerbegehren.info.

number of Polish cities have been ejected in this way.[31] In May 2014, the residents of Krakow voted against the city bidding for the 2022 Winter Olympics and forced the local government to withdraw its bid.[32] In 2017, the PiS government proposed a merger of the Warsaw municipality with its neighbouring suburban communities; realizing that the underlying reasons for the merger were political, residents of twenty-two affected municipalities collected enough signatures to call a referendum and voted against the government's proposal, which was then withdrawn.

In the UK, local referendums became notably more widespread from the late 2000s. Parish councils and residents of a district can formulate neighbourhood development plans, and if they pass an independent check, put these to a binding local referendum. Around eight hundred such referendums took place during the 2010s.[33] Since 2011, any rise in council tax above a set threshold must be approved by a local referendum. In 2012, mayoral referendums were held in England's twelve largest cities; three of these cities (Leicester, Liverpool and Bristol) voted to establish mayors.

The trend is not uniform. Some local authorities have struggled to push national governments to allow more scope for local referendums.[34] Restrictions continue to be severe in Belgium and Spain, even if local authorities here do have formal powers to request a referendum. In Spain, beyond the sensitive issues related to Catalonia and other regions' powers, the central government has been resistant to approving local referendums on development projects and more day-to-day issues.[35] Similarly, the Belgian constitution does not allow for binding referendums due to the prospect of the Flemish-French divide breaking

---

[31] I. Stokfiszewski, 'The rise of Poland's urban movement', *Al Jazeera*, 9 December 2014.

[32] 'Krakove residents vote on bidding for Winter Games', *AP News*, 25 May 2014.

[33] Ministry of Housing, Communities and Local Governments, *Notes on Neighbourhood Planning*, (London: HMG, 2019).

[34] T. Schiller, 'Local referendums: A comparative assessment of forms and practice', in L. Morel and M. Qvortrup (eds), *Routledge Handbook on Direct Democracy and Referendums*, (London: Routledge, 2018).

[35] 'El referendum que negaron a Soto del Real y otras 76 consultas vetadas en democracia', *El Confidencial*, 14 May 2018.

the country apart through a popular vote – although here too some localities have begun to use referendums for very local issues.[36] In sum, trends in relation to referendums are mixed across Europe. The number of local referendums has risen and direct votes have become a more regular aspect of regional and municipal politics. At this level they have become a positive dimension of democratic renewal and supported by forces across the political spectrum. Yet, authorities in general have remained much cooler towards referendums than they are towards participative forums like citizen assemblies. Most centre-left, centrist and centre-right European governments have become more circumspect in backing their use for high-politics issues at the national level, fearing that in the current context such votes would fuel illiberal majoritarianism.

Profile: France

One of the most extensive and important recent examples of citizen participation has occurred in France. Here citizen participation took on the highest-level political significance in the form of a nationwide Grand Débat – perhaps one of the most emblematic cases of democratic renewal in recent years. This was called by President Macron in 2019 in response to weeks of Gilet Jaunes protests against elements of his economic and social reform programme. The Grand Débat and climate assembly that came in its wake did more than perhaps any other initiative in Europe to raise the profile of citizen participation. How far this entailed healthy democratic renewal became an extensively debated and fiercely contested question.

Debates about deliberative participation had been accumulating in the years before Macron's initiative, and this was notable in a state known for its top-down political culture. The Paris municipal administration had been building up a range of local deliberative participation models

---

[36] 'Leuven is not keen on referendums, *Veto*, 4 March 2017.

for several years prior to the Grand Débat. It created youth and neighbourhood councils by sortition with the ability to raise issues on the city government agenda. Other local initiatives spread beyond Paris. In 2014, the urban planning law was reformed to allow and facilitate citizen councils; from then until 2019 over six hundred of these were created by sortition and worked on local planning issues.

A February 2019 report by the French National Assembly detailed a far-reaching expansion of local democratic mechanisms but also noted that relatively small numbers of citizens were taking advantage of these due both to low awareness and the restrictive conditions governing their use.[37] One frustrating experience occurred in Grenoble. In 2016, this city launched a referendum procedure that allowed citizens to sign a petition in an area of the municipal council's competence. If the petition garnered over two thousand signatures, it would be debated in the City Council; if more than 20,000 residents voted in favour, the mayor was obliged to undertake the project.[38] The administrative court then ruled the new procedure was unconstitutional because voters could not impose decisions on a mayor, and the scheme was withdrawn.[39] Citizens were angered and pushed for votes on local issues. This case generated pressure on a powerful, centralized state to allow more popular influence over public-policy decisions.

Against this background of patchy local initiatives, in early 2019 President Macron launched the so-called Grand Débat. This was propelled in part by the Gilets Jaunes protests, covered in the previous chapter. The Gilets Citoyens group emerged out of the protests to work on designing a large-scale participative initiative – a noteworthy link between revolts and structured deliberation. The Grand Débat offered citizens across France the chance to engage in debates and put forward proposals on four topics: environment, democracy, tax and

---

[37] Assemblee Nationale, 'Mission flash sur la democratie local et la participation citoyenne', Communication de Mme Emilie Chalas et M. Herve Saulignac, 2019.

[38] 'Grenoble: le tribunal administratif retoque la democratie a la sauce piolle', *Libération*, 24 May 2018.

[39] 'L'etat veut faire annuler la votation-citoyenne de grenoble', *Le Dauphine*, 5 May 2018.

public services. The government oversaw thousands of town hall and local meetings. It opened *cahiers de doleance* or complaint books in communities across the country. It set up a platform for individuals to submit proposals online; 1.9 million people used this to send in suggestions. In its most deliberative component, a series of citizen assemblies was held towards the end of the process and got randomly selected people to focus on a small number of concrete policy proposals. Independent guarantors or *garants* oversaw many of the meetings. Macron himself participated in several events, engaging with voters on a range of policy detail for hours at a time.

The government set some limits to what it was prepared to consider. It excluded immigration from the Grand Débat's remit. It refused to consider some of the proposals that attracted most online support, including those to repeal same-sex marriage and reinstate a wealth tax. Opposition parties argued the process was cosmetic and too tightly controlled. Even members of the government feared it would simply lead to a wish list of funding demands. The well-off, urbanites prominent in the meetings were very different from the people active in the Gilet Jaunes protests that continued in parallel to the Grand Débat, diluting the crossover between these two routes ostensibly headed towards democratic renewal.[40]

Still, those involved in the meetings reported that people were interested in democratic citizenship, not just the predictable calls for more state funds for jobs and security. Even if the government set the parameters of the Débat, the process spawned many autonomous civil society-led debates and consultations. In this way, it unquestionably galvanized public debate and democratic engagement. While the government rejected a provision for citizens to trigger referendums, it promised to expand the use of referendums at the local level.[41] It introduced a process for randomly selected citizens to sit in the state's

[40] R. Thillaye, 'Is Macron's grand débat a democratic dawn for France?', Carnegie Europe, 26 April 2019.
[41] 'Conference de presse a l'issue du Grand Debat national', 25 April 2019, https://www.elysee.fr/emmanuel-macron/2019/04/25/conference-de-presse-grand-debat-national.

Economic, Social and Environmental Council and widened petition rights. Despite all these gains, however, into 2020 the Débat's wider follow-up remained uncertain. While the government insisted that many of its reform plans mirrored the concerns raised through the Grand Débat, ministries archived most of the ideas proposed by citizens without plans for any action.[42] State authorities remained ambivalent over supporting local citizen assemblies, despite several political lists pushing for these.[43]

In its most concrete follow-on to the Grand Débat, the government established a 150-person, six-month citizen assembly on climate change. This was charged with proposing ideas for how France could meet its emission-reduction targets and used an elaborate process of random selection. The exercise turned into Europe's most high-profile initiative of deliberative participation. The government's tutelage over the assembly was especially marked as it played a prominent role in its launch and in tightly defining its mandate. Alongside the main assembly gatherings, expert consultations and thematic subgroups were held. Climate CSOs were involved, providing a link to organized civil society. Six weekend sessions ran between October 2019 and January 2020, before meetings moved online due to Covid-19. Macron engaged with the assembly and promised that its ideas would be submitted in concrete form to be voted on in parliament and possibly in a referendum too.

The participants pushed hard to widen the mandate handed to them by the government and brought forward ideas related to general economic problems and the Covid-19 pandemic.[44] The assembly presented a package of 149 proposals in June 2020. It suggested only two of these be put to a referendum – proposals for a new crime of ecocide and revision of the constitution to enshrine climate goals. In

[42] C. Dobler, *The 2019 Grand Débat National in France: A Participatory Experiment with Limited Legitimacy* (Berlin: Democracy Reporting International, 2020).

[43] C. Vernaillen, 'French local elections in democratic limbo', Democracy International, 5 June 2020.

[44] Convention Citoyenne, *Coronavirus: 50 propositions de la convention citoyenne pour la sortie de la crise*, April 2020.

this sense, the assembly was more cautious than Macron was about putting the more ambitious ideas to a popular vote. Macron initially agreed to advance in parliament with 146 of the 149 proposals, rejecting lower speed limits, a dividend tax and revision to the constitution's preamble – while suggesting the latter proposal might be put to a referendum. However, the government put legislation to the parliament in March 2021 that included fewer than half the assembly's suggestions.[45] Assembly participants complained and protestors took to the streets, sensing that the president had gone back on his word.

Assessment: Participation's potential and limits

The spread of deliberative participation and to a lesser extent referendums represents a notable development in European politics. Europe has come to occupy a prominent place within a worldwide trend towards both more direct democracy and various forms of consultations, assemblies and citizen petitioning.[46] The Covid-19 emergency caused complications but has not reversed this trend. Many books and articles on democratic renewal have in recent years focused on making the general case in favour of such participative initiatives.[47] However, while many reformers champion this participatory turn, there remain question marks over how valuable the trend has so far been for European democracy. The deepening of participative dynamics is

[45] 'Climat: sept propositions de la convention citoyenne écartées par le gouvernement (malgré la promesse d'Emmanuel Macron)', Franceinfo, 30 September 2020.

[46] D. Altmann, *Direct Democracy Worldwide* (Cambridge: Cambridge University Press, 2011); B. Kaufmann and J. Mathews, 'Democracy doomsday prophets are missing this critical shift', *Washington Post*, 8 May 2018.

[47] H. Landemore, *Open Democracy: Reinventing Popular Rule for the Twenty-First Century* (Princeton, NJ: Princeton University Press, 2020); C. Taylor, P. Nanz and M. Beaubien Taylor, *Reconstructing Democracy: How Citizens are Building from the Ground Up* (Cambridge: Harvard University Press, 2019); J.Gastil and K. Knobloch, *Hope for Democracy* (Oxford: Oxford University Press, 2020); OECD, *Innovative Citizen Participation and New Democratic Institutions: Catching the deliberative wave* (Paris: OECD, 2020); D. Van Reybrouck, *Against Elections: The Case for Democracy* (New York: Seven Stories Press, 2018).

and will be one of the most vital and valuable elements of democratic renewal, but difficulties remain in advancing this area of reform beyond a controlled and relatively bounded form of citizen engagement.

Better deliberation – but with limits

Governments have launched many deliberative initiatives, but these have not become so numerous as to build an all-pervasive democratic practice. The numbers have increased but still amount to a maximum of twenty or so initiatives even in the most committed states – not what could be called a mainstreamed dimension of democratic decision-making. If some supporters see assemblies as a complement to election-based representation and some push them as more of a replacement, in practice they are for now nowhere near the point of becoming the central core of European decision-making and rivalling other democratic processes.

They have mostly been commissioned by public institutions with tight, preset remits. Doubts remain about the fact that governments can easily capture and use these kinds of highly structured, one-off deliberative initiatives for their own ends. Authorities of all political stripes have typically kept their parameters relatively narrow, seeking the benefits of wider participation while preventing this from becoming a radical challenge to governmental power. Organizers tend to run deliberation with a particular agenda or policy output in mind rather than because they want to improve democracy in a general or systemic fashion. As yet, these exercises have not allowed citizens to get issues onto the agenda that governments refuse to address or do not even consider to be important.

Proposals have taken shape to make deliberative participation a more permanent feature of democratic decision-making. The East Belgian model is a vanguard template that opens the door for citizens to propose their own deliberations and to do so on a permanent basis. However, the fact that such a model is still the exception after so many years of innovation is a sobering reminder of the distance left to travel towards widespread democratic renewal. Certainly, little momentum has gathered behind a step up from time-limited, one-off citizen assemblies to permanent citizen chambers embedded within legislative processes – with both methodological and political doubts prevailing over the latter template of reform. Governments and parliaments are still reluctant to let citizens themselves choose the issues on which assemblies are held. Deliberative initiatives have been used mainly to take specific issues out of the standard political cycle, rather than being embedded as a regularized part of such normal politics.

The methodological quality of deliberative participation has improved significantly in recent years. Most citizen assemblies today select participants by random lot, involve experts, move methodically from broad agenda-setting discussions through to more specific decisions on solutions, structure deliberation in way that avoids polarizing debate and get public authorities signed up to consider their recommendations. They have increasingly used a skewed stratification of random selection to bring in disengaged and disadvantaged sectors of society.[48] Contrary to many initial doubts, the evidence suggests that citizens have engaged in these initiatives and have done so in an open-minded way that has generated agreement or at least mutual empathy on many policy issues.[49] Deliberative practitioners have worked hard to maintain such rigorous standards as the number of such initiatives increases and also to design ways of improving the impact of assemblies' recommendations.[50]

Still, the number of EU citizens involved in deliberative participation has been very limited – in most instances, no more than a few dozen people. This leaves most citizens untouched by or even unaware of their increased use. In places with a rich experience in recent deliberative participation, this has not sufficed to prevent illiberal macro-level

---

[48] J. Gastil and R. Richards, 'Making direct democracy deliberative through random assemblies', *Politics and Society*, 41/2 (2013), 253–81.
[49] www.participedia.net.
[50] OECD Report, *Innovative Citizen Participation and New Democratic Institutions. Catching the Deliberative Wave* (Paris: OECD, 2020).

political trends or the rise of far-right parties. Belgium, Estonia and Spain are all prime examples of this. Austrian villages pioneered a whole template of citizen councils to soften tensions over migrant arrivals, and yet this was precisely when the far-right Freedom Party rose to new heights.[51] Participative forums have not provided any decisive antidote to the rise of illiberal populist parties – and this might be beyond what can fairly be expected of them.

The Irish experience is widely lauded as the best-organized use of citizen assemblies, especially because the parliament and civil society organizations were closely involved. Nevertheless, even in this most exemplary of cases some local observers have raised doubts. They point out that Irish politicians were already looking for ways to change constitutional provisions on same-sex marriage and abortion, and that they blocked the assemblies' several other recommendations that did not match their own interests. While those on the winning side of the two referendums argued that the process won widespread legitimacy independent of the outcome, not all those on the losing side agreed.[52] The 2019 proposals for two further assemblies met with more misgivings about the arbitrary way in which the government had selected the issues to be deliberated.[53]

President Macron has probably done more than any other European leader to raise the profile of citizen participation, and yet still riles many with what they see as his hyper-presidential understanding of democracy. For all his promises of bottom-up democratic renovation, Macron had to be pushed into the Grand Débat by the Gilets Jaunes protests. If Macron's main aim in launching the Grand Débat and the spin-off climate assembly was to take the wind out of protestors' sails and channel frustration into a form of participation that he could more easily control, then he probably succeeded. The Débat calmed the

---

[51] C. Taylor, P. Nanz and M. Beaubien Taylor, *Reconstructing Democracy: How Citizens are Building from the Ground Up* (Cambridge, MA: Harvard University Press, 2019).

[52] N. O'Leary, 'The myth of the citizens' assembly', *Politico*, 18 June 2019.

[53] See the *Irish Times* editorial 'The Irish Times view on citizens assemblies outsourcing political decisions', *Irish Times*, 14 June 2019.

Gilets Jaunes revolts and restored the president's flagging popularity. It might be concluded that democratic participation here was both the government's self-interested tactical ploy and a positive case of citizens being placated by the chance genuinely to express their grievances.

Similar concerns emerge from the more general spread of climate change assemblies. While participants in climate assemblies have called for measures to hasten energy transitions, these have mostly been ideas to meet policy aims that governments have defined. Citizens in the French climate assembly pushed in frustration to modify the mandate handed down to them by the government.[54] While many believe that citizens will support more ambitious climate action the more they engage with the issue, it is not clear what happens if and when assemblies come out *against* some types of climate action. Concerns have surfaced over experts' pronounced influence in pushing citizens towards their own preferred outcomes in climate assemblies.[55] Tension can easily open up between the kind of process needed for 'good democracy' and that needed for 'good climate policy'.

From low to high politics?

Given these limitations, the question arises of how the highly positive rise in deliberative initiatives might be taken further in Europe and its impact raised to a higher political level. Experts' focus to date has been mainly on improving the internal processes and methodology of deliberative forums. Most initiatives have been organized around practical challenges that permit constructive solutions, and only limited consideration has been given to participation's role in broader democratic renewal.[56] Currently, discussions about assemblies can feel

---

[54] 'Conventon climat: Les citoyens ont tenu a depassar le mandate de depart', *La Croix*, 9 March 2020.

[55] S. Capstick, C. Demski, C. Cherry, C. Verfuerth and K. Steentjes, *Climate Change Citizens' Assemblies*, CAST Briefing Paper 03 (2020); R. Wilson and C. Mellier, *Getting Climate Assemblies Right* (Brussels: Carnegie Europe, 2020).

[56] D. Caluwaerts and M. Reuchamps, 'Generating democratic legitimacy through deliberative innovations: The role of embeddedness and disruptiveness', *Representation*, 52/1 (2016), 13–27.

disconnected from the political situation of the European countries in which they are being held.

Research suggests that the spread of deliberation within mini-publics has not yet fostered better deliberation within the democratic system or public as a whole.[57] While many assessments suggest that citizen assemblies can have wider positive effects, some experts point out that overall the evidence is mixed and that better methods are needed to ascertain whether mini-publics have any broad impact on citizens' trust in democracy.[58] Detailed evaluations have found that local-level initiatives have differed somewhat between countries, some giving space to social actors and new voices while most limit citizens to more modest managerial debates.[59]

Deliberative participation has commonly taken the form of European governments and local authorities asking citizens for opinions on a specific issue. Much, although not all, of it revolves around debate about projects – what authorities should spend local funds on in certain city locations. It commonly takes places around issues where a one-off choice is to be made. Most political decisions do not take this form, of course, but rather require ongoing attention and a rolling series of trade-offs and are never definitively resolved. The question of how far citizen assemblies can deal with the intricate and complex linkages between different areas of policy remains relatively untested in European countries. To contribute at a higher political level to democratic renewal, participative initiatives will need to move from selective consultation to a regularized co-creation of democratic politics between citizens and political elites.

This relates to a long-running debate about how far deliberative participation can be scaled-up from the local level. Most of Europe's recent deliberative initiatives are locally based, even though

---

[57] N. Curato and M. Böker, 'Linking mini-publics to the deliberative system: A research agenda', *Policy Sciences*, 49/2 (2016), pp. 173–90.

[58] S. Boulianne, 'Building faith in democracy: Deliberative events, political trust and efficacy', *Political Studies*, 67/1 (2019), 4–30.

[59] B. Griessel, 'Democratic innovations in Europe', in S. Elstub and O. Escobar (eds), *Handbook on Democratic Innovation and Governance* (London: Elgar, 2019), pp. 412–13.

national-level initiatives have also emerged. Some governments have attempted to scale-up participation to higher political levels, but such cases have been relatively rare. There is a particularly glaring disconnect between the flourishing world of citizen assemblies and more atrophied debates on EU reforms. How far linkages between the local, national and European levels are actually possible remains subject to lively debate. Some of the foremost experts in participative design warn that scaling-up and politicizing assemblies may risk undermining the very features that make them successful and useful. [60] Chapter 8 returns to this question in its exploration of recent EU reform initiatives.

Referendums – risks and potential

While views on deliberative participation exercises are generally positive, opinions on the use referendums tend to be hesitant and have become more negative in recent years. Many fear referendums are either controlled by elites for their own nefarious ends or used by populists, and neither case is good for democratic quality.[61] However, while governments of contrasting political persuasions have sought to curtail risky direct votes, especially on EU-related issues, some of them seem to acknowledge that citizens do want more direct democracy. Some governments have been more open to developing the use of direct democracy at a local level and for issues beyond inflammable issues of identity.

Intriguingly, while populists have promoted direct democracy, mainstream governments and local authorities have sought to use it in a moderated form as a means of undercutting populists' appeal. While direct democracy's image has suffered in recent years, experts point out that as a wider range of different levels and types of referendums have taken shape, and as best practices have been fine-tuned, so their

---

[60] G. Smith and R. Bechler, 'Citizens' assembly towards a politics of considered judgement. part-2', *Open Democracy*, 27 November 2019.
[61] L. Topaloff, 'The rise of referendums: Elite strategy or populist weapon?', *Journal of Democracy*, 28/3 (2017), 127–40.

impact on democracy has become more varied than the standard fear that they simply give vent to ill-formed, intransigent and intolerant majoritarianism. Quantitative research suggests that the use of referendums in EU states over the last twenty years has in many cases narrowed rather than stirring polarization at local level.[62]

Direct democracy has worked best as a means of incentivizing ongoing and constructive citizen participation, not simply as an occasional means for giving national and EU elites a figurative kicking.[63] At this level, some referendums have been a modest but useful tool of European democratic renewal. Research on recent referendums finds that their use goes well beyond an association with the rise of populism or with illiberal agendas.[64] There is now more focus on ensuring referendums do not undermine constitutional rights or minorities' protection – a major challenge being to ensure that direct votes do not throttle core liberal norms. While citizen assemblies only involve a very small number of people, major political dilemmas often need the kind of mass-based decisions that referendums offer. Still, it remains striking how uneasy most EU governments have become about exploring direct democracy's wider potential.

Connecting democratic channels

Perhaps the most pressing imperative is to dovetail deliberative participation and direct votes with each other and with other areas of democratic reform. For many years now, experts have argued that emerging forms of direct citizen participation need to work in tighter concert with existing channels of representative democracy. Some champions of deliberative initiatives have begun to address

---

[62] S. Vospernik, 'Referendums and consensus democracy: Empirical findings from 21 EU countries', in L. Morel and M. Qvortrup (eds), *Routledge Handbook on Direct Democracy and Referendums* (London: Routledge, 2017).

[63] Independent Commission on Referendums, *Report of the Independent Commission on Referendums* (London: Constitution Unit, UCL, 2018).

[64] K. Collin, *Populist and Authoritarian Referendums: The Role of Direct Democracy in Democratic Deconsolidation* (Washington, DC: Brookings, 2019).

long-standing criticisms that these are often niche initiatives aloof from the core thrust of democratic debates. A growing focus in theoretical work is on how various levels of democratic innovation, including the use of certain types of referendum, are needed to bring out deliberative dynamics that cannot be delivered by stand-alone assemblies.[65] Yet, practical progress in joining together different types of democratic renewal remains limited. In general, efforts across Europe to improve participative, representative and direct forms of democracy are not particularly linked. So-called mixed or blended deliberative forums that include citizens and politicians together have not been a major part of the current participative wave across Europe. The two routes to democratic renewal covered in this chapter should work tightly together – with small-scale deliberation providing detailed, focused problem-solving and referendums a wider decisional legitimacy – yet they have evolved as almost rival communities of democratic experiment. And both participative initiatives and referendum campaigns still tend to frame themselves as a counterweight to parliaments and parties.

Some empirical research on citizen assemblies in Europe reveals that participants themselves are concerned that these bodies might be displacing elected officials and that the latter need to be more engaged in their deliberations.[66] Few policy initiatives in Europe have addressed the difficult questions that would arise should participative initiatives spread more dramatically so that a really significant number of decisions were no longer based on electoral competition – like the question of who would be responsible for the consequences of assemblies' decisions should these go wrong. A standard line is that election-based and randomly selected decision-making logics need to function in tandem, but little practical endeavour has yet worked at docking these strands of democratic organization together.

[65] J. Parkinson, 'The role of referendums in deliberative systems', *Representation*, published online, 6 February 2020.
[66] V. Jacquet, 'The role and the future of deliberative mini-publics: A citizen perspective', *Political Studies*, 67/3 (2019), 639–57.

This matters because at present Europe's emergent deliberative forms of democratic renewal can feel depoliticized. Citizen assemblies individualize citizen engagement, deflecting attention away from collective organizations. Many democracy-focused CSOs across Europe have expressed concern that the attention now given to citizen assemblies unhelpfully draws oxygen away from organized civil society. Mini-publics can cut across the democratic activism coming with increasing dynamism from social movements and protests. In one notable example, many climate protest movements have been critical of recent climate assemblies. While some focus has been given to linking deliberative mini-publics 'upwards' to politicians and state bodies, less effort has been made to link them 'downwards' to mass mobilization.[67] To the extent that they take place largely on governments' terms, formal deliberative initiatives are usually more conservative than the civic activism covered in Chapter 3.

The surge in deliberative assemblies has rightly garnered a great deal of attention and optimism, but deep democratic renewal also requires elements of less bounded and more adversarial contestation. Europe's recent deliberative exercises have aimed to soften the roughest edges of polarized opinions; it remains to be seen how they can prove their worth in areas where democratic renewal requires more not less contestation. Not all major political and identity differences can be neutralized through deliberation, and consensual deliberation can sometimes risk leaving deep-seated power imbalances untouched. At least some democratic renewal must be built around power struggles and divisions, whether rooted in class, material, identity or national divergences.[68] It is important that European governments' controlled opening to participation is not allowed to deflect deeper challenge to their own power and interests. In the ways that civic activism, organized deliberative forums and referendums combine with each other, Europe's

---

[67] Y. Sintomer, 'Deliberative Polls and the Systemic Democratization of Democracy', *Good Society*, 27/1–2 (2018), 155–64.

[68] I. Shapiro, 'Collusion in restraint of democracy: Against deliberation', *Daedaleus* 146/3 (2017), 77–84.

democratic renewal needs to avoid being destructively illiberal at one extreme and overly tame at the other.

Realistic expectations

Overall, it might be said that Europe's participative turn has not sufficed to remedy the adverse macro-trends laid out in Chapter 2, but it has helped prevent popular disengagement from democracy extending even further than might otherwise have been the case. After previously being rather neglected and under-appreciated, different kinds of participative initiatives have come to occupy a prominent place in debates about European democratic renewal. Expectations around such initiatives have risen to extremely high levels. Arguably, the pendulum has swung from neglect all the way over to an uncritical assumption that deliberative citizen initiatives are the major plank in efforts to restore democratic accountability.

Yet, so far, there has been no higher-level 'systems perspective' on the broad political impact of the growth in participative initiatives across Europe.[69] The most-cited big-picture books on democracy in recent years hardly mention or acknowledge the existence of the rising world of small-scale deliberation; and in turn, those immersed in this world tend to act as champions for such initiatives largely disconnected from wider democracy debates. Some experts involved for many years in running such forums warn that they cannot be expected to solve democracy's most high-level problems and that expectations must be kept at a realistic level.[70] The question remains whether these initiatives can feed more naturally into the high politics of democratic reform in Europe without losing their undoubted value in relation to very practical, local politics. If the potential of participative forums is

---

[69] F. Hendriks, 'Democratic innovation beyond deliberative reflection: The plebiscitary rebound and the advent of action-oriented democracy', *Democratization*, 26/3 (2019), 444–64.

[70] A theme in M. Warren, *The Handbook of Deliberative Democracy* (Oxford: Oxford University Press, 2017).

oversold, citizens may become disillusioned. If it is undersold, these forums will remain a niche arena, disconnected from broader political problems of European democracy.

While deliberative forums and local referendums are clearly vital strands of European democratic renewal, they still need to dovetail fully with other areas of much-needed reform. Governments are right to be concerned about direct citizen influence breaching core liberal rights, but they have arguably erred on the side of being overly cautious. European democracy has still to find the right balance of mediated and unmediated citizen engagement, as both types of democratic rebuilding are needed. Participation must be the core axis of political renewal, but it still needs to be designed in a way that improves other forms of democratic accountability, rather than undermining or overshadowing them. While Europe's participative turn is welcome and highly promising, it still needs to act as a catalyst for reforming democracy more widely rather than proceeding as a stand-alone trend.

5

Political party responses: Democratic realignment?

It is widely agreed that political parties are central to Europe's democratic woes. Parties in general seem to have lost their connection with citizens, while those that challenge aspects of liberal democracy have gained ground. Party systems are under strain, presenting serious problems of governability. Many of these systems have become more polarized, as their centre ground has weakened. Many European parties are now driven by cultural-identity issues that often sit uneasily with core liberal rights. This chapter examines what changes have taken shape in response to these problems and concerns. It does not replay the well-known and exhaustively researched malaise of party politics but explores whether any positive adjustments have emerged in European party systems.

The chapter reports on the new political parties that have formed across Europe in the last several years aimed at improving democratic quality and reshaping party politics. It also analyses the efforts of many mainstream parties to isolate and undercut those parties seen as a menace to liberal democracy. Notwithstanding the importance of these twin developments, the chapter argues that the sphere of party politics has so far been relatively resistant to far-reaching pro-democratic change. New parties born with an express focus on democratic renewal have either struggled to gain momentum or have gradually mimicked the old-style politics they once disparaged. And party coalitions that ostracize illiberal-populist parties have either been fragile or brought their own challenges for democratic representativeness. Efforts at democratic regeneration have begun to refashion European party politics, but change in this area has lagged behind other areas of reform. Alongside innovative forms of citizen participation, more effort is also needed to rework traditional party politics as an indispensable part of European democratic resistance and renewal.

New-style parties

Shifts have occurred in many European party systems in recent years. New parties have established a presence and even entered government, innovative coalitions have formed and some historic parties have all but collapsed. Analysts stress that in the aggregate these shifts have not been dramatic and that many core features of European party systems have not changed.[1] Yet, the rate of new party formation accelerated in the 2010s relative to previous decades.[2] This has been a period of unprecedented fluidity in terms of new parties forming and winning seats across European states.

Of course, party-system fluidity is often painted in negative terms as many of the challenger parties are the national-populist parties that oppose liberal values. But, some emergent parties are themselves challengers to the populists. They have formed as self-declared liberal-democratic projects against the illiberal populist wave. In recent years, a raft of new political parties has emerged explicitly as a response to democratic decay. This trend is significant because – contrary to much political commentary – defending and reviving democracy is not simply about traditional, mainstream parties recovering lost ground. Emerging democratic parties are positioned across the political spectrum, although there are probably more of them to the left than

---

[1] F. Casal Bértoa and T. Weber, 'Restrained change: Party systems in times of economic crisis', *Journal of Politics*, 81/1 (2019), 233–48; S. Hutter and H. Kries (eds), *European Party Politics in Times of Crisis* (Cambridge: Cambrdige University Press, 2019).

[2] M. Lisi, 'The impact of the European crisis on party system change: Some comparative reflections', in M. Lisi (ed.), *Party System Change, the European Crisis and the State of Democracy* (London: Routledge, 2018).

to the right of centre. But they all share an ostensible commitment to the kind of participative politics needed for deeper democratic renewal. Probably the highest-profile new arrival has been the La République en Marche (LREM) party that has dramatically shaken up France's party system and has done so from an avowedly liberal and democratic position. LREM took root and grew in record time. It was in some ways an extremely top-down phenomenon, organized to service Emmanuel Macron's presidential bid. In other ways, it resembled a bottom-up movement, growing out of local circles and policy deliberations with ordinary citizens. The party drew heavily on crowd-sourced donations and organized around a decentralized network of local councils where citizens contributed to its early development. These councils engaged with citizens in a range of very informal ways like dinners and youth events to build momentum behind the new party. The very depth of discontent with French democracy and the mainstream parties ensured that much of the 2017 presidential election campaign was about political-system renewal more than traditional left-right issues.

Layers of paradox are apparent in the way LREM has developed. Macron has been a disruptor of the French party system, but in many senses his movement is about defending France's long-standing policy frameworks against more radical parties on the right and left. The party is ostensibly based on the logic of rebuilding bottom-up democracy and also serves a president with a tendency to top-down decision-making.[3] While Macron promised to stay close to the party's local circles and keep them involved in his presidency, he soon drifted away from these bases when in office.[4] He made a point of cutting out and weakening *corps intermediares*, seeking a somewhat populist-style direct link to the population and filling his team with technocrats not local LREM leaders. He instrumentalized LREM as 'the president's party' in a long-standing Fifth Republic tradition and stopped it from decentralizing

---

[3] S. Pedder, *Revolution Francaise: Emmanual Macron and the Quest to Reinvent a Nation* (London: Bloomsbury, 2018).

[4] W.Drozdiak, *The Last President of Europe* (New York: Public Affairs, 2020), p. 56.

into territorial units that might allow rival political leaders to gain their own bases.[5]

Over a hundred members left the party in late 2018 concerned that Macron's extensive use of decrees sat uneasily with the promise to rejuvenate French democracy. A small team of LREM members, nominated by Macron, designates election candidates. To many, the party has become a more passive rubber-stamp for Macron's personal preferences and less of a vehicle for robust citizen participation.[6] By mid-2020, nearly thirty centre-left MPs had left depriving the party of its majority in the lower house. The party then lost ground dramatically in local elections in June 2020. If LREM arrived to protect French democracy, both its cadres and voters have increasingly doubted its claim to enshrine a different style of politics.

Equally enigmatic, Jean-Luc Mélenchon's leftist-populist La France Insoumise also based itself on an ethos of citizen participation and defined itself as a decentralized network rather than standard party. It was formed around locally based *groupes d'appui* rather than mass-membership structures and has created several direct-democracy internal processes. For the 2017 elections, it selected many candidates with no political experience and boasted that these represented ordinary people. The movement's 2019 annual assembly used randomly selected delegates to propose new policy ideas. Still, some of its own members have criticized the party leadership for a top-down style.[7] The party has lost support since the 2017 elections, down to little over 5 per cent in polls by late 2020. Taken together, LREM and France Insoumise have eviscerated the dominance of the Socialist Party and the Gaullist Republican machine and have done so on an express platform of democratic renewal. Yet, both the new parties are highly personalistic and inextricably tied to their respective founders. In response, Place

[5] A. Cole, *Emmanuel Macron and the Two Years that Changed France* (Manchester: Manchester University Press, 2019).

[6] 'En Marche! and France insoumise – "modernity" put to test', *L'Humanite*, 12 June 2017; J. Hamburger, 'Whose populism? The mixed messages of la France insoumise', *Dissent*, Summer 2018.

[7] C. Stangler, 'Rebuilding France insoumise', *Jacobine*, 22 June 2019.

Publique formed as a centre-left party in 2018 that sought to avoid such top-down personality dominance and deepen deliberative democracy, but it has struggled to gain traction.[8]

Another new party that has attracted significant attention is Italy's Five Star Movement (5SM). This novel party movement formed with an aim of shoring up Italian democracy by taking power away from the country's discredited party elites. The party was reticent to place itself on a traditional left-right ideological spectrum, and its concept of democracy leant heavily on notions of direct citizen participation. After entering government in 2018, in coalition with the radical-right Lega, 5SM set up a ministerial department for direct democracy. It used its online Rousseau platform to provide a link between citizens and public-policy decisions (this digital dimension is explored more in Chapter 6).[9] The party took internal votes on whether to enter into government with the Lega, on candidates for the 2019 European elections and on whether to form a new coalition with the Democratic Party in 2019 after the Lega pulled out of government. 5SM is distinctive in having very few mediated structures between the party leadership and its grassroots membership.[10] 5SM leaders pointedly built close relations with the French Gilets Jaunes movement to demonstrate their focus on mass democratic engagement.

The party's positioning in Italy's party system has fluctuated. Its alliance with the Lega from 2018 to 2019 implied a 'challenger' coalition against established parties. This opened the party to charges that it was part of the populist menace to liberal democracy. After switching to a new governing coalition with the Democratic Party, 5SM became part of a more 'establishment' camp pitted against the Lega. In early 2020, Luigi Di Maio stepped down as party leader, feeling 5SM had drifted too far away from innovative forms of democratic participation.

---

[8] J. Hamburger, 'Whose populism? The mixed messages of la France insoumise', *Dissent*, Summer 2018.

[9] D. Loucaides, 'What happened when techno-utopians actually run a country?', *Wired*, February 2018.

[10] A. Seddone and G. Sandri, 'Primary elections and party grassroots: Participation, innovation and resistance', *European Political Science*, published online June 2020.

A divide opened between leftist and more centrist wings as the party struggled with its commitment to a transversal form of unmediated democratic politics. Some of its founding figures pushed to take the movement back to its roots and out of the coalition. Yet party leaders agreed to run a joint platform with the Democratic Party for regional elections, a reversal of the party's initial promise never to ally with mainstream parties. When the government coalition was replaced by a national unity administration in February 2021, outgoing prime minister, Giuseppe Conte took over as 5SM leader, with plans to move the party further in a mainstream direction – triggering a bad-tempered exodus of many party members. If 5SM has undeniably helped reshape one of Europe's most dysfunctional party systems, its own essence has remained inscrutable.

The Greek party system has gone through a decade of convulsions as well. The leftist Syriza formed back in 2004 but gained ground most dramatically after 2010, especially as the socialist PASOK party collapsed. Syriza styled itself as a party movement and promised participative democratic renewal, even if critics decried its leftist populism as a threat to democracy. In practice, the 2015–19 Syriza-led government pursued relatively moderate policies under strict guidance from the EU. It chipped at the edges of some state bodies' autonomy but did not seek to override liberal-democratic checks. Conversely, neither did it fundamentally improve participative politics or reform Greek democracy in the emancipatory ways it had promised. In response, To Potami (The River) formed in 2014 as an alternative party focused on democratic renewal and citizen participation. It finished fourth in the January 2015 elections but then lost support and by the end of the decade was winding up its operations. In 2019, the traditional, conservative New Democracy returned to power, a surprising reversion to pre-crisis politics in what had seemed to be Europe's most upended party system.

There are less high-profile examples of new parties too. In Denmark, Alternative is a green party that emerged after 2013, committed to more citizen participation within the party and in the country more widely. It represented a new kind of leftism based around urban liberals and creative progressives. The party set up its own Centre for Democracy, Policy Development and Public Participation to engage citizens through 'political laboratories' and committed to crowdsourcing new policies. In 2015, it entered parliament with 4.8 per cent of the vote, falling to 3 per cent in the 2019 general elections as doubts grew about what its core policy stances really were.[11] The election of a controversial new leader in February 2020 led to splits among Alternative members, and the party slipped down even below the 2 per cent threshold to enter into parliament.[12] Another example is in Belgium where a new political party Agora, with one seat in the Belgian parliament, set up a randomly selected assembly of Brussels residents in late 2019, with the commitment that its one MP would support the assembly's proposals in parliament.[13] In the Netherlands, new style, anti-racist party, Bij1, won a seat in parliament in the 2021 elections.

New parties committed to democratic renewal have emerged in virtually all Central and Eastern European states. In Poland, the Nowoczesna (Modern) party was set up just before the 2015 elections and won a small number of seats. The party's political programme advocated multiple democratic reforms, based around local participation, decentralization and limiting the powers of the president. The party expressly styled itself as a movement-like party to counter the highly personalistic leadership and hierarchical structures of both Civic Platform and Law and Justice (PiS). With both of these parties having low levels of membership, the Modern party sought to find ways of engaging citizens in party politics. In the 2019 legislative elections, it joined Civic Platform in a coalition, a strategy it repeated in the 2020 presidential contest. The parliamentary elections saw leftist party Razem (Together), that had formed in 2015, and the newer liberal-left Wiosna (Spring) team up together with the Democratic Left Alliance and some small groups to win forty-nine seats in the lower house. Another group

---

[11] H. Freinacht 'The Danish alternative: A party about nothing', *Metamoderna*, 12 May 2017.
[12] R. Min and D. McIntosh, 'Fock off-kilter, claim critics', *CPH Post Online*, 18 March 2020.
[13] 'Citizens assembly will give "unprecedented" boost to direct democracy in Brussels', *Brussels Times*, 17 October 2019.

of reformists registered the Poland 2050 party at the end of 2020 and rose dramatically to prominence in early-2021 opinion polls.

Several new Romanian opposition parties emerged around a narrative of combatting the Social Democratic Party's undermining of democracy. The Save Romania Union (USR) was launched in 2016 by civic activists, while the Party of Liberty, Unity and Solidarity (PLUS) was set up in 2018 by former prime minister and European commissioner Dacian Cioloş. These two new parties formed an alliance for the EU elections on a platform of democratic renewal and grassroots activism.[14] In 2020, this alliance became part of the governing coalition led by the centre-right National Liberal Party and gained weight within this after end-of-year elections. On the left, two new parties – Pro Romania and Demos – formed on platforms of democratic regeneration, although they struggled to gain traction.[15] In Bulgaria, similar issues were taken up by the three-party Democratic Bulgaria coalition that formed in 2018. This won one seat in the EP elections but struggled to gain high levels of support despite the widespread popularity of ongoing protests against the government.

Slovakia's party system has become notably fluid as multiple political projects have sought to push back against the country's illiberal-populist drift. In March 2019, the candidate of Progressive Slovakia (PS), Zuzana Čaputová, was elected president. PS was set up in 2017 as a pro-European social-liberal party, promising a range of democratic innovations.[16] The party system then reconfigured itself further at the March 2020 parliamentary elections. Another new party – Ordinary People and Independent Personalities (OLANO) – emerged as the largest party in these elections. The long-dominant left-populist Smer party was defeated and the PS failed to win any seats. The OLANO

---

[14] G. Reigh, 'What's next for Romania?', *Open Democracy*, 10 July 2019; M. Gascón Barberá, 'Romanian "hipster" party feels ambitious after European poll success', *Balkan Insight*, 18 June 2019.

[15] S. Gherghina and V. Stoiciu, 'Selecting candidates through deliberation: The effects for Demos in Romania', *European Political Science*, 19/2 (2020), 171–80.

[16] 'Čaputová's Progressive Slovakia Party on the rise ahead of EU elections', *Kafkadesk*, 6 May 2019.

party promised democratic renewal through more participation, more direct democracy and anti-corruption measures, although some feared it had a somewhat populist style itself.[17]

In Hungary, the Momentum movement organized protests in 2017 and then formed a new political party promising to restore democratic governance. It defined itself as a centrist party committed to building bridges between different parts of Hungarian society under a 'national project' of resisting Viktor Orbán's authoritarianism.[18] The party's policy pledges included a focus on transparency, giving local government back its autonomy, online debates on new laws and measures against corrupt oligarchs.[19] In addition, the Politics Can Be Different party was founded in 2009 based around a green agenda of injecting citizen participation into the political system; although this party only managed to win 3 per cent of the vote in the 2018 parliamentary elections, it rose to almost 10 per cent in the 2019 EP elections.[20]

More generally, a number of Pirate Parties emerged and gained momentum into the 2010s, mainly in Northern Europe, with an identity based on citizen participation and digital rights. The Pirate Party in Germany did much to popularize LiquidFeedback software, known for allowing users either a direct vote in internal policy decisions or to choose a trusted expert to represent them. Yet, the Pirate Parties phenomenon has petered out across Europe. The German Pirate Party won seats in state parliaments in 2012, but then fell away. The Czech Pirate Party is an exception that has gradually grown to win twenty-two seats in the national parliament and over three hundred in local councils, as well as three MEPs. It pushes for citizen petitions to drive

---

[17] I. Godarsky, 'Slovakia's next Prime Minister: Maverick or saviour', *Reporting Democracy*, 10 March 2020.

[18] R. Heath, 'Hungary's 'hipster patriotts' set sights on Orban', *Politico*, 7 August 2017.

[19] At www.momentum.hu.

[20] V. Vadja, 'Politics can be different: Hungary's Green Party shows the way', *Green European Journal*, 5 January 2015.

new laws, more referendums at national and local level and direct selection of senior party positions.[21]

In contrast to other countries, the UK has been relatively resistant to new parties focused on democratic renewal. Brexit gave rise to several initiatives to found new parties, but these all faltered. A number of MPs discussed plans for a new centrist party but could not reach agreement between those wanting to fight to remain in the EU and those willing to seek a soft Brexit.[22] The Independent Group of eleven MPs that split from the two main parties failed to gain support and then fractured; it failed to win a single seat in the 2019 election and then closed down. On the populist right, both UKIP and the Brexit Party faded, to some extent as their main mission had been accomplished. The 2019 election showed that the country's most convulsive and unsettling period of recent political history failed to shake up the party system.

Instead, innovations in the UK have emerged mainly within existing parties. After 2015, party membership rose dramatically in the Labour Party, the Liberal Democrats and the Scottish National Party, and the main parties have all offered many more direct internal votes in recent years.[23] The Labour Party went furthest in developing new participatory dynamics, in partnership with the left-wing grassroots movement, Momentum. Momentum's community-level organizing got a huge number of young voters to engage in the party through flexible forms of membership. Local citizen meetings proliferated in the party, while the Policy Forum website provided for online debate. For a while, these participatory channels were widely lauded. In light of the party's crushing electoral defeat in December 2019, it seemed clearer that in many ways Labour had turned into a strikingly top-down party under Jeremy Corbyn. As the party moved on to elect a new leader, Momentum's influence and the networks of citizen initiatives lost

[21] At https://www.pirati.cz/program/strana.html.
[22] Michael Savage, 'Dozens planned new centrist party after Brexit, says ex-Tory minister', *The Guardian*, 16 November 2019.
[23] P. Dunleavy and S. Kippin, 'How democratic are the UK's parties and party system', *Democratic Audit*, 22 August 2018.

prominence.[24] Incoming leader Kier Starmer laid out of vision for the party's future that did not focus on new-style citizen participation.[25]

More generally, the Covid-19 crisis in 2020 complicated party-political dynamics across Europe. Many of the new democratic-renewal parties were those that expressed most concern about governments using the pandemic to restrict freedoms and pressed hardest for Covid-19 restrictions to be lifted promptly; in this sense, the crisis gave a further boost to their core mission. Yet in some countries, it was rather the illiberal, hard-right parties that led calls for democratic freedoms to be reinstated – this was the case with the Lega in Italy, the AfD in Germany, Vox in Spain, the Freedom Party in Austria and the VVD in the Netherlands, in particular. Although these parties' discourse of defending democracy was opportunistic, the new context seemed to put some of the newer democratic parties on the backfoot. The 5SM and LREM found themselves under critical pressure for constricting democratic rights, the very opposite of their original democratic rationale. Overall, the Covid-19 adjustment pulled in contrasting directions in different countries: while some of the newer parties found an added motive for their political projects, others were squeezed by traditional parties' call for support to manage the crisis.

Confronting anti-democratic parties?

An equally important question is whether mainstream parties have found the right strategies for confronting extremist, non-democratic parties. For many years, analysts have debated whether democracy is best served by ostracizing or cooperating with such parties. While some studies suggest that a number of populist parties have become more normalized democratic parties as and when they share power

[24] K. Proctor, 'Can Momentum survive after Jeremy Corbyn stands down?' *The Guardian*, 23 January 2020.
[25] K. Starmer, 'A new chapter for Britain', speech, 18 February 2021.

with others, the weight of academic analysis leans towards the conclusion that such cooperation rather drags moderate parties to the extremes.[26] A nuanced line is that context-specific variations across different countries determine whether inclusion or exclusion is the better tactic.[27] I do not replay this long-running debate here, but rather point to recent examples of mainstream parties beginning to deal more robustly with populist-undemocratic parties. This is not a question of such parties being legally excluded from the democratic arena, but of other parties being less willing to do deals with them and making more effort to combat their menace to democracy.

As the 2010s progressed, the general trend seemed to be towards populist parties finding their way into government. Italy and Austria were the most significant cases of this happening in the latter part of the decade. The Danish Peoples Party provided informal support to the government in Denmark, while the True Finns entered government in 2015. In Greece, Syriza brought the right-wing nationalist Anel into a coalition. In Bulgaria, the centre-right GERB party entered into coalition with the United Patriots, an alliance of three nationalist parties that included the far-right Ataka. In 2019, the EKRE party was included in a new governing coalition in Estonia, while the Spanish Vox party was brought in to support several municipal and regional governments. In 2020, the Slovenian Democratic Party took power backed by a coalition of several smaller parties, after having previously been ostracized by the mainstream political groups.

Yet there was also evidence of growing resistance to such inclusion. As illiberal populists have risen under all types of electoral system in Europe, electoral reform does not appear to offer any easy solutions; the focus has rather fallen on parties' tactical choices. Aggregate data shows

---

[26] On the former claim, see H. Kriesi, 'Is there a crisis of democracy in Europe?', Springer Online article, 16 March 2020. On the general overview, see C. Mudde, *The Far-Right Today* (Cambridge: Polity Press, 2019).

[27] F. Casal Bértoa and J. Rama, 'The illness of representative democracy: Is there a cure?', *Journal of Democracy*, forthcoming. See also T.Daly and B. Jones, 'Parties versus democracy: Addressing today's political party threats to democratic rule', *International Journal of Constitutional Law*, 18/2 (2020), 509–38.

how mainstream parties have gradually colluded to a greater extent against illiberal challenger parties. Established parties have closed ranks with each other and managed to protect their own predominance by excluding newer parties from coalition cabinets.[28] In Germany and France, this involved mainstream parties intensifying their already-existing strategies of exclusion; in early 2021, German intelligence services began formal surveillance of the AfD to gauge its possible contravention of the constitution, while the French government closed down the Génération Identitaire movement. In other countries, democratic parties changed course quite dramatically to prioritize the same aim.

In Italy a shift from inclusion to exclusion happened almost by chance – and temporarily. Italy had long been a case of mainstream parties offering more extreme parties a degree of inclusion. In 1994, Prime Minister Silvio Berlusconi included both the Northern League and the neo-fascist Italian Social Movement in his coalition; he included the former again from 2001 to 2006 and 2008 to 2011. After the 2018 election, the 5SM formed a coalition with the now-remodelled Lega. In 2019, Lega leader Matteo Salvini pulled out of the coalition government after a series of disagreements, expecting new elections to be called. The centre-left Democratic Party and 5SM called his bluff by forming a new coalition government. While this opportunity appeared somewhat serendipitously, both the Democratic Party and 5SM were willing to adjust their tactics in order to exclude the Lega – a significant change given that they had previously refused to deal with each other. Still, in February 2021 the Lega found its way back into Mario Draghi's national unity government as the dynamics of intra-party negotiations shifted once again.

In Austria, inclusion began in 1999 when the centre-right Peoples Party entered into coalition with the far-right Freedom Party. After international criticism, this arrangement crumbled and the Freedom

---

[28] F. Casal Bértoa and T. Weber, 'Restrained change: party systems in times of economic crisis', *Journal of Politics*, 81/1 (2018), 233–48.

Party began to lose support. In 2016 elections for the largely ceremonial post of president, the mainstream parties collaborated to support the Green party candidate in a run-off against the Freedom Party candidate. However, after the 2017 general election, the Peoples Party again offered the Freedom Party a place in government. The Freedom Party then shot itself in the foot, when its leader was caught in a set-up related to kickbacks for Russian businesses. At this point, the Peoples Party opted for a strategy of isolating the Freedom Party, with party leader Sebastian Kurz claiming to have regretted the tactic of inclusion. It won new elections in September 2019 and then chose the Green party over the Freedom Party to form a new coalition in early 2020.

Several *cordon sanitaires* tightened against far-right parties during the latter part of the 2010s. In the Netherlands, different Liberal, Labour, Christian-Democrat combinations excluded the far-right Party for Freedom (PVV), and all mainstream parties reconfirmed their refusal to deal with this party after the 2021 elections. As the 2010s unfolded, Belgian parties adhered firmly to a strategy of not including the far-right Flemish nationalist (VB, Vlaams Belang) party within the country's traditionally expansive coalitions; in 2019 and 2020, seven parties combined and took nearly two years to form a coalition so as not to include either VB or conservative New Flemish Alliance (NVA), the two parties that finished first and second in 2019 elections. In Slovakia, the left-populist Smer party sacrificed power in 2020 rather than do a deal with the far-right. The 2019 Swedish elections saw a concerted attempt by mainstream parties to keep the Sweden Democrats out of power – although conservative parties then aligned with the far-right party in criticism of the government's Covid-19 policies. In Greece, the Golden Dawn party was banned outright in 2020.

Influenced by historical experience, Germany's mainstream parties have long been resolute in keeping radical parties ostracized. The Christian Democrats (CDU) and Social Democrats (SDP) struggled to form a coalition after the 2017 elections, but their five months of effort showed heightened determination to keen the AfD surge at bay. Germany's exclusion model was the subject of a dramatic political crisis in early 2020, when a Liberal party (FDP) politician became regional premier in the eastern state of Thuringia with the joint backing of the CDU and AfD. Condemnation of the deal from across the political spectrum forced him and CDU leader Annagret Kramp-Karenbauer to resign. The episode reinforced the redline against dealings with the far-right. While the crisis also spurred some debate about how well the 'grand coalition' approach could deal with the AfD threat in the long-term, by choosing Armin Laschet as its new leader in early 2021 the CDU doubled down on the longstanding and centrist approach.

Other examples have seen more complex shifts. Denmark has been a more varied case, mixing the dynamics of inclusion and exclusion. A Liberal-Conservative coalition had parliamentary support from the far-right Danish Peoples Party (DPP) from the early 2000s to 2011 and then again from 2015 after the DPP climbed to over 20 per cent of the vote. In essence, mainstream parties half-included, half-excluded the DPP. The latter's hard line on migration has clearly been normalized among other parties; conversely, the DPP seemed to become less radical and eschew any fundamental threat to Danish democracy.[29] In 2019 elections, the DPP's support plunged, and the party lost over half its seats in parliament. The victorious Social Democrats formed a 'red bloc' coalition, and the DPP was left weaker and more isolated than it had been for nearly two decades.

In Poland and Hungary, the dynamics were different; with illiberal parties already in power, the issue there was whether pro-democratic opposition parties could coordinate to greater effect. Five Polish opposition parties forged a coalition in early 2019 to challenge the PiS party in European elections. This European Coalition of Opposition Forces won 38 per cent of the vote behind the PiS. For the October 2019 legislative elections, a different coalition formed with the idea of drawing social conservatives away from PiS.[30] Similarly, Hungarian

---

[29] K. Kosiara-Pedersen and P. Kurrild-Klitgaard, Change and stability in the Danish party system', in M. Lisi (ed.), *Party System Change, the European Crisis and the State of Democracy* (London: Routledge, 2018).

[30] A. Szczerblak, 'Can Poland's opposition win this year's election?', EUROPP Blog, LSE, 9 July 2019.

opposition parties joined forces in Budapest's 2019 mayoral election; a reformist candidate duly defeated the Fidesz candidate and quickly moved to consider a range of citizen consultations. In response to Prime Minister Viktor Orbán's draconian Covid-19 emergency law in 2020, six parties agreed to present a common list against Fidesz in the next parliamentary elections.

Profile: Spain

Spain offered one of the most dramatic cases of new party irruptions and party-system renewal during the 2010s. The leftist Unidas Podemos (hereafter, Podemos) and centre-right Ciudadanos emerged and established themselves in a relatively short time frame as influential parties; at times, they came close to overtaking the country's two long-dominant parties, the Socialist Party (PSOE) and conservative People's Party (PP). The new parties' appearance got more people involved in politics and in innovative ways. It stimulated debate and sharpened accountability over corruption. Spain's new parties added vibrancy to democratic debate and their respective leaders were young, modern and eloquent. Rejuvenation of the party system has helped keep Spain's overall democracy scores reasonably healthy. A relatively comfortable two-party system has been shaken up, and all parties forced to seek new ways of engaging with citizens.

However, the Spanish case also shows how difficult it is to break the mould of party politics in ways that genuinely improve democratic quality. The reconfiguration of the party system has ultimately not translated into the qualitative change that the two new parties promised. Indeed, by the end of the decade, the party system was more fractious and seemed to be undercutting governability more than improving the quality of democracy. The difficulties of forming governing majorities meant that in November 2019 the country held its fourth general election in four years. Podemos and Ciudadanos seemed to have contributed to a more combative style of politics, while their initial commitments to citizen participation had given way to hierarchical and personalistic party structures.

In the years following democratic transition, Spain's party system was effectively a two-party national system combined with an array of regional parties whose votes were sometimes essential to the formation of a government. After the country's famed pacted transition, the PSOE and PP alternated in power. They were both implicated in a growing number of corruption cases and seemed powerless in the face of the economic recession that hit from 2009. This opened a window of opportunity for new parties to challenge the bi-party dominance.

Podemos grew out of a broad social movement against austerity during the Eurozone crisis. Spain was one of the most notable cases of protest-based activists ending up in parliament with their own party. This was significant, because in many countries protestors failed to make this transition or chose not to. The Indignados protests brought millions into the streets in 2011 against EU-imposed spending cuts. The movement was initially innovative in its range of practical street actions: protesting, holding community assemblies, blocking evictions, occupying public buildings. Out of this, the new political party took shape, and within a year of its founding in 2014, it won significant representation in the national legislature and the European Parliament. Podemos sought to combine street politics and parliamentary politics – a 'street party' hybrid of horizontal and vertical political strategies.[31]

Through its innovative series of local decision-making forums, Podemos helped get ordinary citizens engaged in politics. It took shape from a collection of local organizations, parties and movements, and this has been integral to its identity and claim to be dedicated to democratic renewal. It organized its internal workings around citizen-led 'circles', both territorial and issue-based. These circles played a big role in setting policies for the 2015 election campaign. With the cost of party membership set extremely low, Podemos resembled an open

---

[31] R. Feenstra, S. Tormey, A. Casero-Ripollés and J. Keane, *Reconfiguring Democracy: The Spanish Political Laboratory* (London: Routledge, 2017).

platform and collection of local groups, more than a traditional party. The party's primaries were limited to members, but membership grew fast, giving these primaries a very open feel.[32]

The party put in place structures reflecting its participative ethos. Members of the party's Citizen Assemblies proposed new policies to the Citizen Council, the party's executive organ elected through an open primary. The Citizen Assemblies had input into decisions over internal positions and election strategies. A Commission of Democratic Guarantees was charged with safeguarding the rights of those registered with Podemos as well as the party's fundamental principles, and included members directly elected though open citizens' primaries.[33] The strong regional component in Spanish politics was a factor that encouraged Podemos to form a loose network of alliances across different territories rather than a single, standard party structure.[34]

Despite having established a core level of support remarkably quickly and with leaders who became prominent fixtures in Spanish political debate, the party struggled to carry forward this momentum in the latter part of the decade. The party declined from 21 per cent of the vote in the 2015 elections to 14 per cent in the April 2019 elections.[35] After the latter elections, the party potentially held the balance of power, but after months of talks it failed to reach an agreement with the PSOE that would enable the socialist party to assume power. Ultimately, the PSOE preferred to call another election rather than offer Podemos a formal coalition. Podemos lost seven MPs in those November 2019 elections and saw its share of the popular vote drop further to just under 13 per cent. With both the Socialist Party and Podemos now on the backfoot, in early 2020 they finally agreed to form a coalition, ironically giving Podemos major influence even as its support declined.

---

[32] G. Cordero and X. Coller, *Democratizing Candidate Selection: New Methods, Old Receipts?* (London: Palgrave, 2018), p. 141.

[33] See www.podemos.info/.

[34] J. Rodríguez-Teruel, A. Barrio and O. Barberà, 'Fast and furious: Podemos' quest for power in multi-level Spain', *South European Society and Politics*, 21/4 (2016), 561–85.

[35] The 2019 figure being in conjunction with leftist party, Izquierda Unida.

Internally, the party has gradually changed, with internal policy-making becoming increasingly top-down. Notwithstanding the various levels of citizen participation, in de facto terms decisions were made by a small group of managers around party leader, Pablo Iglesias.[36] Podemos became more of a traditional leftist party, successful in mobilizing a significant amount of core support, but at the cost of moving away from its initial commitment to a 'transversal' reinvention of party politics. The initial wave of assemblies, community circles and policy-focused *mareas* (literally, tides) dried up somewhat. Levels of participation in internal decisions and policy platforms declined from around 2015.[37] The participative ethos continued more through the municipal initiatives of associated groups like Barcelona en Comun and Ahora Madrid. Ideas related to direct or participative democracy have lost prominence in Podemos' recent national strategies.

Endless personal differences between the party's founders played out in the media. Eventually, splits followed. Failing to convince the party to head towards a more moderate line, co-founder Íñigo Errejón left. He later set up a moderate-left party, Más País that won three seats in the November 2019 elections. In 2020, Podemos' anti-capitalist wing exited the party in protest at it going into government with 'neoliberal' ministers, further fragmenting the left. Indeed, at this stage Podemos moved to adopt more structures of a traditional party, in both its membership and leadership models. In an effort to strengthen its organizational bases, in September 2020 it announced that only those paying a standard membership fee would have voting rights in the policy circles – a move that seemed to undercut the spirit of movement-like, open citizen participation.[38] After poor results in Madrid regional elections in May 2021, Iglesias stepped down as party leader, adding further uncertainty to Podemos' future.

[36] R. Feenstra, S. Tormey, A. Casero-Ripollés and J. Keane, *Reconfiguring Democracy: The Spanish Political Laboratory* (London: Routledge, 2017).

[37] J. Rodrîguez-Teruel, A. Barrio and O.Barberà, 'Fast and furious: Podemos' quest for power in multi-level Spain', *South European Society and Politics*, 21/4 (2016), 561–85.

[38] I. Santaeulalia, 'Podemos se reorganiza como un partido tradicional', *El Pais*, 3 March 2020; L. Tolosa, 'Los afiliados de Podemos pagan desde hoy una cuota de tres euros', *El Pais*, 14 September 2020.

Ciudadanos' evolution has been just as beguiling. Formed as an anti-independence Catalan party in 2007, Ciudadanos then made a jump to the national level and gained traction with notable speed. The party's very name denoted its commitment to a new type of citizen engagement. Although the party did not grow out of the same kind of movement-type identity as Podemos, it stressed a more participative way of doing politics. Ciudadanos was sometimes referred to as 'the Podemos of the right' highlighting an anti-corruption rhetoric and participative politics.[39] The party defined itself as a centrist, liberal party – a potentially major contribution to democratic regeneration in a country that had long lacked a European-style modern liberal party. Ciudadanos used the 'democratic regeneration' leitmotif heavily in the early 2010s, forming a novel 'Citizen Movement' to help it move from being an anti-independence Catalan regional party to a Spanish national party.[40] Its emergence was one of the most notable counterpoints to the standard line that the EU's crisis years had nourished parties only at the extremes of the spectrum.[41]

In practice, Ciudadanos then drifted to the right and adopted more strongly hierarchical party structures. Though Ciudadanos initially promised new forms of participatory democracy – both inside the party and for the political system as a whole – this element increasingly disappeared from its identity. It came to stress its identity as a more technocratic party than one focused on democratic regeneration.[42] After taking power in Madrid's municipal government in coalition with the PP in 2019, Ciudadanos leaders were directly responsible for

---

[39] A. Kassam, 'Ciudadanos, the "Podemos of the right", emerges as political force in Spain', *The Guardian*, 13 March 2015.

[40] J. Rodríguez-Teruel and A. Barrio, 'Going national: Ciudadanos from Catalonia to Spain', *South European Society and Politics*, 21/4 (2016), 587–607.

[41] G. Vidal and I. Sanchez-Vitores, 'Spain – out with the old: The restructuring of Spanish politics', in S. Hutter and H. Kries (eds), *European Party Politics in Times of Crisis* (Cambridge: Cambrdige University Press).

[42] J. Rodriguez-Teruel, O. Barbera, A. Barrio and F. Casal Bértoa, 'From stability to change? The evolution of the party system in Spain', in M. Lisi (ed.), *Party System Change, the European Crisis and the State of Democracy* (London: Routledge, 2018).

actually dismantling the city's recently-formed participative democracy initiatives.[43]

The Catalan crisis had a major impact on Cuidadanos, as this reached a new level of intensity from 2017. The party adopted some of the hardest-line positions against the Catalan secessionists. In doing so, it insisted it was defending Spanish democracy from what it defined as anti-democratic Catalan populists. It insisted that direct rule over Catalonia, giving pro-succession leaders jail sentences and categorically ruling out self-determination were steps needed to protect Spanish democracy. It viscerally opposed the socialist government's offer of dialogue with secessionist leaders. The fact that direct democracy and grassroots engagement became widely associated with Catalan secessionism was one factor that pushed Ciudadanos away from talk of such democratic innovation in favour of a much more status quo-oriented narrative.

The party focused on strengthening Spanish national identity, insisting this was a benign and overdue contribution to democracy. This focus proved popular for some time, but it also dragged the party away from the centre ground. Its leaders adopted a strikingly pugnacious and even inflammatory tone that did much to lower the quality of democratic debate. Party leader Albert Rivera often used quite eye-wateringly bellicose language that seemed to bear little resemblance to the ostensible moderation of European liberal parties. Critics felt this fanned the flames of an increasingly strident political discourse and an intolerant rightist nationalism.

This was a majoritarian more than liberal approach to democracy: Ciudadanos reflected the hard-line hostility towards Catalan secessionists felt by one part of the population, as both it and the pro-independence bloc moved further away from any kind of mutual understanding, compromise or tolerance. Even though Ciudadanos defined itself in opposition to populism, surveys showed that it picked

---

[43] S. Perez, 'El Gobierno de Almeida acaba con un órgano innovador de participación ciudadana creado por Carmena', *El Diario.es*, 2 October 2019.

up a significant degree of its support from voters with 'populist values'.[44] The party even joined a motion in the Madrid municipal parliament to proscribe pro-independence parties. Ciudadanos' support plummeted and the party was left with only ten MPs after the November 2019 elections. Once hailed as one of Europe's brightest democratic stars, party leader Rivera resigned in failure and left politics altogether.

The scale of this implosion was sufficient for some in the party to push for a return to the original focus on liberal rights and democratic regeneration. One group of reformers challenged the new leader-in-waiting, Inés Arrimadas, because she seemed reluctant to agree to the democratic-renewal focus or to decentralize power within the party.[45] However, the party duly elected Arrimadas as leader, despite her close association with the party's rightist drift. While she initially doubled down on her predecessor's hard line and rather shrill truculence, the party repositioned itself to a degree into 2020. It tiptoed back to a more centrist identity on some issues, cooperated with the government on Covid-19 measures and intimated at fostering participation around a network of citizen experts. Still, Ciudadanos' membership declined and criticism grew within the party over an increasingly top-down style of leadership bereft of internal participation.[46] After disastrous results in Catalan and Madrid regional elections in February and May 2021, respectively, Ciudadanos' very survival was now in question.

As Podemos and Ciudadanos lost support, the far-right Vox party grew in record speed from not having a single MP in 2015 to finishing third in the November 2019 elections. This was salutary after many years in which Spaniards had proudly noted that the country lacked a hard-right populist party of the kind gaining ground across Europe.

---

[44] H. Marcos-Marne, C. Plaza-Colodro and T. Freyburg, 'Who votes for new parties? Economic voting, political ideology and populist attitudes', *West European Politics*, 43/1 (2020), 1–21.

[45] 'Los críticos de Cs miden fuerzas para estudiar una alternativa a Arrimadas', *El País*, 24 January 2020.

[46] E. Garcia, 'Un año despues, Ciudadanos pelea por levanter el vuelo', *El Pais*, 8 November 2020.

Vox naturally insisted it was a democratic – or constitutionalist – party, yet its positions clearly menaced core liberal political principles. The party picked up support in 2019 due to its promise to take powers back from Catalonia. Vox's dramatic rise was a reconfiguration of the party system that brought risk rather than opportunity to Spanish democracy.

In sum, Spain shows that party-system regeneration has been possible but difficult to convert into gains in democratic quality. The duopoly of the PP and PSOE has been broken. Podemos and Ciudadanos have given Spanish voters more choice and helped displace a discredited older generation of politicians, especially from the PP. Bottom-up civic participation was paramount in the rise of both these parties. Far from Podemos being an ephemeral pop-up party, a decade on from the Indignados protests its leaders are household names. The new parties have ensured that the country's shocking levels of political corruption are no longer so easily tolerated.

Yet neither party has fulfilled its promise to place democratic renewal at the centre of a new style politics and both have lost support – in Ciudadanos' case, dramatically so. Both built links with new types of movements, privileging these over traditional interest groups, but failed to develop these into radically different internal party dynamics.[47] By 2020, the two 'new' parties had successfully put down strong political roots, yet they had also come to resemble fairly standard insider parties. Voters have come to see them increasingly as part of a discredited party system rather than as challengers to that system. One disillusioned senior figure within Ciudadanos lamented that 'the most disappointing thing is that the new [parties] have ended up exactly like those that already existed'.[48] Ironically, both these supposedly community-rooted parties have become arguably even more top-down and personalized than the old parties.

---

[47] O. Barberà, A. Barrio and J. Rodríguez-Teruel, 'New parties' linkages with external groups and civil society in Spain: A preliminary assessment', *Mediterranean Politics*, 24/5 (2019), 646–64.

[48] E. Garcia, 'Toni Roldan: Una estrategia que va contra los intereses de España no es viable', *El Pais*, 28 July 2019.

The emergence of these and other new parties has impacted governability more than qualitative democratic renewal. Their rise produced a parliamentary arithmetic that made the formation of stable governments more difficult. Spain went for months without a government in 2015 while coalition talks floundered and elections had to be repeated; the same thing then happened in 2019. By 2020, the system housed six national parties and a plethora of regional parties. The progressive coalition that eventually formed in 2020 showed that a new party like Podemos could contribute positively to governability. Yet the bruising experiences of the late 2010s left unsettling doubts over the prospects for healthy democratic renewal.

Assessment: Tentatively unlocking party reform

There has been a moderate degree of change to European party systems in recent years, combined with efforts to reform the internal workings of individual parties. Many core features of European party systems have proven resistant to major changes, and many parties have remained relatively weak in confronting both overreaching executives and illiberal parties.[49] While the entrepreneurial strategies of 'challenger parties' have begun to chip away at the oligopolistic structure of European party systems, in most countries these systems have exhibited notable resilience and continuity.[50] This might be seen as both boon and bane for democracy. Party systems have generally not imploded to an extent that would entail democratic collapse, but they have neutered more positive innovations too.

A number of new parties have formed with an express aim to improve democratic quality. Much analytical work has homed in on the well-established drift away from mainstream centre-left, centre-right

[49] F. Casal Bértoa and Z. Enyedi, *Party System Closure: Party Alliances, Government Alternatives and Democracy in Europe* (Oxford: Oxford University Press, forthcoming).
[50] C. De Vries and S. Hobalt, *Political Entrepreneurs: The Rise of Challenger Parties in Europe* (Princeton, NJ: Princeton University Press, 2020).

and centrist parties and how this has worryingly opened the door for illiberal populist parties.[51] As a flipside of such negative party system fluidity, however, this chapter shows that some new parties have emerged that are avowedly democratic and aim specifically to revive liberal-democratic processes. Democracy has become more central to many parties' internal organization and to their popular mobilization strategies. This trend is not limited to one part of the political spectrum, with examples of new-style democratic-reform parties found on the left, in the centre and, albeit less frequently, on the right. Party engagement with democratic renewal has strengthened.

Some believe there is still little meaningful link between social mobilization and increasingly dysfunctional party politics and that Europe now has a disruptively unmediated 'democracy without politics'.[52] Yet, recent initiatives do reveal efforts to rethink party politics and parties' contribution to democratic quality through better mediated links between citizens and the political sphere. The declining vote share of the traditional party families is neither intrinsically good nor bad for democratic quality; while this trend reflects the rise of some illiberal parties, in some cases it has generated a wider array of democratic choice. Simply 'holding the centre' is not synonymous with upholding democracy even though debates are now often framed in a way that assumes this to be the case. More important is qualitative change, and this heightens the significance of new parties' promises to inject the dynamics of participative citizen engagement into party politics.

Still, many of these new parties have struggled to increase their levels of support or to fulfil their promise of an innovative democratic renewal. Relatively few of the new parties that emerged in the 2010s have achieved really significant electoral success. In most states, there has been only a modest degree of party dealignment without

---

[51] See special edition, M. Caiani and P. Graziano, 'Understanding varieties of populism in times of crises', *West European Politics*, 42/6 (2019), 1141–58

[52] D. Innerarity, 'Democracia sin politica', *El Pais*, 28 Febraury 2014; See also D. Innerarity, *Una teoría de la democracia compleja: gobernar en el siglo XXI* (Barcelona: Galaxia Gutenberg, 2020).

far-reaching system regeneration. This is the case in the Nordic states, Belgium, Germany, Ireland, the Netherlands, Poland and Portugal. All these have experienced more volatile changes in the balance between parties and the formation of new parties, but with significant continuity in the contours of the party system as a whole.[53] While the UK may be going through a realignment of traditional party support bases that could be healthy for democratic pluralism, this is happening without new parties playing any role.[54]

Even where pro-democratic challengers have made dramatic breakthroughs and partially dislodged long-present mainstream parties – as in France, Greece, Italy, Romania and Spain – the democratic innovation part of their mandates has stalled. While many have movement-like qualities and have developed more open internal structures, they have come to mimic the very features of party politics they initially sought to transcend. Ironically, the parties predicated on bottom-up citizen participation have become some of the most top-down, personalistic parties in Europe. Many parties that emerged in the last decade have ended up either looking increasingly like the old parties or have descended into internal wrangling. Far from uniformly worsening governability, some of the new parties have compromised and entered into quite surprising coalitions to help government formation often to the detriment of their ambitious democratic-renewal promises.

Some of the new parties have certainly infused European politics with a looser and more citizen-centred notion of party politics, and in this sense, the 'democracy without politics' charge looks somewhat harsh and overly dismissive of the many real-world efforts to close the gap between grassroots civic engagement and party politics. Yet much research shows that where parties have introduced internal participative processes, these have tended to reinforce party leaderships rather than

---

[53] M. Lisi, 'The impact of the European crisis on party system change: Some comparative reflections', in M. Lisi (ed.), *Party System Change, the European Crisis and the State of Democracy* (London: Routledge, 2018).

[54] P. Norris, 'On dealigning and realigning elections: Is Britain about to experience a Westminster earthquake?', LSE Blog, 13 November 2019.

allow a wider plurality of influences or open-ended forms of party democracy.[55] Some analysts argue that the new-style parties are based around a counter-intuitive fusion of populism with technocratic politics, often sitting uneasily with the promise of bottom-up participation.[56] The shortcomings of the new parties chimes with findings that citizens' satisfaction with democracy has not increased where the number of party choices has increased.[57] Some parties may have become more like movements, but movements have in turn become more like old-style parties.

Apart from new parties forming, there have been some attempts to fashion more overtly pro-democratic alliances. The question of whether mainstream parties should engage or ostracize radical parties has received much analytical attention over many years. The empirical evidence on which of these strategies works best is not conclusive; each strategy can have very different results depending on the specific national context. Yet, the weight of opinion and research has shifted towards the conclusion that offering illiberal parties a share in government normally does not strengthen liberal democracy. While the embrace-or-shun debate is complex, it is significant that many mainstream parties across Europe have moved towards a firmer isolation of hard-right forces.

In a handful of cases, mainstream parties have recently worked together and put aside many differences in order to keep radical parties out of power. This has not happened everywhere, but it is a notable change that has come about as concerns over European democracy have intensified. An intriguing question is whether some European countries may be moving too far to the other extreme of ostracizing parties that do not necessarily represent a systemic threat to democracy. There may

[55] P. Gerbaudo, 'One person, one click: Is this the way to save democracy?', *The Guardian*, 13 February 2019; European Parliament Research Service, *Prospects for E-democracy in Europe Case studies* (Brussels: EPRS, 2018).

[56] C. Bickerton and C. Accetti, *Technopopulism: The New Logic of Democratic Politics* (Oxford: Oxford University Press, 2021).

[57] R. Dassonneville and I. McAllister, 'The party choice set and satisfaction with democracy', *West European Politics*, 43/1 (2020), 49–73.

be strong grounds to exclude parties that do not respect fundamental democratic or liberal rights; it is another matter for mainstream parties to deem parties structurally unfit to participate in government because they dislike their policies.

Most observers have worried that new parties' ability to jostle themselves into the political sphere is what has most unsettled European democracies in recent years. But the reverse is just as pertinent: traditional parties may have colluded not only in the name of defending democracy but also to protect their own positions against challengers in a way that is not beneficial for democratic pluralism. Some efforts to deflate populism actually risk curtailing the competitive democratic debate that is needed to generate more effective policy responses to hard-right democratic threats.[58] In some instances, 'cartel parties' have become even more cartel-like in an attempt to rebut the populists whose very rise is driven by frustration with those same cartel dynamics.[59] In one warning sign of how this can backfire, far-right leader Marine Le Pen was once again gaining ground in French polls during the early months of 2021. While a great deal of focus has been given to anti-establishment or outsider parties, the equally pervasive pathology in European democracy is that democratic parties in general have been resistant to far-reaching change.

Tying these trends together, it is clear that deeper and more innovative change in the sphere of party politics is needed if Europe's emerging democratic renewal is to succeed. While this book foregrounds the need for more unfettered forms of direct citizen participation, it is important not to neglect the vital role of political parties in replenishing the core template of liberal-representative democracy. A spirit of democratic regeneration has found its way into the sphere of European party politics, but in subdued and cautious form. Many analysts believe that in aggregate terms parties and party systems are

---

[58] C. Mouffe, *For a Left Populism* (London: Verso, 2018); in relation to Germany, see S. Berman and H. Kundnani, 'The costs of convergence', *Journal of Democracy*, 32/1 (2021), 22–36.

[59] W. Jacoby, 'Grand coalitions and democratic dysfunction: Two warnings from Central Europe', *Government and Opposition*, 52/2 (2017), 329–55.

still on a downward trajectory, discredited and more distant from voters.[60] While this may well be a sound judgement, there are at least some signs of pro-democratic renewal in party politics whose relevance should not be overlooked as a basis for much-needed further reform. Party reform is underway but as in other areas of change examined through the book, still too timid and controlled to herald far-reaching democratic resistance and renewal.

---

[60] M. Lisi, 'The impact of the European crisis on party system change: Some comparative reflections', in M. Lisi (ed.), *Party System Change, the European Crisis and the State of Democracy* (London: Routledge, 2018).

6

Digital responses: Reclaiming technology for democracy?

Few issues have drawn as much attention in recent years as the political impact of digital technology and social-media platforms. As explained in Chapter 2, a consensus has taken root that the systems and behaviour of large technology companies and foreign powers' digital disruption have combined to menace European democracy. The EU and member state governments have gradually caught up with these challenges – at least in some measure. There have been two strands to their policy responses. One cluster of new policies has focused on curtailing digital activity to limit its negative effects on democratic rights. This strand has included measures to control social-media platforms, address the rights implications of digital technology and build stronger defences against disinformation and external 'influence operations' in European elections.

The second policy strand is a more positive one: EU institutions, governments and civil society organizations have redoubled their efforts to use digital technology as a benign force in improving democratic accountability. Taken together, these areas of change now represent a strong and expanding area of democratic resistance and renewal. Yet questions remain about the balance between the two strands, as European strategies have tilted more towards digital protection than digital empowerment. The result is that more positive and bolder innovations are still needed if the digital sphere is to be reclaimed as a positive tool for rather than danger to European democratic renovation. Explaining how digital issues have become both a stand-alone policy concern and an area that touches upon other arenas of political reform, the chapter links technology trends to the book's wider call for more empowered citizen engagement.

Protecting rights online

European governments have increasingly sought to control and limit the digital sphere's harmful impact on democratic rights. They have instigated several different levels of digital control: efforts to deal with disinformation and hate speech, defences against electoral interference and concerns over privacy infringements. While in many senses welcome and overdue, this cluster of policies has privileged a relatively narrow approach towards democratic resilience. Indeed, many of these European initiatives have either been of modest impact or have even created their own, new risks for political rights.

Targeting the tech companies

Several high-profile European initiatives have aimed to influence the behaviour of tech companies. In 2017, the German government introduced a seminal Network Enforcement Act (or NetzDG) that made the removal of manifestly illegal online content, such as hate speech, mandatory. At the end of 2019, it further tightened legal restrictions against hate speech and right-wing extremist content. In 2018 the UK government introduced tighter laws covering online safety, imposed statutory requirements on companies to uphold 'the norms and rules developed by democratic societies' and set up a rapid reaction unit against disinformation.[1] In the same year, Finland was the first EU country to prosecute those responsible for disinformation and online defamation. In 2019 the Danish government made it a criminal offence to spread disinformation that 'aids or enables' a foreign state to

---

[1] UK Government, *Online Harms White Paper* (London: HMG, 2019), p. 7.

influence political debate.[2] In 2020, the French government introduced a law that obliged online platforms to take down hate speech within 24 hours. Terror attacks in France and Austria in autumn 2020 prompted governments further to strengthen measures against radical online content. Concerns have intensified that these kinds of measure curtail freedom of speech and actually present a new risk to European democratic rights. Several of the new laws appear to have forced a somewhat zealous over-compliance in terms of content limitation.[3] While the German government nominally acknowledged that too much online content was being removed due to the NetzDG, its 2019 upgrade to internet law involved more potential infringements to rule of law and privacy rights with platforms being obliged to reveal users' identities without court orders. The German president hesitated to sign the new laws due to doubts over their constitutionality. In October 2020, the French constitutional court knocked down parts of France's equivalent law for similar reasons. At the same time, civic organizations challenged a new Spanish disinformation law that gave the government extensive powers over online content with little independent judicial oversight.[4] In an ironic twist, in early 2021 the Polish and Hungarian governments proposed measures to prevent platforms removing content, insisting they were defending freedom of speech from a social media bias against rightist-populism.

At the EU level, several strategies have been forthcoming on the issue of disinformation. In 2014, EU Human Rights Guidelines for Freedom of Expression Online and Offline committed the Union to develop policies to protect democratic rights online as much as offline.[5] In September 2018, the European Commission introduced a Code of Practice on Disinformation that pressed private sector companies to work with the EU to remove false information, design tighter rules for

---

[2] https://www.loc.gov/law/help/social-media-disinformation/compsum.php.
[3] D. Kaye, *Speech Police, The Global Struggle to Govern the Internet*, (New York: Columbia Global Reports, Columbia University, 2019).
[4] J. J. Gálvez, 'Ambiguedad contra desinformacion', *El Pais*, 7 November 2020.
[5] Council of the European Union, *EU Human Rights Guidelines for Freedom of Expression Online and Offline*, Foreign Affairs Council, 12 May 2014.

political adverts, exert more control over bots and provide for more open identification online. The EU strategy put more responsibility on major online platforms to direct advertising away from sites spreading disinformation, make political advertising more transparent, address the issue of fake online identities and empower users to report disinformation. The EU also increased funds for fact-checkers and developed toolkits for media literacy.[6]

The main thrust of most EU action has focused on pressuring and constricting tech companies. The General Data Protection Regulation (GDPR) began to operate as a constraining tool over the use of data. In February 2020, the Commission published a digital strategy that stressed the need for more open data to be used for public benefit beyond tech companies' control. It promised high impact projects putting billions of euros into data-sharing infrastructure and 'common data spaces' across Europe.[7] Member states also launched plans for a European cloud computing initiative, Gaia-X, in an effort to wrest back control from tech companies. Angela Merkel argued that defending democracy required the EU to exercise 'digital sovereignty' and to regain control over data from US tech giants. [8]

In 2020 the EU drew up tougher guidelines to control platforms' actions in the Covid-19 pandemic, and the virus gave a further prompt towards formal EU regulation of the tech sector. A Commission communication on disinformation in the context of Covid-19 committed to the use of restrictive instruments, as health related disinformation became a serious concern.[9] At the very end of 2020, the Commission introduced two important initiatives. A European Democracy Action Plan promised more EU coordination and capacity-building against

[6] European Commission, *Tackling Online Disinformation: A European Approach*, COM (2018) 236.

[7] European Commission, *Shaping Europe's Digital Future*, COM (2020) 67; European Commission, *A European Strategy for Data*, COM (2020) 66.

[8] G. Chazan, 'Angela Merkel urges EU to seize control of data from US tech titans', *Financial Times*, 13 November 2019.

[9] European Commission and High Representative of the Union for Foreign Affairs and Security Policy, *Tackling Covid-19 Disinformation: Getting the Facts Right*, Join (2020) 8.

disinformation, a new law mandating transparency in online political advertising and stronger support for media pluralism as a bulwark against distorted online information.[10] In parallel, a Digital Services Act threatened the large platforms with fines if they failed to provide more information on their online content moderation and promote trustworthy sources; its aim was to move from platforms' self-regulation to the tougher notion of 'co-regulation' between them and democratic authorities.[11] In parallel the British government forwarded similar measures and planned a wide-ranging Online Safety Bill.

The general focus of these national and EU-level measures has been on getting tech companies to introduce technological changes to overcome online harm and distortions to democracy. They have pushed for what has become a standard menu of reforms that has included ways to filter content without outright censorship, programmes for weeding out extremist content and bots, more transparency of algorithms, user alerts of questionable sources and claims, algorithms to detect disinformation, and automated content diversification that gives users a range of views. In the context of this book, it is notable that the EU institutions and national governments have pushed hard for these 'tech fixes' but not always for flanking improvements in underlying democratic process to protect online rights.[12]

Electoral interference

If one target has been the tech companies, another has been external powers' digital attacks on European democracy. Most specifically, European governments have stepped up their defences against election meddling. French authorities defended robustly against attempts to disrupt and influence the 2017 election, with the media not giving

---

[10] European Commission, *On the European Democracy Action Plan*, COM (2020) 790/3.
[11] The EU's information page on the DSA is https://ec.europa.eu/digital-single-market/en/digital-services-act-package.
[12] European Commission, *Technology and Democracy: Understanding the Influence of Online Technologies on Political Behaviour and Decision-Making* (Brussels: Joint Research Centre, 2020).

airtime to hacked information from Emmanuel Macron's campaign. The French government ordered 'false news' to be removed during the election campaign, especially where there was reason to suspect foreign actors were behind this. Building on these moves, Macron proposed a European Agency for the Protection of Democracy aimed at protecting elections from hacking and disinformation. Even if Macron's proposal did not materialize in quite this form it galvanized EU initiatives that moved in a similar direction.

Other member states also adopted defensive measures. The Netherlands adopted new cyber-defence capabilities for elections and banned electronic vote counting as protection against possible electronic interference. Germany boosted cyber defences in the run up to its September 2018 elections. That same month, Sweden sought to protect its election with a national counter-disinformation initiative. In the UK, the government set up an initiative to counter disinformation and boost cyber defence after the 2017 election and then launched a Defending Democracy programme against electoral interference in July 2019. In July 2020, a high-profile report of the British parliament's intelligence and security committee on Russian influence operations berated the Conservative government for still not treating this problem with sufficient funding or commitment, noting that intelligence agencies had been reluctant to be dragged into what was for them the unfamiliar territory of domestic elections.[13] On the back of the debate and pressure this report generated, the government debated new powers for the intelligence agencies to defend elections and also mooted possible new capacities for the UK Electoral Commission in this area. By 2021 it was planning to criminalize some external actions against UK democratic processes.[14]

The 2019 European elections saw the EU introduce a range of initiatives against outside interference. The European Parliament set up

---

[13] UK Parliament Intelligence and Security Committee, *Russia* (London: House of Commons, 2020), p. 10.

[14] Her Majesty's Government, *Global Britain in a Competitive Age: The Integrated Review of Security, Defence, Development and Foreign Policy* (London: HMG, 2021), 74–5.

a committee on Foreign Interference in all Democratic Processes in the European Union. A European election cooperation network set up a 'rapid alert system' within the European External Action Service. This created a network of member state officials charged with coordinating responses to external threats. The EU promised significant funding to protect against external electoral interference and to link its work with the G7 Charlevoix Commitment on Defending Democracy from Foreign Threats.[15] The 2019 EU elections passed without massive disruption, although they were subject to some external disinformation efforts.[16] As concerns persisted, the 2020 Democracy Action Plan proposed a new mechanism to boost electoral resilience against cyberattacks, limits on micro-targeting in EU election campaigns and measures to limit external support for European political parties.[17]

The concerns over electoral integrity have become a more central part of the EU's wider cybersecurity policies. While most elements of cybersecurity extend well beyond this book's remit, there are some overlaps: European cybersecurity resources have increasingly been deployed in a way that relates to democratic resistance. In May 2019, the EU introduced a new sanctions regime that allows it to impose restrictive measures against individuals and entities implicated in cyberattacks including interference against European democratic processes. This was invoked for the first time in July 2020 against Russian, Chinese and North Korean entities and hackers. Several new or upgraded bodies including the European Agency for Cybersecurity, the European Centre of Excellence for Countering Hybrid Threats and the European Digital Observatory have all increased their focus on electoral interference, alongside their work on the more standard areas of cybersecurity. In December 2020, the Commission raised the possibility of a sanctions

---

[15] Council of the European Union, *Conclusions of the Council and of the Member States on Securing Free and Fair European elections*, 6753/1/2019; European Commission, *Action Plan against Disinformation*, COM (2018) 36.

[16] European Regulators Group for Audiovisual Media Services, *Report of the Activities Carried Out to Assist the European Commission in the Intermediate Monitoring of the Code of Practice on Disinformation* (Brussels: ERGA, 2019).

[17] European Commission, *On the European Democracy Action Plan*, COM (2020) 790/3.

regime against states practising disinformation attacks on European democracy, potentially adding a highly political complement to the cybercrime sanctions.[18] In the cyber domain, security and democracy policies have increasingly overlapped with each other.

At a relatively small scale, the EU set up its so-called StratCom initiative in 2014 to monitor Russian influence operations. Its budget was set at a modest level of around a million euros a year before increasing to five million in 2019. StratCom works in particular on correcting disinformation and producing good news EU stories in the Russian language media in member states and non-EU Eastern European countries. It has been driven mainly by concerns over Russian actions in the eastern neighbourhood but has increasingly gained a remit related to democracy within EU states too. Stratcom's operations were extended to some North African states and the Balkans in 2019. Still, the programme has remained relatively small-scale and several member states have been reluctant to give it full political backing out of a desire to reduce geopolitical tensions with Russia.

Surveillance and the Covid-19 apps dilemma

Quite separate from external influence operations and disinformation, in 2020 a very specific challenge emerged in relation to government surveillance and the tracing apps designed to contain the Covid-19 pandemic. Debates over surveillance technology and process-tracing tools in the Covid-19 crisis intensified concerns over privacy as a core element of democratic rights. The pandemic somewhat altered the state-private sector equation on this: the tech companies, especially through an Apple-Google collaboration, devised what they insisted were privacy-first apps with safeguards to protect users from states using information in an expansive and intrusive fashion. Several

---

[18] E. Zalan, 'EU Commission plans sanctions on disinformation', *EU Observer*, 4 December 2020.

European governments initially pushed the companies to relax these privacy requirements for access to their apps' data.[19]

Yet as the pandemic evolved, governments shifted position. After initially considering centralized tracing apps that would transmit information to a single state-managed database, European governments switched to decentralized systems where data was shared only among users of an app and not with state authorities. Denmark, Germany, Ireland, Italy and the UK made this move, for example. The shift was in part due to the technical difficulties of countries developing their own apps separate from the tech companies, but popular pressure over privacy issues was also a factor. France was the outlier, launching a state-managed centralized app in June 2020, although the French government insisted rights-protection guarantees were built into its systems through randomized identities and limits on state bodies' access to information. In general, nearly all European states' apps ended up being voluntary and time-limited and promised to use data only for health purposes.[20]

The Commission set criteria suggesting that tracing apps should not use geolocation data and be prevented from being used for any purpose other than Covid management; it insisted that these standards helped rein back member states' apps.[21] European apps were not as intrusive as those used in several Asian states; nor were they as effective, with relatively low take-up rates among the population. Concerns over privacy persisted and several states' apps were found to breach GDPR privacy restraints. One notable legal case found that the UK government had failed to undertake a privacy assessment before launching its app.[22] Yet, citizen and civil society concerns over digital surveillance made

[19] P. McGee and H. Murphy, 'Coronavirus apps: The risk of slipping into a surveillance state', *Financial Times*, 27 April 2020.

[20] P. O'Neill, T. Ryan-Mosley and B. Johnson, 'A flood of coronavirus apps are tracking us. Now it's time to keep track of them', *MIT Technology Review*, 7 May 2020.

[21] A. Hern, 'Surveillance a price worth paying to beat coronavirus, says Blair think tank', *The Guardian*, 24 April 2020.

[22] J. Miller and E. Solomon, 'Germany launches coronavirus app to immediate criticism', *Financial Times*, 16 June 2020.

governments more attentive to privacy rights and meant that tracing apps remained low profile. Beyond the Covid-19 crisis, these same concerns were evident in a 2020 Commission white paper on artificial intelligence (AI) that focused heavily on protecting citizens' rights from new surveillance technology.[23]

Digital activism 2.0

While much attention has centred on these different levels of control over digital technology, a broader and more positive agenda of digital empowerment has also revived in the last several years. Policymakers and politicians claim to realize that overly strict online controls can easily become an additional problem for democracy. Many illiberal populist parties have complained that governments are trying to silence their views online and this risks boosting their popularity. Alongside efforts to influence online content and actions, multiple actors have sought to bolster the positive democratic potential of digital technology. Although this has not attracted the same high profile as authorities' battles against tech giants, disinformation and election interference, such digital activism stands to be equally consequential for democratic quality over the longer term.

In recent years, an intense wave of digital initiatives has gathered momentum. This constitutes a second phase of digital activism. The first phase began in the early 2000s and elicited much optimism that it would be the central pillar of democratic renewal. A period of cyber pessimism followed as the downsides of technology became more evident. What might be described as a digital activism 2.0 has now begun to emerge in response to these problems, with more multifaceted features than the digital activism 1.0 of the early 2000s. It is instructive

---

[23] European Commission, *White Paper on Artificial Intelligence: A European Approach to Excellence and Trust*, COM (2020) 65.

to distinguish the several types of emerging digital empowerment that can be identified across Europe.

Government digital petitions

A first type of initiative is the government instigated online petition. These have multiplied in number in recent years across Europe. There has been a dramatic spread of so-called e-government and most member states have introduced online petition mechanisms. Latvia's ManaBalss. lv online petitioning platform has become a widely emulated leader in the field. This is normally cited as the highest impact e-petition mechanism, with two-thirds of petitions reaching the required one million signatures to generate new laws. Created in 2011, Manabalss. lv has generated proposals on property taxes and budget reforms, overturned anti-human rights legislation and has inspired new laws on a stricter ethical code for MPs and the use of synthetic drugs.[24]

The Finnish government has a unit working to extend e-democracy; between two and three million people visit the government's online e-petitions every year, in a country of five million. A petition portal supports the government's goal of finding innovative ways to develop public services, connecting civic reformers with government officials. Moving in a similar direction, in 2018 the Danish parliament introduced a platform that allows citizens to make legislative proposals if they gather fifty thousand signatures for their ideas.[25] In Austria, since 2018 support for citizen petitions can be registered electronically.

The British parliament has begun to implement a wide range of measures using digital platforms to give citizens more participation in parliamentary debates and closer contact with politicians.[26] It created its own petitions website where citizens can draft and support

[24] Citizen initiatives' platform, ManaBalss.lv.
[25] 'A new initiative from the Danish Parliament gives Danish citizens a direct role in the democratic process', Danish Parliament, 1 February 2018.
[26] UK House of Commons, *Open Up! Speaker's Digital Democracy Commission* (London: House of Commons, 2015).

initiatives for the parliament's consideration. If a petition gets ten thousand signatures, the government will respond; if it gets a hundred thousand signatures, there will automatically be a parliamentary debate on the initiative. Issues that have been debated in parliament through this route include limiting media bias, making online homophobia a criminal offence and enacting stricter dangerous driving laws.[27] The most popular electronic petition to have been submitted to the UK parliament was the one calling on the government to stop Brexit.[28]

City level platforms

A second type of initiative is the kind of online platform increasingly offered and used by municipal authorities in numerous European cities. The Decide Madrid portal has engaged citizens through votes and proposals on new local laws, consultations and debates. During the city government's 2015–19 mandate, this portal received 26,000 citizen proposals, making the platform one of the most heavily used citizen input platforms anywhere in the world. Still, only two proposals garnered the threshold minimum support – one relating to pollution and one on public transport tickets. Only 1 per cent of proposals even got to a thousand online endorsements, way short of the nearly thirty thousand needed. Apart from the two successful cases, only two others attracted even half the endorsements needed. The platform's organizers lamented that they were held back by the Spanish state's reluctance to allow binding local referendums to legitimize and take forward citizen ideas. Despite this, Decide Madrid got people debating online, while also attracting the attention of institutions all around the world. The portal also allowed for some open collaborative online editing of legislative proposals.[29]

Barcelona's portal Decidim has developed as part of a wider programme of the city taking back control of data. The city

---

[27] A running list of petitions is at Petitions debated in Parliament, UK Parliament.

[28] H. Cheung, 'Do petitions ever work?', *BBC News*, 26 March 2019.

[29] Facts on the Madrid experience can be found in MediaLab, *Future Democracies: Laboratory of Collective Intelligence for Participatory Democracy* (Madrid: MediaLab, 2019).

administration's approach has moved from e-government to wider online participation, with more use of open data. A key development has been Decidim's expansion into smaller Catalan towns. The portal's architects say around two-thirds of city-level proposals have come from citizens in recent years; closing streets off to traffic is a prominent example. A Participation Lab Network has moved participative digital infrastructures into schools, youth centres and libraries. The municipal council has begun investing in training, so more citizens know how to use these tools. Increasingly the platform is organized in a way that allows citizens to propose their own ideas for participation, with officials then helping them to set up such initiatives. Coordinating 1200 local administrative entities, the Barcelona administration has worked to knit all this together into a larger scale Network of Open Government.[30]

Athens City Council created its SynAthina platform after the financial crisis to link citizens together and give them input into the provision of public services and self-help schemes in the midst of cutbacks and shortages. Citizens submit policy proposals and voluntary activities on the SynAthina website and get connected to relevant sponsors, business representatives, governmental and non-governmental agencies that will assist them in their efforts.[31] The activities that SynAthina volunteers have organized over the years range from operating soup kitchens to administering refugee-integration campaigns.

The City of Paris has developed a space called the Civic Hall to bring together technologists, experts and community members for solving civic problems in innovative ways and creating new modalities of democratic participation.[32] The City of Grenoble has financed Grenoble CivicLab, a space that brings together citizens, entrepreneurs and NGOs to develop digital tools for tackling urgent social, environmental

---

[30] This paragraph draws on author conversations with Decidim's designers in January 2020.
[31] Summarized on Urban Sustainability Exchange, SynAthina: a social innovation platform.
[32] Information is on the Paris city government webpage, 'La halle civique dans le 20e: l'innovation democratique a desormais son lieu', at https://www.paris.fr/pages/la-halle-civique-dans-le-20e-l-innovation-democratique-a-desormais-son-lieu-5609/.

and economic challenges.[33] In 2020 many city governments launched platforms specifically to collect citizen input on the management of Covid-19. Grenoble ran a notable Voisins Voisines platform to organize a mutual aid system for the crisis. Milan city hall developed an especially notable range of online Covid-19 initiatives.[34] Indeed, nearly all cities with online participative platforms used these to collect requests for assistance and to organize community distribution by citizens at some point in the pandemic.

These municipal level initiatives are closely associated with a focus on open data. More open data rules have increasingly been built into digital processes in municipal administrations so that data becomes openly available to citizens on procurement contracts, for example. There is now a general movement across Europe among city administrations to try to take data out of companies' control, keeping citizens' data private from companies and making service providers' data public. This represents an emergent 'data commons' aimed at using digital information to solve problems related to service provision.

Civil society digital activism

A third level of innovation is the digital activism led by civil society, a range of grassroots initiative seeking to use technology to increase citizen participation and monitoring of government decisions. This is an area of even greater dynamism than the innovations in e-petitions and city-level platforms. One EU-funded database lists over two thousand civic initiatives that have commenced in the field of 'digital social innovation'.[35] Many of these operate at the European level. CitizenLab has developed a platform to help local governments consult citizens. WeEuropeans undertook large-scale social-media consultations across

---

[33] Information at www.grenoble.civiclab.eu, 'Citizen-driven initiatives for tomorrow's smart city'.
[34] Information at https://www.grenoble.fr/1700-voisins-voisines.htm, 'Grenoble voisins, voisines'.
[35] The database is at https://digitalsocial.eu.

Europe to devise an EU reform agenda focused on democracy. The European Citizen Action Service created a DigiDem initiative to get more citizens pursuing their rights online.

Other initiatives focus on monitoring and pressuring national politicians. The early pioneer apps like Loomio and LiquidFeedback have given rise in more recent years to an almost limitless number of similar platforms for monitoring, debating and decision-taking. The Raoul Wallenberg Algorithm initiative tracks whether leaders' statements are compatible with positive democratic values. In Spain, the Osoigo platform allows citizens to submit questions to Spanish politicians. In the UK, Mysociety has pioneered the WritetoThem and FixmyStreet digital initiatives. The similar TheyWorkForYou site helps citizens keep tabs of how MPs vote. The SmartGov app also hosts online debates between citizens and legislators. In several locations digital tools are being used to form 'civic networks' that link residents, activists and local officials to debate solutions to neighbourhood issues.[36] A group of civil society organizations launched the Good Web Project to cooperate with government institutions to ensure greater online transparency over algorithms and content management, with the aim of making the internet 'compatible with liberal democracy'.[37]

Efforts have been made to connect citizens with parliamentarians. In France, the Parlement et Citoyens platform was conceived by the civil society organization Cap Collectif to allow citizens to feed ideas into new laws being debated in the National Assembly. It has gained over twenty thousand registered users and has fed citizens' suggestions into draft legislation on a regular basis; one of its key features is that each consultation is supported by a particular MP to ensure that online deliberation filters into parliamentary debate.[38] The Your Priorities application has been used in Estonia, Iceland and Romania, enabling

---

[36] M. Leong, 'Civic networks: A new paradigm for online citizen engagement', *Apolitical*, 4 December 2018.

[37] https://demos.co.uk/project/the-good-web-project/.

[38] J. Simon et al., *Digital Democracy: The Tools Transforming Political Engagement* (London: Nesta, 2017), pp. 24–8.

citizens to debate online with other civic and political actors, and then to link such debates to mainstream political processes.

Such innovations have proliferated in the Central and Eastern European states where democratic quality has been most worryingly under threat. In Poland, civic-tech experts launched a Personal Democracy Forum to explore how to enhance the democratic impact of digital technology. Also in Poland, Akcja Demokracja was set up in 2015 to organize nationwide advocacy campaigns and mobilized thousands of people by combining online petitioning with mass protests on issues like environmental protection and judicial independence. In Romania, DeClic has become the country's leading platform for online campaigning; it makes a virtue of combining online and offline activism. Several civil society initiatives have begun using Blockchain to bring politicians and citizens into more regular interaction.

One highly controversial civic initiative was Tsunami Democratic in Catalonia. This used Telegram and coded messages to generate a tsunami-like momentum among protestors, especially at the micro level of community clusters. It provided for real-time coordination of protests and was based around similar technology used by democracy activists in Hong Kong. The app got caught up in the politics of Catalan independence. Supporters of the independence parties saw the informal group and app as a major boost to democracy and as a necessary tool for circumventing state repression. Nearly half a million people joined the group's online platform. The group insisted it was peaceful, and its immediate aim was simply to push the two sides to engage in dialogue; its most prominent hashtag was #Spainsitandtalk. Spanish politicians and officials in Madrid insisted these online activities represented a threat to Spain's democratic constitution and invoked antiterror laws to insist that operators close down the app.[39]

One type of digital activism that has expanded especially fast is that of fact-checking. A network of independent fact checkers formed across

---

[39] J. Faus and B. Carreño, 'Spain closes Catalan protest group website and probes riots', *Reuters*, 18 October 2019.

Europe, called the Social Observatory for Disinformation and Social Media Analysis (Soma); this later morphed into the European Digital Meda Observatory that began work on June 2020.[40] The number of civil society fact-checking initiatives in Europe doubled between 2016 and 2020.[41] Some examples are listed in Table 6.1. One type of activism in this sphere focuses on how official fact-checking efforts themselves infringe freedom of expression and fail to stay impartial. Nineteen European organizations formed the FactcheckEU platform. Unlike Soma, these refused official funds as they charged the Commission and the European Parliament (EP) with pushing mainly for anti-EU stories to be revised.[42] Article 19 has been critical of the EU's focus on content removal and restricting online speech and began a project to make sure that European governments' counter-disinformation efforts respect the freedom of expression. The European Digital Rights Initiative focuses on how government-mandated content removal risks undermining freedom of expression. EU DisinfoLab has shone a spotlight on how the EU's own interests dilute its willingness to take down some fake news sites.

A still different kind of civic digital initiative multiplied during the Covid-19 pandemic. Many civic groups found ways during the Covid-19 lockdown to 'protest' online, by flooding social media with messages and digitally mimicking the route of marches. Many groups found using online 'gatherings' enabled them to reach new audiences among house-bound ordinary citizens.[43] Hundreds of Covid-19 hackathons took place; there were few civic organizations that did not organize some form of digital activity along these lines. Groups ran dozens of Slack community-sharing initiatives to coordinate responses to the health emergency and help deal with life under lockdown – examples, among thousands, included the Tech4Covid19 movement in Portugal and the

---

[40] See www.edmo.eu.
[41] K. Bontcheva and J. Posetti (eds), *Balancing Act: Countering Disinformation while respecting Freedom of Expression* (Paris, UNESCO, 2020), p. 128.
[42] 'Now is the time: the journalists fighting fake news before the EU elections', *The Guardian*, 16 May 2019.
[43] B. Bonfert, 'Organizing under lockdown: Online activism, local solidarity', *Roar*, 9 April 2020.

Table 6.1 Fact-checking digital initiatives

Country	Platform	Objectives	Website
UK	Full Fact	Fights misleading information	https://fullfact.org/
Slovakia, Czech Republic, Poland	Demagog	Project of the SGI Institute to control veracity of politicians' statements	https://demagog.sk
Romania	Factual	Monitors bribes and elections and undertakes fact-checking. Run by Funky Citizens	https://www.factual.ro
Italy	Pagella Politica	Political fact-checking site	https://www. pagellapolitica.it
Austria	Mimimaka	Fact-checking, especially focused on Facebook hoaxes in German and Dutch	https://www.mimikama.at
Croatia	Faktograf	Fact-checking website founded by civic groups	https://faktograf.hr
France	Captain fact	Collaborative fact-checking platform	https://captainfact.io
Germany	Correctiv	Non-profit newsroom that focuses on abuses of power through fact-checking work	https://correctiv.org
Greece	Fact Checker	Independent fact-checking site with a focus on pseudoscience and medical fraud	https://www.factchecker.gr

Lithuania	Debunk	Site launched by local media sites seeking to collaborate with society and the state to fight against disinformation	https://debunk.eu
The Netherlands	Nieuwscheckers	Fact-checking civic initiative	https://nieuwscheckers.nl/
Spain	Minsiterio de la Verdad Newtral	First fact-checking site in Spain to debunk fake news. Example of new, software-driven fact-checking online initiative	https://www.miniver.org http://newtral.es
Scotland	The Ferret Fact Service	First Scottish non-partisan fact checker. Checks statements from politicians, pundits and prominent public figures	https://theferret.scot/ferret-fact-service/
Czech Republic	Czech Elves	Dedicated to rooting out and debunking Russian propaganda and disinformation	https://www.codastory.com/disinformation/volunteers-fight-disinfo-czech-republic/
France	Newsguard	Tracks the veracity of online news outlets, giving these a reliability ranking	https://www.newsguardtech.com/

Compartimos Barrio site in Madrid. The EU drew up a database and Civic Hall compiled a Coronavirus Civic Tech Field Guide that listed the hundreds of digital citizen initiatives that sprang up related to Covid-19, in what became perhaps the most intense period of online organizing and mobilization.[44]

Digital party platforms

In a final type of incipient digital democracy, some political parties have developed platforms to guide their decision-making. The general emergence of new political parties was assessed in Chapter 5; here their online elements merit specific mention. A small number of new 'digital parties' were built around digital democracy from their inception – a different matter from existing parties adding a few online tools to their traditional processes. These parties burst to prominence without the large and costly institutional structures that traditional parties require, relying instead on looser notions of membership through online participation. Their digital democracy was tailored to a specific segment of society: young, educated people that are highly connected through social media but otherwise increasingly excluded from societal opportunities.

The best-known example of a digital party is the Five Star Movement (5SM) in Italy. At its creation in 2009, the 5SM was fairly empty in terms of preconceived ideology; the remit was to be responsive to what its online base asked of the party. The party's online Rousseau platform, launched in 2016, has got tens of thousands of previously politically unengaged citizens contributing towards public-policy decisions. The platform allows for participative internal party decision-making and for users to propose and jointly edit new legislation. Dozens of proposals that participants launched online have made it into the party's manifestos.

---

[44] Civictech.guide: coronavirus; See https://joinup.ec.europa.eu/collection/digital-response-covid-19/useful-information-and-resources.

Yet the platform has also underpinned a top-down style of leadership. The party leadership has often framed debates online in a way simply to clear its own proposals. Most online votes have been a confirmatory vote on the leadership more than a deliberative debate over democratic alternatives. The numbers participating in online discussions about new laws reached an apparent ceiling and in recent times have fallen. Participants have complained that there is no clear link between online deliberations and the proposals eventually selected by the party leadership.[45]

The prominent role of the digital platform has displaced party workers. The 5SM is based on a small leadership combined with a large base of online sympathizers and not much in between. This means there are few internal voices to challenge the leadership based on coherent ideological alternatives. Being so responsive to the online base means the 5SM can swing between relatively progressive positions, say on climate issues, to populist positions on immigration and the EU. Moreover, Rousseau has suffered from security problems with several hacking incidents and questions exist over its use of personal data; it was subject to the first case in which EU data protection laws were used against a political party. The 5SM has increasingly taken up a more standard form of 'managerial politics' using offline political strategies[46]; by April 2021 it seemed like the party and the Rousseau platform were set to part ways from each other.

In Spain, Unidas Podemos has followed some of the same logic, albeit not to the same extent as the 5SM. It launched a Reddit forum entitled Plaza Podemos that soon attracted several hundred thousand users. Many ideas in its election programmes came from online crowdsourcing. Yet, as in the 5SM, most online votes have rubber stamped the leadership's positions. A citizen initiative mechanism on Plaza Podemos has such a high threshold that no proposal has ever made it to a membership vote. While the party exudes the same kind

[45] P. Garbaudo, *The Digital Party* (London: Pluto Press, 2019), p. 131.
[46] P. Garbaudo, *The Digital Party* (London: Pluto Press, 2019), p. 91 and p. 102.

of social media identity as the 5SM, digital decision-making has not become quite so central to its identity. The party's various affiliates have gained power at local level and build their legitimacy there through a mix of online and traditional on-the-ground politicking.

The techno-optimism that underpinned digital parties' creation remains, but it has withered somewhat. As of 2020, the most digitalized parties had lost support rather than rising inexorably. Rather than being a harbinger of future party politics, the self-styled digital parties remain an exception not the norm. They have not given rise to a large number of imitators, even if most of Europe's older parties now have some form of online discussion portal. The 5SM has been fairly unique in how core the digital dimension was to its democratic claims. Others that showed signs of taking steps in the same direction have to some degree relented. For instance, the tone of the Labour Party leadership contest in 2020 centred on returning to more traditional political forms after the Corbyn-Momentum years and the early-2010s talk of online democracy was strikingly absent from candidates' pitches. Innovations in digital activism inside parties have been significant, but they have yet to become a dominant feature in European party politics as a whole.

Profile: Estonia

Estonia offers some of the best practice in the field of digital governance: the government is widely seen to have taken on tech for community aims and is generally transparent in how it uses citizen data. As online platforms have become mainstream and increasingly used across the country, they have opened highly political debates about Estonian democracy. The country has been at the frontier of not only digital developments but also the thorny political dilemmas that come with them.

Estonian digital innovations go back quite some way to the early 2000s, with several e-petitioning, e-voting and online crowdsourcing initiatives attempted before 2010. The big upgrade came with the

Rahvakogu or People's Assembly initiative in 2013 that was a response to a party-funding scandal and ended up generating fifteen major legislative proposals through online debate. This exercise led to the creation of a permanent digital portal Rahvaalgatus.ee in 2016. As noted in Chapter 4, this enables Estonian citizens to propose and co-draft initiatives to be submitted to the parliament. The parliament has to process every appeal with over a thousand signatures. Through these provisions, around thirty collective proposals have been sent to the parliament through the portal; four have become laws.[47]

The initiatives have allowed citizens to voice their opinions on a regular basis; those involved in running these initiatives argue that the spirit of online input and debate has become a normalized part of Estonian democracy. The political parties were somewhat unsure about the moves but got involved in part to stop a separate sphere of e-democracy developing as a rival to the parliament. Public authorities made a big effort to close the divide in digital use between different parts of the population, including through extending free internet access and e-government services to the most remote communities and also having the state and social-media platforms working in partnership in schools and other public places.

E-voting has increased gradually since it was introduced in 2005; in 2019, around 44 per cent of citizens voted online in the national elections and around 47 per cent in the EU elections. Estonia has several units within government working on AI and its impact on governance processes. The momentum on e-government has gathered pace, mainly in relation to the transparency of government policies and the wider availability of open data. Online input into participatory budgeting has grown dramatically across twenty cities, this now very much a mainstream part of local decision-making. The government's online consultation platform has also evolved, although it still has a

---

[47] A summary of the Estonia case is given on the OECD Open Government website, https://oecd-opsi.org/innovations/collective-addresses-and-rahvaalgatus-ee-nudging-the-parliament-of-estonia-to-more-openness-and-accountability.

relatively low number of regular, registered users, despite attempts to make it more accessible and user friendly.

While Estonia's online petition initiative was one of the earliest and remains one of the most highly regarded, frustration has grown that its impact has not expanded more significantly. The tools have proven useful and used by citizens for very concrete service provision questions, without permeating political practice in general or in an overall sense getting citizens more engaged in core democratic processes. In an attempt to rectify this, public authorities have more recently looked to use online tools together with offline processes, supporting the latter to work in parallel with e-petitions and the like.

However, recent proposals to revive and upgrade the use of e-petitions have been controversial and have engendered debate at the highest political level. Estonia has world-renowned experiences in e-government, but digital activism in the civic sphere has struggled to keep pace. The fact that online petitions have generated no more than a handful of new legislative proposals has led a number of parties to call for ways of ensuring they get a better political response. The coalition government that took office in 2019 promised to provide for referendums where parliament failed to act on petitions that collected the requisite number of signatures – although it remained unclear exactly how this would be taken forward.

This idea became highly politicized because most pressure came from the far-right EKRE party, as part of its broader drive for more direct democracy. The party was given the post of digital minister when it entered into government. Many suspected that EKRE pushed this idea mainly as part of its attempt to weaken or circumvent parliament. Mainstream parties feared that this would set up a strand of direct popular legitimacy that would confuse and cut across the channels of representative democracy, and they sought to dilute the plans. EKRE pushed to get citizens to use online petitioning to call for more frequent referendums where it believed the state institutions were out of line with public opinion. The most significant issue in this regard was that of same-sex marriage, where the party wanted to mobilize citizens through e-democracy tools to push back against government proposals for legal civil partnerships. In addition, EKRE pushed in government for a directly elected president as another attempt to offset the parliament with competing channels of direct popular legitimacy.

In sum, plans for the political use of digital tools have retained momentum in Estonia but have also become gradually more infected with tensions and sensitive debates at the political level. Digitally driven direct democracy became associated with the EKRE party's radical and illiberal agenda. As the country's two mainstream parties formed a new coalition in early 2021 and pushed EKRE aside, it was unclear how this might affect the direct- and digital-democracy agenda; one immediate move was the cancellation of a 2021 referendum on same-sex marriage. Those involved in the country's internationally famed e-government and e-participation initiatives say the unresolved question is whether Estonia can or even wishes to move to a phase of deeper digitally enabled democracy: for a decade the country has been at the forefront of using technology to improve decision-making and public debate, but it has yet to move beyond the ethos of online petitioning and consultation to make democratic politics digital in a full and systemic sense.[48]

Assessment: The right ingredients for digital democracy?

While the EU institutions and national European governments were slow to address the downsides of digital technology, they have in recent years begun to do so. In a multipronged set of responses, European governments have begun taking measures to influence the operations of tech companies and social-media platforms, and also to protect democratic processes from outside digital disruption in its many forms. In many areas such as regulation and election-defence, the EU

---

[48] Information from meetings with Estonian E-government Academy and Praxis institute, Tallinn, October 2019.

has leapfrogged most other powers around the world, including the United States.[49] In this progress there has been a shift from state-based cybersecurity to protecting European citizens' digital rights.

Control with openness?

The EU institutions and European governments have been most active in the sphere of regulation and other attempts to limit the harmful impact of digital platforms. Most new initiatives focus on a standard menu of options: better monitoring of illegal content, control over the way data is used, efforts to tackle abuses and hate speech online and enhancing e-privacy.[50] While European policies have undoubtedly begun to bear down on the most serious forms of digital harassment and violence, they have shied away from far-reaching online deterrence to defend democracy. While the new rules have exerted some leverage over the tech companies, these companies are still not subject to strong democratic accountability. Policy interventions still need to be more assertive when it comes to requiring transparency and accountability for the content-shaping algorithms that dictate what users see and profile extreme content because this gains more internet traffic. European policies still need to make a move from encouraging aspects of online transparency to crafting full and effective accountability over platforms. To protect European democracy, policies are needed to reshape the way platforms work far beyond the removal of content or correcting already-posted disinformation.

If EU regulatory action still needs to be strengthened, however, the reverse danger has surfaced of new rules stifling pluralism. As European regulations and pressures on tech companies have intensified, so concerns have taken shape over freedom of speech. As new laws make

---

[49] E. Brattberg and T. Maurer, *Russian Election Interference: Europe's Counter to Fake News and Cyber Attacks* (Washington, DC: Carnegie Endowment for International Peace, 2018).

[50] U. Pachl and P. Valenti (eds), *A Human-Centric Digital Manifesto for Europe* (Brussels: Open Society European Policy Institute, 2019).

tech companies more heavily responsible for illegal content, so these companies have erred on the side of caution by taking down much content that runs any risk of being deemed unacceptable. The EU Code of Practice appeared to have a chilling effect on the freedom of speech, and CSOs have criticized early drafts of the DSA for opening the door to further constriction.[51] Policymakers' intent may not be anti-democratic but the focus on online restrictions can easily be instrumentalized by forces that do want to narrow democratic freedoms.[52] The mounting disquiet over unregulated social media spaces has bred an inverse risk of online restrictions becoming *more* severe than those guiding offline debate. If disinformation has come to menace the exercise of democratic rights, so too have many European governmental *counter-disinformation* measures.

As online content cannot be fully controlled, policies can most usefully shine a stronger light on where information is coming from.[53] From a democratic perspective, the pressing need is not so much to take content down but providing more explanatory background to contentious material. A more democracy-sensitive approach would lie in giving citizens more choice in whether and how they use algorithms or even allowing users to build their own algorithms so they and not the tech companies decide what they get to see online. EU institutions and some European governments have indeed begun to adopt this kind of narrative about transparency and choice and to move beyond the focus on regulatory limitations.[54] This is especially important as the problem has shifted from egregiously untrue, extreme content to more

---

[51] A. Kuczerawy, 'Fighting online disinformation: Did the EU Code of Practice forget about freedom of expression?', forthcoming in *Disinformation and Digital Media as a Challenge for Democracy*, European Integration and Democracy Series, 6. https://ssrn.com/abstract=3453732.

[52] J. Pamment, *The EU Code of Practice on Disinformation: Briefing Note for the New EU Commission* (Washington, DC: Carnegie Endowment for International Peace, 2020), p. 11.

[53] P. Pomerantsev, *This is Not Propaganda: Adventures in the War against Reality* (London: Public Affairs, 2019).

[54] Annenberg Public Policy Center of the University of Pennsylvania, 'Freedom and Accountability: A Transatlantic Framework for Moderating Speech Online', 16 June 2020.

subtle anti-democratic narratives that cannot be dealt with through legislation.[55]

The overall European policy mix entails a curious and intricate balance. If one priority is more privacy, another is more openness. European strategies promise more data privacy but also more open data. How far open data can help revive democracy remains unclear. Initiatives that have pushed forward a more publicly open use of data are a boon for open governance on some local services, like decisions over procurement contracts. Whether this valuable boost to accountability translates into generalized citizen engagement in pluralistic, competitive democratic decision-making is for now more debatable. The push for more open data has rightly attracted a great deal of hopeful attention in the last few years, but the challenge remains of linking this with more traditional strands of democratic reforms.

In sum, the EU and national governments have done much in recent times that helps contain the influence of tech companies. Partly due to these policy responses, European citizens are more aware today of disinformation. Indeed, this has become one of the most exhaustively publicized themes in recent years and is hardly an underappreciated risk anymore. In addition, the focus on defending online privacy rights has sharpened, especially in light of debates over Covid-19 tracing apps. How far these important shifts necessarily help shore up European democracy is still unclear.[56] Despite the numerous European policy responses, online risks to democracy remain acute.

Mission creep in external digital defence?

The same question of balance is relevant to initiatives aimed at protecting European elections and democratic integrity from harmful outside attacks. The EU institutions and national governments

---

[55] H. Margetts, 'Rethinking democracy with social media', in A. Gamble and T. Wright (eds), *Rethinking Democracy* (Chichester: Wiley, 2019), p. 116.

[56] T. Garton Ash, R. Gorwa and D. Metaxa, *Glasnost! Nine ways Facebook can make itself a better forum for free speech and democracy*, Oxford-Stanford Report, 2019.

have moved with unprecedented speed to release a plethora of new strategies and documents on different aspects of externally generated disinformation and they increasingly justify this new activity with a 'defending democracy' narrative. Although this is undoubtedly a strong and necessary strand of democratic resistance, it has been easier for governments to focus on protecting democracy from outsiders than to rectify their own democratic shortfalls.

While they target external threats, European governments' own use of digital surveillance has continued to increase rather than diminish. Data suggests that internally generated online undemocratic discourse has become more widespread in Europe than interference in democratic process and disinformation coming from external actors.[57] Government capacities in the EU to monitor online content are among the highest in the world.[58] Policies have focused heavily on external threats to elections when interference comes from a wider range of actions and discourse. Increasingly problems derive from subtle forms of information laundering rather than really outlandish external hacking – which means the European policy toolbox needs constantly to catch up with the evolving nature of online distortions. The EU and member state governments still need to look beyond external disinformation and fake news at these broader, endogenous risks.

Much of what the EU does in this field tends to equate 'defending democracy' with 'defending the EU from unfair criticism'. The approach often blurs what is democracy-threatening disinformation with what is simply a different set of opinions and outlooks – whether coming from Russia or from within Europe. Russian, Chinese and other interference is not the cause of European democracy problems, but a factor that amplifies the underlying causes that already exist. Only a modest amount of democracy-rebuilding can be achieved by rebutting external

---

[57] S. Feldstein, *How to Tackle Europe's Digital Democracy Challenges* (Brussels: Carnegie Europe, 2020), citing data from the Digital Society Project.
[58] See data from V-Dem's Digital Society project, www.digitalsocietyproject.org.

criticisms and influence operations.[59] Moreover, geopolitical interests have acted as a counterweight on EU policies: despite all the action plans and internal processes created, many European governments have been reluctant in practice to push back with coercive policy instruments against states guilty of external influence operations due to their wider political and commercial priorities.[60]

Positive digital renewal?

As the policy focus has shifted towards top-down efforts to regulate tech giants, this has diverted governments' attention away from the kind of bottom-up, citizen-driven technology that prioritizes individuals' democratic empowerment. Policies have understandably focused mainly on protecting digital rights through countering disinformation and companies' control over data.[61] Yet in terms of rebuilding democracy, the more positive agenda of digital empowerment is just as important. This is because online distortions like disinformation are not so much the cause of democratic erosion as its symptoms: democracy-by-regulation can only be an extremely partial strategy.

Some strands of more positive digital activism have begun to gain new momentum in recent years across Europe. The chapter adds to debates in this sphere by offering a typology of an emerging digital activism 2.0, including e-petitioning, digital municipalism, civil society initiatives and e-parties. Still, these varied initiatives have not yet gained a constant and regular impact over democratic decision-making.[62] Critics suggest that e-petitions and local-level digital portals have

[59] M. Meyer-Resende and R. Goldzweig, *Online Threats to Democratic Debate: A Framework for a Discussion on Challenges and Responses* (Berlin: Democracy Reporting International, 2019).

[60] J. Pamment, *The EU's Role in Fighting Disinformation: Taking Back the Initiative* (Washington, DC: Carnegie Endowment for International Peace, 2020).

[61] K. Bontcheva and J. Posetti (eds), *Balancing Act: Countering Disinformation while respecting Freedom of Expression* (Paris: UNESCO, 2020).

[62] S. Coleman, *Can the Internet Strengthen Democracy?* (Cambridge: Polity Press), p. 72.

begun to individualize citizen input in ways that undermine collective deliberation.[63]

Many online platforms are still used more by professionally interested stakeholders than citizens at large. E-participation initiatives still struggle to generate a sense of popular ownership over decisions where they are not well linked to formal policy agendas. [64] Such tools may have given a false illusion of real citizen input in European states where governments are becoming less democratic. Digital consultations and petitions have clearly not been enough to stop citizens feeling frustrated enough to take to the streets in more direct forms of political engagement. While the case of Estonia offers an impressive and promising experience, it remains some way ahead of most other European states in e-governance. And even in this country, e-democracy has become embroiled in political disputes, reflecting a complex and perhaps unsettling relationship between digital participation and hard-right populism.

The most promising area of democratic renewal has come instead from the large number of more bottom-up and citizen-led digital initiatives. These have mushroomed in number and begun to try innovative ways of reshaping politics – beyond formal institutional digital initiatives. Their tangible impact on policies may be mostly modest, but they do reflect an interest on the part of democratic reformers to explore more open-ended uses of digital tools. Such dispersed activism has become a meaningful counterweight to tech giants' concentration of knowledge and social control. It is at this level that citizens and civic organizations have begun to push back against the digital dexterity of illiberal and anti-democratic actors. In line with the book's running concern with citizen-centred democratic renewal, it is surely this kind of embryonic digital civics that most needs to be intensified as a valuable strand of democratic potential and change. Yet

---

[63] G. Berson, 'E-Estonia the ultimate digital democracy', *Medium*, 4 November 2018.

[64] For one such mixed assessment, see J. Simon, T. Bass, V. Boelman and G. Mulgan, *Digital Democracy: The Tools Transforming Political Engagement* (London: Nesta, 2017), pp. 24–8.

while EU leaders increasingly push tech companies to assume greater responsibility, their own support for critical digital empowerment so far remains circumscribed.

What longer-term vision?

Overall, the patterns of digital democratic resistance and renewal are varied across Europe. In some instances, European citizens and tech companies are working together to make states more accountable. In other instances, states and EU institutions are cooperating against tech companies. Yet in a more generic sense, the confluence of state and tech company surveillance works against citizens' democratic empowerment. The positive dynamics of digital renovation have intensified across Europe but still struggle to outweigh these more negative developments. With technology intrinsically neither good nor bad for democracy, the crucial issue is whether democratic actors can be more effective in matching their practical digital strategies to very specific reform requirements across the multiple democratic functions of scrutiny, representation of interests, citizen engagement and deeper deliberation. [65]

While European digital strategies have moved up several gears in recent years, they are still predominantly reactive and concerned with limiting immediate risks and threats. A longer-term outlook will also be needed. There is of course much speculative thinking about where digital technology is likely to take democracy. It could push politics towards an extreme form of individualized marketing as politicians use digital tools to tailor messages to each citizen, in a turbo-charged Schumpeterian model of democracy devoid of ideological solidity. Many fear tech companies taking over government functions and having the power to exclude citizens from basic services. Some predict that AI and algorithms will eventually make political choices for

---

[65] A. Jungherr, G. Rivero and D. Gayo-Avello, *Retooling Politics: How Digital Media are Shaping Democracy* (Cambridge: Cambridge University Press, 2020).

citizens, with profound implications for the whole notion of liberty. Algorithmic governance might reflect citizen preferences, but without being participative. [66]

For this book, the germane point is that there is still no clearly defined European strategy on these kinds of futuristic dilemmas. Policymakers admit that European policies still lack a positive vision of the internet's role in democracy. Problems with platforms' business models have arguably been conflated with the essence of digital technology itself. Policy debates to date have erred in starting from certain blanket approaches towards tech models rather than from an understanding of the detailed challenges facing democracy that digital means can either help solve or make worse.[67] The EU and its member states have moved far in recent years in grappling with digital-democracy issues. Their next step will be fully to integrate technology into a long-term democracy strategy – as opposed to bolting select democracy concerns onto their technology policies.

---

[66] J. Susskind, *Future Politics* (Oxford: Oxford University Press, 2018).

[67] H. Kundnani, *The Future of Democracy in Europe: Technology and the Evolution of Representation* (London: Chatham House, 2020).

7

EU responses I: Taking on illiberal democracy?

Democratic resistance and renewal are not only a matter of reform efforts within states but also of relations between European countries. Sitting atop local and national responses, another arm of democratic resistance comes from EU efforts to confront governments guilty of the most egregious infringements to democratic quality. Some national governments and the EU institutions have gradually exerted a greater degree of pressure on governments in Hungary, Poland and several other counties too. In addition, they have begun to explore a wider range of options for defending core democratic values more generally, including initiatives to redirect funds away from governments guilty of anti-democratic steps and towards civic actors committed to upholding democracy.

Taken together, these measures reflect an incipient change. The crisis of European democracy has forced the EU to move towards fulfilling its earlier promises to be a gatekeeper of democratic norms. Although the EU helped galvanize democratic transitions in many countries before they became members, in the 2010s it did not work well as a safety net against democratic regression for its own member states. It has now begun to pay more attention to this challenge. However, concrete EU policy responses have so far been partial and have generally had modest impact. The chapter delves into the complex explanations for this limited policy adjustment.

Rule of law crisis

One level of EU response to the continent's most undemocratic developments has focused on the rule of law. The European Commission initially broached rule of law problems through a so-called Cooperation and Verification Mechanism (CVM) applied to Bulgaria and Romania after their accession to the Union. Under this mechanism, the EU held back structural funds to Bulgaria in 2008 and Romania in 2011. Still, the overall policy response under this instrument was partial and did not stop democratic backsliding in the two countries. As pre-accession conditionality disappeared, the EU struggled to deal with actors that challenged democratic norms. EU funds sometimes unwittingly fed corruption as local political actors sought to control the rents coming from such huge injections of money.[1]

In 2014, the incipient creep of 'autocratic legalism' led the Commission to introduce what it called a Rule of Law Framework.[2] This provided for various stages of response to rule of law infringements: in a first stage, a dialogue between the Commission and the offending government; in a second stage, concrete Commission requirements for policy and legal changes in the member state in question; and after that the possibility of the state's voting rights being suspended under Article 7 of the treaty. This third step could be triggered by one-third of member states, the Commission or the European Parliament. In a complex decision-making process, a qualified majority was needed to impose sanctions for legal infringements, a four-fifths majority to decide that fundamental EU values risked being breached and unanimity actually to take steps against the flouting of those values. The Council started its own annual Rule of Law Dialogue, with member states seeing this as a cooperative, peer-pressure approach to offset the Commission's potentially punitive framework.

---

[1] A. Mungiu-Pippidi, *Europe's Burden: Promoting Good Governance Across Borders* (Cambridge: Cambridge University Press, 2019).

[2] K. Scheppele, 'Autocratic legalism', *University of Chicago Law Review*, 85 (2018), 545–83

Hungary. Developments in Hungary provided the stiffest test for the EU's resolve. Under Prime Minister Viktor Orbán, the Hungarian government gradually assumed almost full political control over the judiciary. Yet, the Commission did not activate its Rule of Law Framework. Over the course of many years, the EU prevaricated in taking punitive measures against Orbán's government. While Orbán used EU funds to finance his autocratic system of patronage and overtly rubbished the very notion of liberal democracy, he received no more than an occasional slap on the wrist from the Union. The European Parliament voted to trigger Article 7 against Hungary (only) in 2018, but governments in the Council did not bring the motion to a vote.

Instead, the Commission launched successive infringement procedures against Hungary in the European Court of Justice (ECJ) – that is, legal cases related to measures contravening very specific EU laws. These have been taken inter alia on migrants' rights, several elements of the government's civil society restrictions and its measures against the Central European University. The Commission used this legal route selectively; there were many Hungarian government laws where EU action could have been taken but was not. The Commission declined, for instance, to use EU laws against a government-controlled media body created in 2018, despite this infringing media independence rules.[3] Each time the ECJ was called to rule on infringement procedures, it found in favour of the Commission. Yet tangible follow-up was not always apparent or was fairly soft – for instance, allowing Hungary to compensate sacked judges rather than reinstate them. Invariably Hungarian authorities entered into dialogue with the Commission over what changes might be negotiated to overcome EU concerns, pushing back unfavourable action.

A drawn out saga unfolded over ruling party Fidesz's membership of the European People's Party (EPP). For many years, the EPP shielded Orbán from harsher EU measures. In 2019, the government's poster campaign against the Commission president Jean-Claude Juncker

---

[3] Q. Aries, 'Europe's failure to protect liberty in Hungary', *The Atlantic*, 29 December 2019.

triggered a belated reaction from EPP members; twelve centre-right parties called for Fidesz to be expelled. The EPP voted to suspend the party, but only on a temporary basis. As part of the face-saving formula, a committee of wise men was called to look into Fidesz's compliance with EPP values. To many, this looked like a tactical move merely to deflect criticism of the EPP during the 2019 European elections while leaving the door open to bring Orbán back in soon after.

After these May 2019 European elections, the EPP indeed allowed Fidesz back into its meetings, and its seats counted towards the EPP plurality in the new parliament. Yet the fact that the EPP leader, Manfred Weber, did not get selected to be Commission president, despite being the candidate of the party that won most seats, was related in part to widespread unhappiness at his failure to confront Orbán. Conversely, Hungary and other Central and Eastern European states were able to prevent the post from going to Frans Timmermans, the commissioner responsible for invoking legal measures against rule of law backsliding. This paid off as the new Commission seemed to adopt a more emollient approach when it took office in late 2019. While incoming EPP head, Donald Tusk, promised a hard line against Orbán, at the beginning of 2020 the party agreed to keep Fidesz suspended rather than expelling it.

Pressure then mounted against Orbán, however, in the wake of his highly authoritarian Covid-19 emergency measures. Thirteen member states issued a critical statement against these; six others then aligned themselves with this. Another letter came from eleven leaders of conservative parties insisting Fidesz now be ejected from the EPP; yet, centre-right parties in Germany, France, Italy and Spain did not sign this. Toughest pressure came from a group of five Nordic countries – Denmark, Finland, Sweden and non-EU Iceland and Norway – who pressed the Council of Europe for concrete action against Hungary.[4] Feeling greater pressure, Orbán removed Covid-19 emergency measures in June 2020, although he retained many additional executive powers.

[4] 'Hungary summons Nordic diplomats over rule-by-decree row', Euractiv.com, 12 May 2020.

The prime minister's increasingly blatant and confrontational disregard for democratic values then pushed this saga to its denouement in March 2021, when the EPP agreed new rules that effectively forced Fidesz out. This was an emblematic, if gravely overdue, move of democratic resistance.

Poland. The Law and Justice (PiS) government has moved in a similar fashion to exert political control over the judiciary in Poland. After taking power in 2015, it changed the rules governing the Constitutional Tribunal, the National Council of the Judiciary and the Supreme Court in an attempt to gain control over the appointment of judges and a range of other matters. It placed its supporters in key positions in important judicial bodies and put the courts of general jurisdiction under strict control of the Minister of Justice. The Supreme Court fought to retain autonomy, and in 2019 it ruled that the National Council of the Judiciary was no longer independent. In response, the government made it illegal for judges to overrule the Council, in what amounted to a direct attack on the Supreme Court.

The EU's position towards Poland gradually became tougher and moved several steps beyond the pressure brought to bear on the Hungarian government. Unlike in Hungary, the Commission activated the Rule of Law Framework quickly in Poland, in early 2016, only a few months after the PiS's election. It then proceeded through the three-step procedure to activate Article 7 in December 2017. However, the necessary support was lacking among member states to move this forward and the motion lingered in the Council.

With the Article 7 option ineffective, the Commission took a more legal route. Up to early 2021, it launched four infringement proceedings against the Polish government. Two of these related in 2018 to the lowering of Supreme Court judges' retirement age, that the government imposed to force out the head of the court. The ECJ ruled that the government's changes were illegal; the Polish government complied after a first ruling but then backtracked, triggering a second case. In a third case, in April 2019 the Commission launched proceedings against the new disciplinary regime that allowed the government to remove judges from office simply for questioning its judicial reforms. The ECJ ruled that this regime amounted to politically motivated intimidation of the judiciary and ordered the Polish government to retract the measures. Instead of complying, in a remarkably brazen move the government tightened measures to penalize judges that applied EU rulings over national ones.

In a fourth case that began in April 2020, the Commission took further action in relation to the government's use of the National Council of the Judiciary against the Supreme Court. The ECJ again ruled against the Polish government on this matter; the Commission instructed the government to close the chamber down and referred it to the ECJ again in March 2021. The main judicial bodies in Europe pushed for action against the PiS government, while the president of the ECJ insisted the PiS's legal measures were incompatible with EU membership. Judges from around Europe joined Polish protestors, while the European judicial authorities council moved to expel its Polish member. A number of member states' courts began to refuse cooperation with Polish courts, for example on extradition requests.[5]

Notwithstanding the significance of this pressure, the new Commission refrained from opening more infringement procedures where they would have been warranted or adopting more severe punitive sanctions to force the Polish government to comply with ECJ rulings. While President Macron had been the leader most openly critical of the PiS, he now homed in on geopolitical concerns and offered new strategic cooperation with the Polish government through a revival of the Weimar Triangle format. On a trip to Poland, the French president said he would 'lecture no-one' and that the rule of law issue was not a bilateral concern for France.[6] Member-state governments were reluctant to act because they sought Polish concessions on other policy issues. After the PiS-endorsed President Duda was re-elected in

---

[5] Letter from the Judicial Networks to President Von der Leyen, 21 February 2020.
[6] R. Momtaz, 'Macron plays it pragmatic with Poland', *Politico*, 2 April 2020.

July 2020 and the administration reiterated its refusal to comply with ECJ rulings, EU governments were still unwilling to adopt punitive measures.

While Hungarian authorities deflected pressure to some degree because they were willing to make tactical changes, their Polish counterparts were not. Orbán moved more cautiously initially using his supermajority in parliament to legitimize his illiberal moves, whereas the PiS was more openly confrontational. Another difference was that the EPP offered protection to Orbán until 2021, while the PiS was not a member of the centre-right group. Yet beyond the tactical differences, in Poland as in Hungary, member states have remained reluctant to take an overtly confrontational or political approach. Pressure has come from the ECJ issuing legal judgements on very detailed judicial matters, not from governments acting to uphold democracy more broadly.[7]

Other cases

While Poland and Hungary have attracted nearly all the attention in debates over EU rule of law measures, several other countries have also been subject to mounting pressure. In *Romania*, in 2019 the Commission reacted to the social democratic government's dilution of anti-corruption measures, by threatening to invoke the Rule of Law Framework for only the second time and intimated that it might deny Romania entry into the Schengen area and even invoke Article 7 sanctions.[8] Unlike in Poland and Hungary, this pressure seemed to elicit some positive outcomes. Romanian courts removed legal measures against Laura Kovesi, head of the country's main anti-corruption body. The Socialist and Liberal groups in the European Parliament moved to suspend their Romanian members. These measures worked in tandem with the domestically driven changes and protests covered in Chapter 3.

---

[7] C. Closa, 'The politics of guarding the Treaties: Commission scrutiny of rule of law compliance', *Journal of European Public Policy*, 26/5 (2019), 696–716.

[8] L. Pech, V. Perju and S. Palton, 'How to address rule of law backsliding in Romania', *Verfassungsblog*, 29 May 2019.

In a referendum, over 80 per cent of Romanians voted against amnesties and pardons for those involved in corruption cases. At the end of 2019, the social democratic administration lost power and the incoming centre-right government committed to restoring the rule of law.

A similar debate flared up more obliquely and briefly in relation to *Malta*. Backing up large-scale protests on the island, the Commission threatened to invoke the first stages of the Rule of Law Framework in an effort to push the Maltese government into implementing judicial reforms. The Venice Commission had been calling for changes for some time to ensure full independence of the prosecutor's office to take forward an investigation into the murder of journalist Daphne Caruana Galizia. The Commission, the EP and national government leaders all pressured Prime Minister Joseph Muscat to resign, although it was unclear exactly what action they threatened with firm intent. After Muscat left office, the Commission stepped back from taking any measures. The prime minister's resignation led to promises of reform and forestalled any significant EU action, even though the change in leader did not shortly resolve systemic rule of law deficiencies.

In *Bulgaria*, EU responses were far slower and less decisive. In this case, the EU got caught firmly on the wrong side of local pro-democracy pressures. At the end of 2019, the Commission concluded that Bulgaria had progressed on judicial reform and might soon graduate out of the CVM.[9] This decision was despite Bulgaria dropping on nearly all democracy indicators in the late 2010s and came only half a year before protests erupted against rising corruption, rule of law breaches and democratic decline. In summer 2020, Bulgarian protestors expressly targeted EU institutions in the country and appeared with banners accusing the Union of funding corruption and turning a blind eye to nepotism. While several EU ambassadors in Sofia spoke out in favour of the protests, no concrete EU measures were forthcoming. In the

---

[9] European Commission, 'College meeting: Cooperation and verification mechanisms for Bulgaria and Romania,' EU Commission Press, 22 October 2019.

European Parliament, the EPP continued to provide the ruling GERB party with firm support.

Tougher EU instruments

As the 2010s progressed, it gradually became clear that the rule of law crisis was no longer a case of one or two problematic cases or anomalies but entailed a more widespread rise of 'legal nationalism'.[10] In response, beyond the debates about Article 7 and the measures relating specifically to Poland and Hungary, the EU has moved to develop a number of other strategies and instruments to defend European democracy.

The 2014 Rule of Law Framework did not work as a full-spectrum defence of democracy, but an ad hoc and post facto response mechanism. Several member states expressly curtailed its scope for either competence or substantive reasons. In April 2019, the Commission published a first communication on a more ambitious rule of law mechanism. This gave a fairly generic list of criteria for a more effective framework, including the need for the EU to react more quickly, understand country situations better, build more capacity on rule of law issues, agree on firmer, common rule of law definitions, increase funding for rule of law priorities, and work with national judicial institutions.[11]

In July 2019, the Commission published a second communication with its final set of proposals. It suggested an annual Rule of Law Report for all member states; by examining all countries, it was hoped this would neuter complaints from Central and Eastern European countries that they were targeted more critically than others. The Commission called for the new framework to have a much broader mandate to

---

[10] I. Bond and A. Gostynska-Jakubowska, *Democracy and the Rule of Law: Failing Partnership?* (London: Centre for European Reform, 2020); A. Magen and L. Pech, 'The rule of law and the European Union', in C. May and A. Winchester (eds), *Handbook on the Rule of Law* (London: Edward Elgar, 2018).

[11] European Commission, *Further Strengthening the Rule of Law within the Union*, COM (2019) 163.

monitor election manipulation, media pluralism and corruption too. It raised the idea of suspending sectoral cooperation and promised more frequent infringement proceedings to protect the rule of law. It accepted that the experience of problems in Hungary and Poland highlighted how the EU needed to move faster to pre-empt problems in other countries.[12]

Member-state support for the Commission's proposal intensified. EU affairs ministers representing ten member states coordinated in mid-2019 to back firmer action. A joint Franco-German statement pushed for new action; the French and Dutch parliaments in particular pressed for stronger action on rule of law backsliding in member states. In late 2019, justice ministers from Germany, France, Italy, Spain, Belgium and Luxembourg met to plan new rule of law responses; this was the first time that justice ministers had sought to claim a role for themselves on this issue. Some member states also suggested that the so-far low-key Fundamental Rights Agency might be given a more political mandate to help monitor democratic erosion.

The Commission duly presented its new Rule of Law Report at the end of September 2020. This noted concerns across all member states and assessed at least some democratic developments beyond a narrow interpretation of the rule of law, for instancing tracking freedom of expression and media pluralism. Compared to most democracy indices (those presented in Chapter 2) the report was soft on democratic deficiencies, especially outside Eastern Europe. Its assessment was broadly upbeat and dwelt far more on states' promised institutional improvements than on their shortfalls. And the report did not promise concrete policy changes.[13] Still, the exercise deepened debate on democracy across Europe. In Spain, for example, the government was stung by the report's criticisms of political control over the judiciary and ditched a controversial plan to appoint new members of the high

---

[12] European Commission, *Strengthening the Rule of Law within the Union: A Blueprint for Action*, COM (2019) 343.

[13] European Commission, *2020 Rule of Law Report: The Rule of Law Situation in the European Union*, COM (2020) 580.

judicial council without aquiescence from the main opposition party (although the two main parties still insisted on sharing out places on the council rather than allowing this to decide appointments free of political considerations).

Meanwhile, more specific ideas took shape for stricter democratic conditionality to be attached to EU funds, based around an initial 2018 Commission proposal. Germany, Sweden, the Netherlands and Finland supported the idea. France was initially against but changed its position as President Macron ostensibly made defending democracy a priority. The Commission pushed the idea of 'reverse majority voting' so that a majority would be needed to block aid cuts rather than approve them. The Council Legal Service questioned the proposal's legality, doubting whether the Commission had established sufficiently clear and objective criteria for cutting funds.[14] Moreover, several member states remained less than fully convinced about the wisdom of highly political conditionality, beyond the predictable objections from Poland and Hungary.[15]

The issue then came to a head at the end of 2020. With Poland and Hungary in line to receive significant funds from the new Covid-related, 750 billion-euro Recovery and Resilience Facility (RRF), fierce debate ensued about rule of law conditions being attached to this and the EU's 2021–7 budget. At their July 2020 summit leaders agreed that the new funds would come with rule of law conditionality. With Hungary and Poland threatening to withhold approval of the new budget, member states accepted what was effectively a significantly diluted version of the Commission's 2018 proposal. This provided for aid reductions where rule of law deficiencies directly affected the management of EU funds, but not in response to general attacks on judicial independence or democratic rights. The mechanism would not be subject to the 'reverse

---

[14] M. Blauberger and V. van Hüllen, 'Conditionality of EU funds: An instrument to enforce EU fundamental values?', *Journal of European Integration*, published online 8 January 2020.

[15] I. Bond and A.Gostynska-Jakubowska, *Democracy and the Role of Law: Failing Partnership?* (London: Centre for European Reform, 2020).

majority' idea, making it easier for states to block sanctions. After brief consideration of using 'enhanced cooperation' rules to create a new fund that would entirely bypass Hungary and Poland, member states decided it was more important to keep the EU formally together on issues related to post-Covid-19 rebuilding.

The EP then toughened the mechanism, insisting on time limits to prevent the Council delaying decisions and a remit that covered broader rule of law problems beyond the management of EU aid. The Hungarian and Polish governments objected and vetoed the new budget in November 2020. The Netherlands and the Nordic states dug in their heels for tougher conditionality, arguably both a principled position on democracy and a tactic to hold up the recovery funds that they had been reluctant to support. Other member states sought a compromise in order to unblock the RRF. In December 2020, leaders agreed to refrain from applying the mechanism until the ECJ had ruled on its legality and firmer guidelines developed for its application. The Hungarian and Polish governments claimed victory and lifted their veto. Other governments and the Commission also claimed victory, noting that the mechanism's text had not been diluted.

Whatever the correct interpretation, the key factor was still whether the Commission would be more willing politically to invoke the new measures than it had been to use its existing rule of law powers during the 2010s. In March 2021, the Commission indicated that it would be, and that it was already looking at ways of holding back funds if trends in states like Hungary and Poland continued in a negative direction.[16] Adding to the pressure, a cross-party coalition in the European Parliament threatened to take the Commission to court if it failed to take such action.

---

[16] S. Bodoni and Z. Simon, 'EU takes aim at Hungary and Poland with new rule-of-law powers', *Bloomberg*, 19 March 2021.

EU values funding

As problems deepened in multiple member states, many in the EU realized that the Union needed a broader strategy beyond infringement proceedings related to specific legal issues. An increasing number of voices suggested that the EU needed a more positive and proactive approach to supporting pro-democracy actors, especially in the member states with the most serious democratic deficiencies. Alongside the debates about sanctions and conditionality, the EU has begun to explore ways more actively to build up the capacity of democratic voices so that they are better able to resist the assault against liberal norms.

The Commission has gradually increased its use of cohesion and structural funds for rule of law strengthening. Such funding has generally not been overtly political. Initiatives supported by cohesion funds have mainly aimed to build legal capacity rather than touching on the sensitive issue of judicial independence, and they cannot go directly against the will of member state governments. In addition, the Commission offered funds through its Europe for Citizens fund and its Rights, Equality and Citizenship programmes. The Europe for Citizens initiative awarded an increased four million euros to civil society projects in 2018, many of which were more political than in previous years by being directly aimed at building networks of democracy activists.[17] The Commission also funded an increasing number of individual democracy-related research projects. One illustrative example was the Commission-funded Future Government 2030+ project that ran from 2017 to 2019 and that engaged citizens across member states to rethink the future shape of government, together with design experts.[18]

In general, however, the degree of funding directed at defending democracy within the EU has remained limited. A striking paradox

---

[17] Europe for Citizens. Democratic engagement and civic participation, detailed at https://eacea.ec.europa.eu.
[18] European Commission, *The Future Government 2030+* (Brussels: European Commission, 2019).

has been noted: the EU funds a large number of initiatives outside the Union in support of pro-democracy actors but has not supported the same kind or range of projects within the EU itself. As part of its external relations, the EU has several decades of experience supporting democracy across the world, with yearly budgets into the hundreds of millions. Most member states also fund their own bilateral democracy initiatives abroad – including those very states whose own commitment to democracy has been most in question. These efforts outside the EU have run ahead of initiatives funded within the Union itself.

Governments in Greece, Italy, Spain and Portugal have enacted some anti-corruption measures as part of the EU-led stress on debt reduction that began during the Eurozone crisis. However, in many cases local political authorities have introduced these grudgingly, and the nature of pressure coming from the EU troika has militated against citizens taking the lead role or ownership over such good governance reforms. The EU has not backed up its austerity conditionality with a more positive funding support for 'integrity champions' to help them battle for improvements on democracy, corruption and rule of law issues.[19] When opposition mayors from Bratislava, Budapest, Prague and Warsaw pushed for the EU to give them direct funding as 'islands of democracy', the Union lacked the mechanisms to respond.

In fact, in this period, the most active support for defending democratic values in the EU came from outside the Union in the form of funding from Norway and European Economic Area (EEA) states. In the 2010s, the so-called EEA-Norway grants scheme was the biggest funder for democratic rights in EU member states. This scheme provided 160 million for the five years from 2009 to 2014 and a similar amount for 2015 to 2020. As of 2019, it had over a thousand projects running in fifteen member states, including most Central and Eastern European states, Spain, Portugal and Greece. Unlike EU funding, the Norwegian scheme had an overtly political tenor and was more directly

---

[19] A. Mungiu-Pippidi, *Europe's Burden: Promoting Good Governance Across Border* (Cambridge: Cambridge University Press, 2019), p. 127.

related to democracy problems; it was striking that no EU member state developed any similar kind of support programme for democracy activists. As political conditions worsened, EEA-Norway funding ceased to Hungary in 2014. In Poland the scheme sought to divert funds into civil society organizations; where the government insisted on too tight control of the money, projects were suspended.

It was against this backdrop that ideas surfaced for a so-called 'values strand' to EU funding. After long internal debates and motions in the European Parliament, the Commission proposed a 642 million-euros Rights and Values programme within the 2021-7 budget. It presented this as a major step forward in the Union's ability to defend European democratic values. The Commission's July 2019 rule of law communication insisted that the Rights and Values programme must be used to support civil society organizations working on rule of law issues.

Critics were unimpressed, however. They noted that the Commission's proposals simply repackaged and grouped together existing initiatives – the Europe for Citizens and the Rights, Equality and Citizenship programmes. The total was fifty million euros less than these existing funding programmes. Funds would be only to implement EU law and policy, not human rights and democracy more broadly. They would only be available for EU-level groups, disqualifying Europe's most dynamic grassroots organizations. The initiative did not prioritize support specifically for those CSOs targeted by national governments' restrictions on civil society. Most of the funds would go to cultural and historical projects that had nothing to do with political problems. Critics lamented that this was not a meaningful reaction to democracy problems across Europe.[20]

The European Parliament called for a more ambitious 1.8-billion-euro instrument with a much broader mandate. It wanted funds redirected to the most sensitive concerns in states where democratic values were

---

[20] I. Butler, *Analysis of the Commission's Proposal for a Rights and Values Programme* (Brussels: Civil Liberties Union for Europe, 2018).

under threat and for the fund to be able to support democracy activists without governments' approval. In July 2020, member states agreed to the Rights and Values programme along these lines, but reduced the EP's figure back down to 842 million euros. However, with the EP then digging in its heels, governments increased that figure to 1.6 billion euros in November 2020. This dramatic doubling was a significant boost for democracy and human rights work, even if it remained unclear exactly how the funds would be used and whether support would find its way to the most dynamic and outspoken pro-democracy actors across the continent. Commission officials drawing up detailed programming for the new fund in early 2021 certainly promised more of a focus on grassroot civil society, but the programme contained many other aims not related to democracy as such.[21] Separately, the new European Democracy Action Plan promised increased support for media literacy, citizen participation and protection for journalists.[22] Table 7.1 outlines the EU funds related to democracy and civil society.

Assessment: The foothills of change

The EU and its member states have been slow and lacklustre in their efforts to resist the most serious cases of democratic regression in Europe. Much debate about democracy in Europe has centred on the EU's reluctance to take firm, punitive measures against those member state governments most clearly threatening democratic values. The EU failed to push back firmly when governments in Hungary and Poland began openly to challenge the norms of liberal democracy. This reluctance did much to foster a feeling that the basic democratic credentials of the whole European project were beginning to tread water.

Not only did the EU fail to react promptly to resist democratic unravelling in Hungary and Poland, this failure seemed to encourage

---

[21] https://civic-forum.eu/press-release/civic-organisations-to-secure-a-historic-victory.
[22] European Commission, *On the European Democracy Action Plan*, COM (2020) 790/3.

Table 7.1 EU civil society and 'values' funds

European Citizen Fund (2014–20)
➤ Democratic engagement and civic participation
  • Civil Society Projects, Town Twinning and Networks of Towns
➤ European remembrance
  • Celebrates EU values and diversity
  • Reflects on different historical perspectives
  • Commemorates the EU's defining moments
Funds: 188 million euros

Rights, Equality and Citizenship Programme (2014–20)
➤ Combats all forms of discrimination and promote gender equality
➤ Supports Roma inclusion
➤ Helps citizens and consumers to exercise their rights
➤ Promotes children's rights
➤ Fights violence against women, young people and children
Funds: 439 million euros

Rights and Value Programme (2021–7)
➤ To promote equality and rights
➤ To foster citizen engagement and participation in EU 'democratic life'
➤ To fights violence, especially against children and women
➤ To 'protect and promote EU values'
Funds: 1.6 billion euros

Sources: https://ec.europa.eu/info/sites/info/files/infographics_final_04102019.pdf.

illiberal forces elsewhere in Central and Eastern Europe. One imbalance was striking: the EU has been extremely strict, many would say even draconian, in its use of economic conditionality and insistence on austerity cuts. Yet, it has been unable or unwilling to be firm in its use of political conditionality – that is, conditionality in defence of what are supposed to be the EU's core democratic values.

There were several explanations for this limited reaction. The EU as a whole was not set up to deal with democratic decay in its member states, as it had not expected that it would be confronted with such a problem and was clearly caught unprepared. It was then difficult to devise effective policy mechanisms. While some approaches could function well, the most severe democracy-defence mechanisms could be blocked precisely by those governments guilty of undermining democratic quality. Yet, ultimately the caution reflected a lack of strong political will on the part of most European governments. Behind a tendency to blame weak EU instruments, most member states and indeed parliamentarians have been unwilling to put democracy above a range of other policy priorities and interest calculations.

If the Commission was slow in reacting to the most serious cases of democratic erosion in Hungary and Poland, member states were even more reluctant to take action. Few of them wholeheartedly supported the Commission when it did take action, and several actively tried to block or at least dilute its responses. Governments did not want to rock the boat and cause frictions that would rebound on cooperation in key policy areas like Eurozone reforms or migration. Elites still tend to think in terms of how the EU helps to manage interstate relations more than they focus on democratic norms. Meanwhile, even though the European Parliament as a whole called for tougher policy responses, political groups there clearly put narrow self-interest before democratic principles, sheltering their own members from sanction even where manifestly guilty of major democratic abuses.

To a modest degree, interest calculations have begun to shift. Most member states profess to recognize that they can no longer duck these democracy problems as they impact on their own self-interest in the EU's wider legitimacy and success. The governments that previously opposed Commission action, or were at least unenthusiastic about this, have begun to realize that democratic erosion has in some countries reached the stage where it endangers the integrity and functioning of the whole Union. Governments and the Commission have realized that some action is necessary as democratic regression begins to unsettle the whole EU project, even if they still fear that too much pressure would also be destabilizing.

The Commission, the European Parliament (EP) and member states have gradually increased pressure against governments in Hungary and Poland and begun to lean hard on a small number of other governments too. The party groupings in the EP have, albeit grudgingly and incompletely, begun to take some action against their own members. Still, the measures adopted so far are not of game-changing significance. The level of support for resistance against democratic regression has undoubtedly increased, and the Commission has increasingly found ways of taking governments to task for legal infringements without member-state unanimity. However, the overall level of democratic resistance in these measures is still more cautious than assertive. The focus in 2020 on Covid-19 funding sharpened debates over the EU's rule of law instruments but also introduced other priorities that cut across democracy concerns.

The Commission has applied pressure in relation to fairly narrowly drawn legal issues rather than as a wholesale defence of democracy. These rule of law issues are where the Commission has a legally grounded framework for taking action and where it has been able to issue very detailed reform prescriptions. However, the downside is that the Commission's approach formally frames the problem as one of governments' actions impeding the smooth functioning of the EU and not one of democratic regression more widely defined.[23] At the end of 2020, governments effectively dodged responsibility for deciding on rules-of-law conditionality and passed this issue to the ECJ. While the ECJ has played a vitally important role, the legal route has become a substitute for the much-needed, fully political approach to democracy.

Increasingly, the EU institutions and member states have realized that the focus on very specific rule of law questions is a relatively narrow prism through which to safeguard European democratic values.[24] While the debates over Article 7 in Poland and Hungary have received most attention at a policy level and amongst analysts, a range

---

[23] Expert Group of the Friedrich Ebert Stiftung, *The Other Democratic Deficit: A Toolbox for the EU to Safeguard Democracy in Member States* (Berlin: FES, 2018), p. 19.

[24] Breugel event online, 'How can Europe uphold its democratic values while fighting Covid-19?', 14 May 2020.

of other EU instruments has also begun to take shape. For now, these have progressed only to modest degrees and the Commission still lacks a full toolbox applicable to democratic issues – and especially one that is relevant beyond the most problematic cases in Central and Eastern Europe.[25] Yet, innovations like the Rights and Values programme may gradually be opening the way to a more comprehensive EU approach to the core political aspects of democratic regression.

The intensification of EU pressure has not been entirely without effect. Some governments have responded to the pressure against them by backtracking on at least some of their anti-democratic measures. Arguably, EU-level attention has given oxygen to local democrats. One poll asked citizens in fourteen member states whether they thought the EU protected their rights from their own governments' illiberal 'excesses'. In four states, citizens agreed this was indeed the case: Romania, Spain, Poland and Hungary.[26] The combination of EU pressure and protests does seem to have pulled Romania in particular back from major democratic decay. Yet, Viktor Orbán and the PiS are still in power and have hardly converted to liberal democracy. Recall that the data presented in Chapter 2 shows that many other member states, including in Western Europe, now suffer rule of law deficiencies and yet these have not appeared on the EU's radar screen at all.

One shortcoming is that EU debates have been very 'instrument' based, structured around what articles and legal processes the EU has at its disposal, rather than working upwards from a mapping of where and how locally driven reform momentum is likely to accumulate. While much focus has been on the need for tougher measures against governments moving in an undemocratic direction, very top-down and punitive measures rarely unlock major change on their own. Some argue that democratic backsliding in Eastern Europe has far more to do

[25] L. Pech and D. Kochenov, 'Strengthening the rule of law within the European Union: Diagnoses, recommendations, and what to avoid', Reconnect policy brief, June 2019.

[26] I. Krastev, S. Dennison and M. Leonard, 'What Europeans really wanted: five myths debunked', ECFR, 16 April 2019.

with deeply rooted values among even mainstream liberal-democratic parties than the weakness of EU measures.[27] Sanctions and critical pressure tend to work where they lock onto bottom-up, domestic trends and alliances. Tougher, top-down responses may be warranted, but a still unmet challenge is to connect such EU measures to the kind of citizen-centred, civic politics that other chapters in this book stress as most vital to qualitative democratic renewal.

In sum, the last several years have seen some upgrades to EU democracy efforts, although these still fall short of game-changing democratic resistance. Notwithstanding all the limitations, it is significant that the EU has begun to define itself in more tangible ways as a protector of democracy. The very scale of democratic decay has forced it do so. This is a major shift, but one that still has a long way to go if it is to help rebuild European democracy in any major fashion. A vital question is how the increasingly politicized debates over EU democracy-defence measures relate to other arenas of democratic renewal – a complex issue explored in the book's conclusion.

[27] J. Dawson and S. Hanley, 'Foreground liberalism, background nationalism: A discursive institutionalist account of EU leverage and democratic backsliding in east central Europe', *Journal of Common Market Studies*, 57/4 (2019), 710–28.

8

EU responses II: Towards a democratic union?

Beyond the efforts to resist direct instances of democratic rollback, a final strand of debate relates to the EU's more general democratic vitality. A long-present concern is that the structure of European integration has hollowed out democracy within member states, while giving citizens only limited means of directly holding EU institutions to account. As this much-dissected problem has worsened in recent years, efforts have taken shape to make the EU more democratic. If the previous chapter focused on the EU's democratic resistance, this chapter outlines more positive EU initiatives aimed at its democratic renewal. At the most overarching level, EU leaders and institutions have increasingly committed to reforming the basic contours of European integration to make it more democratic. More specifically, there have been efforts to strengthen the EU's participative, parliamentary and party-political dimensions. The chapter unpacks these different advances towards a more democratically open EU while showing that reforms have remained tentative. While the tone of debate has undoubtedly changed, European integration still needs to be democratized beyond a few highly circumscribed democracy initiatives and modest institutional tweaks.

Reform promises

Analysts generally concur that European integration has increasingly placed strains on democracy within EU member states. Although the Union's much-dissected 'democratic deficit' has existed for many years, there is widespread agreement that it has worsened in recent years. Measures taken during the Eurozone crisis after 2010 transferred powers to the EU-level with little effective democratic control.[1] When Greek voters chose an anti-austerity government, the EU actually tightened austerity requirements. The European Central Bank became the most powerful actor in deciding the fate of the euro without any efforts to introduce democratic accountability over its decisions. More broadly, the expanding role of specialist functional agencies in the EU has increasingly favoured technocracy over democracy.

From a variety of analytical perspectives, writers have stressed how far the EU has gradually moved into sensitive political areas in a way that undercuts local channels of democratic legitimacy.[2] Even where national-level democracy indicators may paint a relatively reassuring picture in many member states – as outlined in Chapter 2 – citizens have increasingly felt that they lack influence over decisions taken at the EU level. Democratic shortfalls at the EU and national levels have increasingly reinforced each other.[3] Scholars argue that recent European

---

[1] C. Crouch, *The Strange Non-Death of Neo-Liberalism* (Cambridge: Polity Press, 2011).

[2] F. Schimmelfennig, 'Liberal intergovernmentalism and the euro area crisis', *Journal of European Public Policy*, 22/2 (2015), 177–95; C. Hobson, D. Hodson and U. Puetter, 'The new intergovernmentalism: European integration in the post-Maastricht era', *Journal of Common Market Studies* 53/4 (2015), 703–22; F. Schimmelfennig, 'What's the news in "new intergovernmentalism"? A critique of Bickerton, Hodson and Puetter', *Journal of Common Market Studies*, 53/4 (2015), 723–30; R. Bellamy and D. Castiglione, 'Three models of democracy, political community and representation in the EU', *Journal of European Public Policy*, 20/2 (2013), 206–23; C. Bickerton, *European Integration: From Nation-States to Member States* (Oxford: Oxford University Press, 2014); J. Caporaso, M. Kim, W. Durrett and R. Wesley, 'Still a regulatory state? The European Union and the financial crisis', *Journal of European Public Policy*, 22/7 (2015), 889–907; V. Schmidt, *Democracy in Europe: The EU and National Politics* (New York: Oxford University Press, 2006).

[3] C. Kreuder-Sonnen, 'An authoritarian turn in Europe and European Studies?', *Journal of European Public Policy*, 25/3 (2018), 452–64.

political trends are best interpreted as populations' reaction to a loss of control over major and intrusive EU-level decisions.[4] Others suggest that a lack of fully flexible forms of EU cooperation has militated against democratic legitimacy.[5]

As the Eurozone crisis abated, there was more debate about EU reform. The Commission's March 2017 *White Paper on the Future of Europe* offered a number of future scenarios based on different levels of integration.[6] The newly elected President Macron called abrasively for deeper integration to overcome the 'leprosy' of Eurosceptic nativism.[7] In 2019, the French government published proposals for a 'European Renaissance' based on a mix of deeper institutionalized integration, new intergovernmental agencies to address specific policy challenges and two-speed integration to leave behind those not adhering to democratic values.[8] Macron's proposals attracted notable pushback from Germany, the Netherlands, Poland and others, supporting a less centralized model of integration.[9]

At a summit in Sibiu in May 2019, EU leaders were due to map out a comprehensive plan to relaunch the European project. While they did not do so, they agreed to an agenda for the next five years that promised democratic reform. The summit's ten commitments included promises to bring the EU closer to its citizens, while the Union's new *Strategic Agenda 2019-2024* reinforced the focus on democratic reform.[10] Taking office at the end of 2019, new Commission president Ursula von der

---

[4] C. Bickerton, 'Beyond the European void? Reflections on Peter Mair's legacy', *European Law Journal*, 24/4-5 (2018), 268-80; J. Zielonka, *Counter-Revolution: Liberal Europe in Retreat* (Oxford: Oxford University Press, 2018); R. Cohen, 'It is time to depopularize "populist"', *New York Times*, 14 July 2018; H. Kundnani, 'Liberalism's betrayal of itself – and the way back', *The Economist*, 14 February 2019.

[5] F. Schimmelfennig, 'Is differentiation the future of European integration?', in B. Fagersten and G. von Sydow (eds), *Perspectives on the Future of the EU* (Stockholm: Swedish Institute for European Policy Studies, 2019); J. Fossum, 'Democracy and differentiation in Europe', *Journal of European Public Policy*, 22/6 (2019), 799-815.

[6] European Commission, *White Paper on the Future of Europe*, COM (2017).

[7] A. Jamieson, 'Macron warns "nationalist leprosy" threatens Europe', *NBC News*, 5 November 2018.

[8] E. Macron, 'For European Renewal', Elysée, 4 March 2019.

[9] A. Kramp-Karrenbauer, 'Getting Europe right', CDU, 9 March 2019.

[10] European Union, *Strategic Agenda 2020-2024* (Brussels: EU, 2019).

Leyen promised a two-year Conference on the Future of Europe, a 'push for European democracy' and also appointed a new commissioner specifically responsible for democracy. [11]

The Conference on the Future of Europe was set to open in May 2020, and its remit included a focus on reforming EU integration to improve democratic accountability and participation. Some governments and EU institutions wanted an ambitious agenda that foregrounded democracy issues, while others wanted a narrower focus on a select number of policy issues only. Governments in the Council agreed a more cautious approach to the democracy strand than that advocated by the Commission and EP.[12] Even as Covid-19 changed governments' priorities, the conference's democracy remit formally remained, although its launch was delayed until May 2021 by the pandemic and then by wrangling over who should chair the exercise.

The summer of 2020 was dominated by negotiations over the Recovery and Resilience Facility (RRF) and new EU budget. Beyond the rule of law mechanism – covered in Chapter 7 – there was no EU democratic upgrade as part of this package, despite the huge financial commitments, the Union's new ability to raise debt on capital markets and plans for new EU-level carbon and digital taxes to cover part of the spending. France and other member states expressly sought to keep the RRF separate from the EU budget partly to avoid lengthy democratic checks. The RRF was embedded within the so-called European Semester giving the Commission prime influence over recovery plans and was adopted under legal procedures that limited the EP's role.[13] While member states agreed to consult civil society actors on how funds would be spent, their follow through on this was patchy.[14] As

[11] U. von der Leyen, *A Union That strives for More: My Agenda for Europe: Political Guidelines for the Next European Commission 2019–2024* (Brussels: European Commission, 2019).

[12] Council of the European Union, *Conference on the Future of Europe* (Brussels: Council Secretariat, 2020).

[13] F. Costamagna and M. Goldmann, 'Constitutional innovation, democratic stagnation?', *Verfassungsblog*, 30 May 2020.

[14] G. Negri, 'Civic space under Lockdown', in *European Civic Space Watch 2020: Stories from the Lockdown* (Brussels: European Civic Forum, 2020).

governments submitted their RRF project plans to the Commission in early 2021, the lack of transparency in this process triggered severe political tensions, especially in Italy and Spain. The funding package did not include any EU-level coordinated plan to reinstate the democratic rights that governments had abridged in order to fight the virus.

By this stage, a robust consensus had taken shape that a more openly democratic model of EU integration was required, and yet this remained a promise rather than actual. Several crises have crowded democracy issues from the EU agenda. Just as a promising conversation was opening about the democratic components of EU integration, the Covid-19 pandemic turned policymakers' attention elsewhere. As in the Eurozone crisis, the new recovery funds were decided behind closed doors by governments, in marathon summit sessions bereft of citizen involvement. While the crisis-management imperative was understandable, the sizable resource transfers agreed in the wake of the pandemic surely increased the need for more effective democratic oversight. Each successive EU crisis has left in its wake a starker mismatch between deeper economic cooperation and more limited democratic processes.

The EU and citizens' engagement

With major reform of European integration as a whole proving so difficult to unlock, many in the EU institutions have begun to explore more targeted and specific ways to give citizens greater engagement and voice. Several layers of democratic participation have gained momentum.

European Citizens' Initiative. The European Citizens' Initiative (ECI) is often presented as the Union's main direct democracy tool, although in fact it is for petitioning, not direct popular votes.[15] Since

---

[15] A. Lieninger, 'Direct democracy in Europe: Potentials and pitfalls', *Global Policy*, 6 (2015), 17–27.

it was introduced in 2012, the ECI has had a relatively limited impact. Needing one million signatures across seven different countries, very few ECI campaigns have met the criteria to proceed. From 2012 to 2020, only five initiatives collected sufficient support, on water rights, animal testing, abortion, minority rights and pesticides. Only in two cases (on water and pesticides) did the Commission respond by revising its legislation and then in only a limited way. Another initiative against an EU-US trade deal collected the one million signatures, but the Commission ruled it inadmissible on the grounds that it had no power to stop the trade agreement. In 2019, three new ECIs were registered on carbon pricing, plastics and agriculture.

Reflecting all these shortcomings, the EU agreed to a series of reforms to the ECI that came into force in 2020. The EP would now debate successful ECIs in order to help get them onto the policy agenda. The ECI process was made easier to use, and the scope for eligible initiatives was slightly widened through so-called partial registration. The changes did not go as far as campaigners sought, however. In 2021, the Commission refused to follow through on another initiative that succeeded in gathering one million signatures, this one on minority linguistic rights. The ECI has remained a relatively marginal instrument, not widely known among the European population. It still cannot be used to broach far-reaching democratic change or any institutional modifications that would require treaty change.

Citizen Dialogues. The Commission has developed a series of Citizen Dialogues that take the form of Commissioners attending meetings with citizens to debate and explain EU policies. The Commission began these events in what it labelled the European Year of Citizens in 2013, and then Commission president Jean-Claude Juncker made participation in such dialogues an obligation for all Commissioners.[16] The number of these dialogues increased fairly dramatically: 53 were held in 2015, 73 in 2016, 317 in 2017 and over 600 in 2018. By the Sibiu

---

[16] European Commission, *A Europe That Delivers: Institutional Options for Making the EU's Work More Efficient*, COM (2018) 95.

summit in May 2019, just over a thousand dialogues had been held involving approximately 200,000 citizens.

As the dialogues evolved over time, they became more interactive and gave more space to citizens to set the agenda. They ostensibly became increasingly 'two-way' and less exclusively about the Commission simply explaining and defending EU policies. Rather, citizens were encouraged to present their own ideas. Local politicians and mayors also began to take part.[17] Moreover, in parallel to the events with Commissioners, the Committee of the Regions organized around two hundred of its own citizen dialogues outside capital cities.[18] The Eurocities forum ran over three hundred dialogues at city level, so-called Cities4Europe events. In 2016 the European Space Agency gathered citizen input into its activities, and in 2020 the Commission launched several other citizen dialogues on the future of its research programme and on the European Green Deal.

European Citizen Consultations. As the Citizen Dialogues are still largely informal consultations, policymakers have acknowledged the need for more structured forms of participation. President Macron proposed what he initially termed a convention to give citizens a say over the EU's future. This was modified into a series of European Citizens Consultations (ECC). The ECC process ran from mid-2018 to mid-2019. Around 1700 events were run, 1100 of which were in France. The Commission also ran an online questionnaire until the Sibiu summit in May 2019 that was designed by a Citizens Panel and attracted 87,000 submissions.

The ECCs were a significant exercise but suffered multiple shortcomings. They lacked a common format across member states, and there was much confusion about what really counted as a consultation. Governments exerted firm control over the process and tended to

---

[17] European Commission, 'Europe in May 2019: Preparing for a more united, stronger and more democratic Union in an increasingly uncertain world: The European Commission's contribution to the informal EU27 leaders' meeting in Sibiu on 9 May 2019', p. 44.

[18] Future of Europe, 'From Local to Europeans: Putting citizens at the centre of the EU agenda', European Committee of the Regions, 2020.

rebrand many standard, pre-organized events as counting towards the ECC process. The largest share of 'consultations' was actually fairly standard seminars or conferences with panels of expert speakers.[19] The ECCs had no transnational dimension; events were organized on a purely national basis and often turned into debates about domestic politics. In general, there was no preselection of participants to ensure representative samples of citizens. The impression was that many states were going through the motions so as not to refuse Macron's idea but without putting a lot of effort into doing anything new or intensive.[20]

There was little concrete follow-up to the ECCs. The Commission drew a familiar and predictable conclusion that the consultations showed deeper, across-the-board integration was needed.[21] The EU institutional system was not set up to incorporate the ECCs into a programme of democratic reform. The process was supposed to feed into leaders' discussions at the Sibiu summit, but this did not happen.[22] While a majority of citizens participating in the ECCs called for a new process of ongoing consultations, governments refused to contemplate such a step and also rejected calls for a citizen assembly at the end of the process to decide on further democratic engagement.[23]

Citizens and the Conference on the Future of Europe. In 2020, the focus shifted to how citizens might be involved in the Conference on the Future of Europe. The Council, Commission and European Parliament agreed on the importance of giving citizens direct participation in this conference. Still, they had contrasting ideas of how this should

---

[19] Gobierno de España, 'Consultas Ciudadanos sobre Europa celebradas en España 2018', Madrid, 2019.

[20] C. Stratulat and P. Butcher, *The European Citizens' Consultations: Evaluation Report* (Brussels: European Policy Centre, 2018).

[21] European Commission, *Citizens' Dialogues and Citizens' Consultations: Progress Report* (Brussels: European Commission, 2018)); European Commission, *Citizens' Dialogues and Citizens' Consultations, Key Conclusions* (Brussels: European Commission, 2019)).

[22] P. Butcher and C. Stratulat, *Citizens Expect: Lessons from the European Citizens Consultations* (Brussels: European Policy Centre, 2019).

[23] R. Youngs et al., *Six Ideas for Rejuvenating European democracy* (Brussels: Carnegie Europe, 2019).

be achieved. Most cautiously, governments in the Council called for citizen panels to be organized around the EU's already-agreed Strategic Agenda, with the largely functional aim of strengthening popular buy-in to specific areas of policy cooperation.[24] Governments rhetorically supported citizens' involvement but did not clearly support the use of full randomly selected assemblies with real power over the conference's output. Those in the Commission charged with this democracy remit worked up more ambitious plans to have citizens proactively setting the conference agenda through a transnational assembly, national forums and a fully participative online platform. Many MEPs wanted to go a step further and give citizen panels a more formal and not merely advisory role.

Eventually, the Council, Commission and EP compromised on a model positioned between the maximalist and minimalist agendas. Citizen panels at the national and European levels, together with a digital platform, would generate a report with recommendations, albeit without any guarantee these would be taken on board. While this represented a notable set of commitments, there was no focus on designing a permanent EU citizen forum that would continue to sit after the Conference, despite pressure for this from the Committee of the Regions, the Economic and Social Committee and others.[25] Governments also sought to limit CSOs' role in the conference plenary; in frustration the Civil Society Europe alliance opened its own parallel conference involving seventy-five civil society networks. It seemed that member states' aim was to use democratic participation to enliven the Conference, rather than use the Conference to deepen democratic participation.

[24] Council of the European Union, Conference on the Future of Europe – Council agrees its position, press statement, 24 June 2020.

[25] K-H Lambertz and L. Jahier, 'Bringing the EU closer to its citizens: The call for a permanent mechanism for structured consultations and dialogues with citizens', European Economic and Social Committee and European Committee of the Regions Non paper, 14 December 2018.

The EU and parliamentary democracy

Alongside these different avenues of citizen participation, the parliamentary dimension of EU democracy has shown a similar mix of renewal and thwarted ambition. The EP has long struggled to gain democratic credibility. It has been effective as a lobby for European integration but has provided a weak transmission belt between voters and EU decision-making. The EP's shortcomings became even more notable during the multiple crises of the 2010s. These crises shone a sharper spotlight on the EP's lack of connection downwards to citizens and upwards to executive decision-making. In the 2014 EP elections, turnout plummeted to a new low.

The main innovation for reviving the EP's democratic credentials was an agreement that the lead candidate of the winning party in European elections would become the Commission president – the so-called spitzenkandidaten system introduced in 2014. This did not succeed in bringing more citizens out to vote as they were either unaware of the system or unconvinced that it would make the EP more responsive to their concerns. The system also did not generate anything like a normal process of parliamentary accountability over EU executive decision-making.[26]

As the 2019 elections approached, many politicians talked of the need for democratic reform to empower the EP and tighten its link to citizens. Some governments argued that granting the EP more powers was key to turning back the tide of political illiberalism. They proposed giving the EP full powers to propose legislation, select the executive and hold this to account.[27] President Macron pushed for so-called transnational lists to have candidates campaign for votes on a pan-European basis and not just in their own countries. His party's election

---

[26] S. Russack, 'EU parliamentary democracy: How representative?', in S. Blockmans and S. Russack (eds), *Representative Democracy in the European Union* (Lanham, MD: Rowman and Littlefield).

[27] One example being then Spanish foreign minister, J. Borrell, 'Por un relanzamiento europeo', *El Pais*, 9 May 2019.

manifesto proposed an EU petition facility that would allow citizens to initiate legislative proposals in the EP. Yet the EP itself rejected transnational lists in early 2019, as MEPs saw Macron's proposal as a self-serving tactic to help him create a European En Marche against the existing party blocs.

The 2019 elections awoke considerable interest among European voters and the election campaign was more Europeanized than previously: in each member state significant coverage was given to debates unfolding in other EU countries. The Commission and EP made a concerted effort to frame the campaign in terms of local everyday issues rather than Brussels-centric institutional debates. The turnout was 51 per cent, the highest since 1994 and the first time since then that this figure had increased from one election to another. Perhaps most significantly, the 2019 elections seemed to present voters a clearer set of policy choices between Eurosceptic populist parties and the mainstream pro-European parties.

All this generated much talk about a new era for the EP. Yet, the positive momentum did not result in qualitative democratic reform. After the elections, the focus switched quickly to the traditional and rather unedifying horse-trading for top EU jobs. Ultimately governments decided who got which post, cutting across EU-level parliamentary democracy. Not one of the lead candidates that stood in the elections was offered a job. The EP party blocs failed to unite to safeguard the spitzenkanditaten arrangement; ultimately the centre-right European People's Party preferred to have a conservative as Commission president who had played no part in the election rather than a lead candidate of another party. Party self-interest prevailed over the ostensible means of connecting the EP more directly to voters.

Indeed, the process was so unsatisfactory that it focused minds on the need for reform. Liberals in the EP promised to bring forward a whole programme for democratic renewal. Von der Leyen promised to give the EP the right of legislative initiative. Still, by 2021 it was not clear that the EP was on course to play a stronger role in European democracy. After the 2019 elections, the pro-European parties doubled down on a 'hyper-coalition' against Eurosceptic parties, consolidating the chamber's very binary divide. MEPs were still nervous about shifting from the comfort of this grand coalition to a clearer dynamic of democratic alternation that might make the EP clearer and more relatable to voters. Many of them still feared that transnational lists would distance politicians even more from local communities, while several states like Germany also continued to have misgivings about such reform options. These issues and possible reforms did not figure explicitly in the starting agenda of the Conference on the Future of Europe, with many member states reluctant to consider the formal treaty change that would be needed to enhance the EP's role in democratic renewal.

In parallel to debates in and about the EP, more attention has also been given to getting national parliaments better connected to EU decision-making in recent years. The Lisbon treaty introduced the 'yellow card' procedure that enabled national legislatures to comment on Commission proposals, but this was used only three times in the following decade and to no great effect. During his term as Commission president, Jean-Claude Juncker promised to upgrade the role of national parliaments, and in 2018 a task force proposed reforms to get them more involved in drafting EU legislation.[28] Two 'conferences' grouping together MEPs and national MPs were set up: one on foreign policy and one on economic coordination. In 2017, President Macron proposed a joint parliament of MEPs and national MPs to oversee Eurozone reforms. In at least some member states – Austria, Denmark, Germany and Greece – parliamentary scrutiny of EU affairs increased during the Eurozone crisis.[29]

---

[28] European Commission, *Active subsidiarity: a new way of working, Report of the Task Force on Subsidiarity, Proportionality and 'Doing less more efficiently'*, (Brussels: European Commission, 2018).

[29] See country chapters in S. Blockmans and S. Russack (eds), *Representative Democracy in the European Union* (Lanham, MD: Rowman and Littlefield, 2019); A. Pysgkas, *From the 'Democratic Deficit' to a 'Democratic Surplus': Constructing Administrative Democracy in Europe* (Oxford: Oxford University Press, 2017).

Overall, however, concerns have grown over the 'de-parliamentarization' of EU matters.[30] The Conference of Parliamentary Committees for Union Affairs (COSAC) was created in 1989 to bring national politicians and MEPs together but has made little impact.[31] National parliaments can object to EU laws only on the narrow grounds of subsidiarity; they cannot suggest new ideas or laws but only comment on Commission proposals. Several national parliaments have pushed recently for more use of a so-called 'green card' process as a means to make their contribution more proactive.[32] This still faces resistance from the Commission and EP, however, as they are reluctant to share their current monopoly on introducing legislation and fear that Eurosceptics might gain a wrecking role through national parliaments.

EU party politics?

In a final strand of EU debates, support has grown for a more Europeanized form of party politics. A mismatch has opened up between the national basis of party politics, on the one hand, and crucial decisions being taken at the EU level, on the other hand. Debate has intensified over the need for a more genuinely transnational or pan-European party system as a key ingredient in democratic resistance and renewal. Party politics remains much less Europeanized than civil society, and this reduces parties' ability to hold EU decisions effectively to account.

There is a long history of attempts to develop fully fledged political parties at the European level – so-called Euro-parties – and these have been subject to exhaustive academic enquiry over many years.

---

[30] T. Raunio, 'The role of national legislatures in EU politics', in O. Cramme and S. Hobolt (eds), *Democratic Politics in a European Union under Stress* (Oxford: Oxford University Press, 2015).

[31] A.Gostyńska-Jakubowska, *The Role of National Parliaments in the EU: Building or Stumbling Blocks?* (London: Centre for European Reform, 2016).

[32] A. Gostyńska-Jakubowska, *Boosting the Role of National Parliaments in EU Democracy* (Brussels: Carnegie Europe, 2019).

Despite having been given formal treaty recognition and a regulatory framework, Euro-parties have struggled to gain influence. They are essentially federations or umbrella groupings of national parties. They serve as organizational structures in Brussels but do not compete in elections; this is the preserve of national parties that then group together in the European Parliament. Euro-parties' functions remain limited and are not directly comparable with standard political party functions in structuring voting patterns, mobilizing members, presenting coherent programmes or holding executive decisions to account. Few voters are even aware of their existence. National parties have been decidedly ambivalent about the Euro-parties developing any stronger agency.

In the last few years, efforts have been made to boost pan-European party politics. Nearly all Euro-parties have introduced membership for individual citizens, although national parties retain most influence over their internal decisions.[33] President Macron toyed with the idea of creating a pan-European En Marche, but this did not prosper in part due to established centrist parties in other states. Eventually, a rather strained alliance formed between En Marche and the existing ALDE liberal group; they joined together in a renamed political group, Renew Europe, after the 2019 elections. This did not function smoothly as a single party, and significant policy differences opened up between different liberal parties. Even pro-European liberalism remains very much centred around national political parties.

Several pan-European parties have run in EP elections since the early 2000s but without winning meaningful support; however, in 2019 two Euro-parties, Volt and Diem25, attracted much more attention than these previous attempts. Defining itself as a post-ideological movement, Volt has over 25,000 members. Its agenda is based heavily around new forms of participative democracy. The party was created in 2017 and ran in the 2019 elections in eight member states. It has a central entity and national chapters that conform to the overall programme with

---

[33] S. van Hecke, *Reconnecting European Political Parties with European Union Citizens* (Stockholm: International IDEA).

country variations. The party won one seat in the 2019 EP elections and three seats in the 2021 Dutch elections. The second party, Diem25 launched in 2016, explicitly aimed at democratizing the EU institutions after the experience of the financial crisis in Greece and other countries. Diem25 is a pan-European movement but also incorporates national and subnational groups. It set up 'European Spring' as a vehicle for the 2019 election campaign to include new parties, Alternative in Denmark and Razen in Poland. Diem25 defines itself as a mix of social movement and political party, harnessing the grassroots activism that emerged as a response to the financial crisis.

Diem25's complex structures combine national groups and a European movement. Most internal decisions are taken on a pan-European basis and sortition is used for some party posts. It is an unusual combination of localism, radical activism and top-down dynamics that are reliant on one well-known face – founder Yannis Varoufakis, former Greek finance minister. Diem25 failed to win a seat in the 2019 elections. It was created as a fairly top-down project, based on the aim to forge a European-wide party and then build this down into local communities. Interestingly, although Diem25 leaders initially rejected the concept of national political parties, they then formed a national branch in Greece, MeRA25, and ironically succeeded there in a way they did not at the transnational level. While it is still strongly pan-European, Diem25 has developed more of a policy focus on the national level.[34]

These trends have engendered some degree of pressure for reform. Debate has opened up about changing current EU funding and electoral rules that disadvantage Euro-parties. Many argue that if a supplementary transnational list is agreed for the next EU elections, then it would become logical to introduce rules to favour pan-European parties to take on a more prominent role. Debates have begun within

---

[34] B. De Cleen, B. Moffitt, P. Panayotu and Y. Stavrakakis, 'The potential and difficulties of transnational populism: The case of the Democracy in Europe Movement 2025 (DiEM25)', *Political Studies*, 69/1 (2019), 146–66.

the EP on other prospective reforms too: for spitzenkanditen to be the leaders of their respective Euro-parties, for Euro-parties be in charge of filling the transnational list and for an alignment of national and Euro-party platforms. Some Euro-parties are beginning to consider the same kind of innovative membership and citizen participation schemes that the newer national parties are built around. Still, governments and national parties remain ambivalent about these kinds of changes and the rise of Eurosceptic opinion has caused some national parties to distance themselves from their respective Euro-parties.[35] As in other areas of reform, momentum has gathered behind a possible renewal of EU-level party politics without this having yet produced far-reaching change.

Assessment: European democratic momentum?

After years of growing concern that the EU's institutional features were compounding a certain democratic disconnect from citizens across the continent, policymakers have begun to consider ways of giving citizens more democratic input into EU decision-making. While this denotes an awareness of the need for democratic renewal, however, improvements to the EU's democratic quality have so far been modest at best. Worthy initiatives and debates have increased the profile of democratic shortcomings at the European level, but these are scattered first steps rather than an all-consuming dynamic capable of rejuvenating democracy. They still feel remote from the concrete democratic deficiencies picked up in the indices outlined in Chapter 2.

On the EU model. European leaders have begun to consider reforms to the EU that might contribute more positively to democratic renewal. However, the basic, core model of integration remains largely the same, for now. In practice, there has been no major leap forward in

---

[35] See C. Kolster and H. von Homeyer, *Pan-European Parties in a Time of Resurgent Nationalism* (Brussels: German Marshall Fund, 2019).

EU integration, yet nor have the calls for a more flexible and open EU resulted in any major, tangible change in the integration model. The EU has still not found a route that preserves interstate solidarity while also amplifying democratic choice.[36]

High-politics challenges have generated a more disruptive form of politicized debate and nudged the Union out of its habitual technocratic mode.[37] This has begun to drive a search for channels through which such politicization can be more smoothly and constructively channelled at the EU level. Yet, so far concrete changes to achieve this aim remain relatively muted. Elites are still wedded to a top-down model that is about controlling and managing interstate relations more than any pan-European citizen empowerment, and the Covid-19 crisis has for now reinforced this dynamic.

Differences have grown over what kind of EU would best help defend and deepen democratic quality. Some governments have made efforts to deepen EU cooperation, while others have advocated a more flexible and less centralized model of integration. The push for deeper integration shows that EU policymakers and many national politicians and writers are still minded to double down on a strategy of overcoming Euroscepticism through 'more Europe' instead of rethinking democracy.[38] When leaders talk increasingly about 'European sovereignty' they mean formal institutional and not popular sovereignty. They typically conflate defence of the EU with defence of democracy.

One challenge to such reasoning is that divisions across Europe over democracy do not neatly map onto the battle between national populists and pro-Europeans. There is a lot of anti-EU voting that is neither populist nor politically illiberal, and those arguing that

---

[36] R. Bellamy and S. Kröger, 'A democratic justification of differentiated integration in a heterogeneous EU', *Journal of European Integration*, 39/5 (2017), 625–39.

[37] L. van Middelaar, *Alarums and Excursions: Improvising Politics on the European Stage* (London: Agenda, 2020).

[38] U. Guerot, *Why Europe Should Become a Republic! A Political Utopia* (Bonn: J. H. W. Dietz, 2019); Y. Mounk, *The People vs Democracy: Why Our Freedom Is in Danger and How to Save it* (Cambridge, MA: Harvard University Press), p. 96.

deeper integration is in itself a defence of democracy still have not taken this on board.[39] Reading public opinion and what it implies for EU-level democracy is far from straightforward. In recent years most populations have become more supportive of EU membership, but significant majorities in all states say they want powers returned from the EU to national level.[40]

For now, differences between member states have prevented the EU either from moving dramatically forward or becoming a looser and more flexible organization. A truly reshaped EU model would offer citizens additional forms of democratic influence from those available at national and subnational levels, and far from being distant and opaque, it would perhaps even appear more open than nation-state processes. On this metric, progress has been negligible. Many agree the status quo of European integration is unsustainable, yet because governments disagree on which way to move, it endures.

On citizen consultations. Analysts have argued that the EU needs an open form of participation, as replicating the formal democratic structures of the nation state at the European level is not feasible.[41] While an important area of growth, so far the EU's various consultations fall short in the degree and type of democratic participation they offer. While policymakers increasingly realize that the EU institutions need to reach down more effectively to citizens, this still tends to be equated with 'explaining the EU' to ordinary people. Many initiatives have not been structured to provide deep and ongoing democratic interaction. Data shows that ordinary citizens still wield little leverage through these initiatives compared to the influence of large civil society organizations

---

[39] L. Dijkstra, H. Poleman and A. Rodriguez-Pose, *The Geography of EU Discontent* (Brussels: European Commission, 2018), p. 9.

[40] Pew Research Centre, *In Western Europe, Populist Parties Tap Anti-establishment Frustration but Have Little Appeal across Ideological Divides* (Washington, DC: Pew, 2018), p. 50.

[41] J. Habermas, *The Crisis of the European Union* (Cambridge: Polity Press, 2012); U. Beck and E. Grande, 'Cosmopolitanism: Europe's way out of crisis', *European Journal of Social Theory*, 10/1 (2007), 67–85; J. Dryzek, *Global Deliberative Politics* (Cambridge: Polity Press, 2006).

in formal partnerships with the Commission.[42] Revealingly, in long-running debates about a 'European public sphere' this is generally equated with Europeanized media debates and not Europeanized citizen participation.

Ambitious ideas have been debated for citizen-triggered EU-level referendums, especially through the ECI, as well as for a permanent EU-level citizen assembly with a wide political remit.[43] Yet these have for now not advanced. The dynamics that explain the limits to participatory initiatives at the national level are even more apparent at the European level. EU elites and governments have acknowledged the need to give citizens some voice to deflect discontent but have been reluctant to open up European-level democratic participation in a way that could put at risk their own power and policy agendas. One leading voice in EU and French participation points out that at the EU level citizen forums still need to feed far more comprehensively into formal institutional processes.[44] It is not clear that citizens' role in the Conference on the Future of Europe rectifies this. Instead of waiting a long time to run a modest number of citizen panels under the rather set-piece rubric of this conference, the EU could have already embarked on a more effective but understated path of establishing dense networks of assemblies at multiple levels across Europe around day-to-day issues.

On the EU and parliamentary democracy. The EP elections of 2019 were widely interpreted as good news for European democracy. The elections stopped the long rot of declining participation and revealed the limits to populists' appeal. They certainly opened the doors to the EP playing a greater role in European democratic resistance and renewal. Yet, they have not led to really ambitious reforms or changes to the

---

[42] T. Persson and K. Edholm, 'Assessing the effects of European Union funding of civil society organisations: Money for nothing?', *Journal of Common Market Studies*, 56/3 (2018), 559–75.

[43] A central theme running through A. Alemanno and J. Organ (eds), *Citizen Participation in Democratic Europe: What Next?* (Lanham, MD: Rowman and Littlefield, 2020). See also F. Chevenal, *European Union and Direct Democracy: A Possible Combination?* (BEUCitizen project, 2016).

[44] G. Ricard-Nihoul, *Representation Et Participation: Reinventer La Democratie Europeenne* (Paris: Notre Europe, 2020), p. 19.

EP's functioning. Political dynamics within the EP have not changed in a way that delivers qualitative improvement in democratic debate. Parliamentarization of EU-level democracy has not advanced in part because the Commission is still a nominally above-the-fray guardian of EU rules, not a fully political executive-like body that reflects voting outcomes and that the EP holds politically to account.

Absent a decisive breakthrough in the EP's democratic impact, increased attention has been given to making national parliaments more effective in linking citizens to EU decision-making. Analysts, politicians and policymakers have come to stress the importance of rooting European democratic renewal in national channels of democratic representation as a way of helping states better manage interdependence.[45] However, while EU leaders have talked about the importance of strong national parliaments, they have also not advanced far in this area. National parliaments remain secondary players in European integration. In practice, most governments seem hesitant to promote their own parliaments as fuller democratic players at the European level. The EU has ended up arguably caught between fully Europeanized and nationally rooted parliamentary democracy.

On EU-level party politics. Efforts to better fuse national and EU-level party politics have begun to gain momentum and represent a potentially vital strand of democratic renewal. Euro-parties face enormous challenges in an EU-system structured to their disadvantage. Yet, the need for Euro-parties is at least now more firmly on the agenda and for the first time several embryonic pan-European initiatives are

---

[45] R. Bellamy, *A Republican Europe of States* (Cambridge: Cambridge University Press, 2019); P. Manent, *Democracy without Nations: The Fate of Self-Government in Europe* (Wilmington: ISI Books, 2013); D. Innerarity, 'What must be democratized? The European Union as a complex democracy', in S. Champeau, C. Closa, D. Innerarity and M. Poaires Maduro (eds), *The Future of Europe: Democracy, Legitimacy and Justice after the Euro Crisis* (London: Rowman and Littlefield); D. Innerarity, 'Transnational self-determination: Resetting self-government in the age of interdependence', *Journal of Common Market Studies*, 53/5 (2015), 1061–76; K. Nicolaidis and R. Youngs, 'Europe's democracy trilemma', *International Affairs*, 90/6 (2014), 1403–19; T. Hüller, 'Out of time? The democratic limits of EU demoicracy', *Journal of European Public Policy*, 23/10 (2016), 1407–24.

beginning to make headway. Party politics still needs to be brought into line with the locus of much decision-making at the EU level. Without such alignment, democratic accountability will be curtailed and distorted. While much focus has been on transnational lists, these are an institutional tweak and a poor substitute for a fully developed European-level party politics. The EU's multiple crises have made this clear and helped galvanize activists into forming pan-European party initiatives. Yet this fragile momentum will need much political backing from the EU and governments if it is to be extended and endure.

In sum, efforts at democratic reinvention have gained a prominent place on the EU's agenda, although far-reaching change is yet to happen. Reform efforts have begun to improve EU democracy both vertically (through citizen input) and horizontally (through representative institutions' role relative to executive bodies), although the Union still falls short on both these axes.[46] In very broad terms, the EU is still more drawn to controlled consensus-formation than open-ended pluralism. The EU institutions still tend to talk about improving democratic legitimacy in terms of 'good' policies more than democratic process.[47] Assessments of these EU reform efforts conclude that new avenues of democratic empowerment have opened up, but barriers against their effectiveness remain significant.[48]

At present, the EU has opened an interesting range of consultations and debates, but these do not add up to a powerful or purposive strategy of democratic renewal. Beyond the EU's various 'fast-burning crises' the issue of democratic legitimacy is one of the 'slow-burning crises' that persist.[49] Seeking to retain primary influence and a controlling hand on the tiller of integration, governments and the EU institutions

---

[46] J. Fossum, 'Addressing the right problems, with the right instruments, at the right time: Reflections on the Conference on the Future of Europe', *Der Europaische Foderalist*, 25 July 2020.

[47] European Commission, *A Europe That Delivers: Institutional Options for Making the EU's Work More Efficient*, COM (2018) 95.

[48] D. Levi-Faur and F. van Waarden (eds), *Democratic Empowerment in the European Union* (Cheltenham: Edward Elgar Publishing, 2018).

[49] L. Seabrooke and E. Tsingou, 'Europe's fast- and slow-burning crises', *Journal of European Public Policy*, 26/3 (2019), 468–81.

have so far declined to follow through on their many promises of European-level democratic reform. In the extreme circumstances of the Covid-19 crisis, they seemed set to veer even further towards a technocratic style of EU governance. Elites' inability to reform the EU brings to mind a cardinal lesson from history: in Europe's bloody past, the retreat of political openness within states has invariably strained relations between them.[50]

[50]   S. Jenkins, *A Short History of Europe from Pericles to Putin* (London: Viking, 2018).

9

Pathways to rebuilding European democracy

For over a decade, the apparently parlous state of European democracy has engendered intense analytical and political concern. A number of issues have become something akin to signature debates for European political analysis: the roots and reach of a populist surge, the malaise of party politics and representative institutions, the recurrent difficulties of reforming the policies and institutional structures of the European Union, and most recently the political impact of Covid-19. Deliberation and research on these questions have produced contrasting conclusions on the state of European democracy. Many see the risk to democracy as truly grave and alarming, while others are more sanguine. Yet, while such judgements diverge, there has been wide agreement that what needs assessing, measuring and explaining is the depth of democracy's crisis.

This book has not sought to add to this well-worked question, but rather to move analysis in a different direction. It does so without any intention of implying that European democracy is in robust health. Instead, its starting point is the contention that fuller analysis is needed of the *responses* to democracy's troubles. The book has offered an empirical look at what kinds of reform are being enacted in practice across Europe. It adopts this focus because European democracy is currently being reconstructed and fine-tuned through a rich array of practical initiatives. Much analysis looks conceptually at the competing merits of different models of democracy; but it is equally important to delve into real-life democratic resistance and renewal as these filter back with profound implications into conceptual and normative questions.

The book's core findings can be summarized in three telegraphic headlines. First, multiple layers of democratic resistance and renewal have become firmly established features of European politics, although the general tenor of democratic change remains relatively cautious. Second, significant forces have both prompted governments, political parties, civil society and EU institutions to pursue democratic initiatives and simultaneously restrained their approach to rebuilding democracy. Third, a more ambitious and comprehensive agenda of political reform is needed and the many initiatives pursuing different types of democratic defence and innovation still need to cohere together.

Democratic innovation

Multiple actors across Europe have in the last several years developed initiatives designed to halt and reverse the continent's democratic erosion. Most analysis still overlooks the depth and breadth of these pro-democratic counterpoints to democracy's travails. Many publications lay out recommendations to shore up liberal democracy, but these are invariably framed as ideas for countering an overwhelmingly dominant momentum of democratic deterioration and make little or no mention of positive innovations actually underway.[1] Other analyses are framed as generic critiques of populism and why its appeal may prove ephemeral; again, this is a different focus from looking at the purposive strategies of those already seeking active forms of democratic restoration.

A prevalent analytical orientation is that anti-democratic dynamics are clearly dominant and that an 'anti-liberal consensus' has taken root across the European Union.[2] This book reveals evidence that is more

---

[1] Examples include comprehensive reports such as N. Eisen, A. Kenealy, S. Corke, T. Taussig and A. Polyakova, *The Democracy Playbook: Preventing and Reversing Democratic Backsliding* (Washington, DC: Brookings, 2019); Berggruen Institute, *Renewing Democracy in the Digital Age* (Los Angeles: Berggruen Institute, 2020).

[2] I. Krastv and S. Holmes 'How liberalism became the "God that failed" in Eastern Europe', *The Guardian*, 24 October 2019.

nuanced and mixed. If there has been an anti-liberal backlash against the liberal consensus, so there is now a gathering democratic backlash against Europe's anti-liberal forces. The very fact the liberal democracy no longer seems quite the natural or default state of affairs has helped galvanize many into more concerted action. In political science, analysts often stand back from day-to-day events and assess crises as moments of positive opportunity for overdue change. Even if this might sound overly sanguine in Europe's current context, it certainly is the case that democracy's recent troubles and fragility have given birth to new ideas and raised levels of reform commitment. The demise of ebullient liberal teleology has actually helped generate more committed actor-driven democracy strategies.

Changes on the democratic and anti-democratic sides of the policy equation have often mirrored each other. If democratic erosion has proceeded though undramatic step-by-step increments, so has its reverse-image counterpart of European democratic renewal. Many democratic experiments and initiatives have been low-key and have not attracted media headlines as much as the high-profile instances of leaders behaving in egregiously illiberal ways. Yet, they have been significant enough to help explain why the figures measuring democratic quality presented in Chapter 2 have not fallen more dramatically.

Overall trends in democracy are the result not only of anti-democratic threats but also of pro-democratic dynamics, with the variation between European states' respective democratic trajectories being the combined product of these negative and positive factors. It might be said that European politics are now subject to a push and pull between democratic rollback and democratic revival.[3] Much commentary and analysis in recent years has been framed in terms of illiberal forces being on the front foot and holding all the strong cards,

---

[3] For a similar argument against 'overly schematic' views on democratic backsliding and recognition that different directions of political change have occurred simultaneously, see L. Cianetti and S. Hanley, 'The end of the backsliding paradigm', *Journal of Democracy*, 32/1 (2021), 66–80 and 68.

while democrats are on the defensive. In truth, both have developed new strategies, with each reacting to the other's advances.

The foregoing chapters show that the trend has been remarkably multifaceted. Table 9.1 summarizes the actors involved and their multiple tactics and means of democratic action. Protests have spread as a bottom-up, spontaneous and relatively unstructured form of democratic resistance. National governments have formulated and made available numerous initiatives for direct citizen consultation and participation. Many political parties across Europe have reformulated the way they work with the need for democratic renovation in mind. Civic engagement has also taken shape in a new type of digital activism. Some notable efforts have been forthcoming at the EU level to dissuade governments from undermining democracy, to open up the core model of European integration and to improve accountability over the Union's decision-making. Meaningful change is afoot at multiple levels across Europe.

All this means that democratic rebuilding has myriad features. It contains top-down and bottom-up elements. It is political and civic, formal and informal, local and Europe-wide. Some of it has been about strengthening liberal constitutional guarantees, some of it about parliamentary democracy, some of it about direct citizen engagement, some of it about reforming political parties and some of it about

Table 9.1 Democratic actors and actions

Actors	Tactics and tools
Citizens	Mass mobilization
Civil society organizations	Civil society actions
Political parties	Small-scale deliberation
National governments	Referendums
European Union	Party realignment
	New political parties
	Digital regulations
	Digital empowerment strategies
	EU consultation and reform
	Punitive measures to defend democracy

developments in the digital sphere. In academic usage, the terminology of democratic 'innovations' tends to be applied narrowly to forms of deliberative and consultative initiatives; this is unfortunate as the range of ongoing effort and experimentation across Europe encompasses a far wider range of actors and democratic methods.

This multiplicity of resistance and renewal is conceptually significant as it stands somewhat at odds with many analytical debates. Analysts tend to posit one variable as being crucial in deciding democracy's fate, whether this be citizen deliberation, protests, party-system changes, the fate of populist parties, digital technology or EU reforms. A comparative perspective weighing strategies across these different arenas is invariably missing. Yet, in practice, the agenda of European democratic resistance and renewal has been eclectic rather than moving democracy decisively in the direction of one sole model of democracy.

While noting general patterns of change, the book also reveals that the balance between different strands of democratic renovation has differed across EU states. If Chapter 2 pointed out that there is no single trend of democratic regression, so the book's subsequent chapters reveal that there is no single pattern of democratic renovation. Some EU governments have opened up to new forms of participation, but others have been reluctant to do so. In some states, democracy is hindered by stifling state control, while in others ungovernable pluralism seems to be the greater peril. In a number of countries, party systems have begun to realign, while in others mainstream coalitions have hunkered down in even more self-protective fashion. In some, the EU dimension is seen as crucial to repairing democracy, in others it is seen more as a source of democratic dysfunction. This variation means that a simple, uniform analytical framework of democratic renewal is likely to remain out of reach.

If the rising tide of reform efforts is encouraging, it has been insufficient fully to reverse or restore democracy's fortunes. The preceding chapters stress that in each area of reform, the limits to change are also striking. Citizen-led democratic activism has stirred but has also often been frustratingly directionless and has faced major obstacles since the Covid-19 pandemic hit. Governments and the EU institutions have kept direct forms of democratic engagement within relatively controlled parameters. In becoming a more structured world of professional initiatives, participative-deliberation risks losing its identity as a self-critical vanguard probing for ambitious, open-ended change. Formal participative deliberation has entailed well-structured policy influence but involving only a handful of citizens; protests have conversely involved millions of European citizens but with fairly sporadic political traction.

The same limitations appear in party politics. New political parties ostensibly centred on democratic renewal have invariably flattered to deceive, falling short of their emancipatory potential. New policies in the digital sphere strain to keep up with the governments and companies bent on using technology to distort more than replenish European democracy. The EU's endless promises of and plans for democratic reform have often withered on the vine of institutional resistance. If a spirit of European democratic renovation has gathered steam, its momentum is still fragile.

Bottom-up energy, top-down caution

Of the different areas of pro-democratic pushback, the strongest dynamic has been the incremental expansion in civic participation. Conversely, the arena of party politics has probably been most resistant to far-reaching, qualitative reform. This means that the leading edge of European democratic renewal is what might be termed an incremental civic empowerment – a mirror image of the executive aggrandizement that analysts use to describe contemporary democratic decay.[4] This is all the more encouraging because the democracy indices presented in Chapter 2 struggle fully to incorporate these kinds of participation and

---

[4] N. Bermeo, 'On democratic backsliding', *Journal of Democracy*, 27/1 (2016), 5–19.

direct democratic engagement, meaning that such widely cited figures arguably downplay a number of positive trends in European democracy. A downward shift in forms of accountability has gained traction. Behind the many reform efforts underway across Europe is an interest in citizens gaining greater direct hold over public decisions. Underneath the news cycles focused on crisis moments and the populist surge, there are structural shifts pushing in the direction of more participation and accountability. Indeed, those concerned with limiting democracy are often seeking to push back this tide. From a broader historical perspective, it has been argued that state power has long been checked by bottom-up pluralism in Europe, leaving space open for this democratic resistance.[5]

Bottom-up renewal has entailed mass mobilizations of large numbers of citizens, while organized civil society activism and mini-publics involve smaller numbers of people around particular policy questions. There is long-running academic debate over which is more valuable – mass engagement, intermediary civil society bodies or small-scale deliberative forums. In practice, multiple types of civic engagement have proliferated, each bringing distinctive ingredients to the table of democratic renewal. Some recent European political trends are about reasoned deliberation on fairly specific policy issues, others about fluid and less scripted citizen pressure.

This core civic sentiment has prompted different kinds of democratic innovation including online petitions, participative assemblies, consultations and local referendums. The common thread linking these is an ethos of bringing democratic control and monitoring down to the apocryphal ordinary citizen. This denotes a move from passive to *active* democratic engagement. This is a common spine of recent political developments, evident in the spiralling number of pro-democracy protests, citizen assemblies and civil society initiatives but

---

also in moves to build a spirit of active citizenship into more traditional democratic channels like political parties and parliaments.

While citizens mobilize, governments' role has been more circumspect. If citizens look to counter governmental power, formal actors have supported more cosmetic changes. Governments and European-level institutions have pursued controlled forms of democratic renewal that reduce any risk of their own interests and policy preferences being challenged. Curiously, many governments have narrowed and modestly widened democratic space at the same time. Government driven top-down measures have responded to bottom-up pressure and have so far mainly tinkered around the edges of democratic erosion. The preceding chapters show this has been true of governments across the political spectrum. Government approaches have been too technocratic and controlled to free democracy's captured institutions and are out of synch with what drives the search for bottom-up renewal.

The general move in the direction of participatory initiatives appears to be the form of democratic renewal that all different actors support – leftist, centrist and rightist, governments, organized civil society and social movements, local community groups and pan-European bodies. These are also the kind of initiatives that have retained most momentum in the trying circumstances of Covid-19. It is important to clarify that the trend of formative participation has been stronger than that of directly democratic voting; the expansion of citizen engagement has not been reflected in a spread of direct democracy in the form of high-level referendums. This again reflects the way that governments and public authorities have sought to temper the degree of uncontrolled or adversarial confrontation involved in democratic renewal.

The paradox of democratic renewal

The foregoing chapters reveal a mixture of calculations both pushing governments and other actors towards democratic renovation and pulling them away from reform commitments. This is in part because the overwhelming focus on populism, nativism and illiberalism in European debates has complicated and cut across debates about democratic quality and democratic reform. This has produced a kind of *paradox* of democratic renovation.

On the one hand, the illiberal-populist surge has motivated many actors to embark on democratic reform strategies. After illiberal-populist parties rose rapidly and caused much soul-searching surprise in the early 2010s, democrats began a fightback. Many elements of democratic resistance have been framed very directly as a riposte to illiberal-populist parties, leaders and social trends. Mainstream centre-left and centre-right governments and elites have seen democratic renovation as a means of holding illiberal or populist challenges at bay. They have often adopted populists' hard-line positions on individual policy issues like migration, while confronting these forces more firmly in the defence of political-liberal values at a systemic level.

On the other hand, the very same illiberal-populist surge has acted as a constraining factor. Governments, EU institutions and even some civil society activists have been cautious about extending democratic innovation and experimentation too far, precisely because of the support that illiberal-populist parties have built up. This is most true in respect to new ideas for direct democracy and citizen participation. It is also seen in the persistence of a largely top-down EU integration model. Populists' rise has discredited at least some forms of direct democracy, as it has intensified fears that direct popular voice is today more of a danger than fillip to liberalism.

Some evidence casts doubt on how far governments, EU institutions and mainstream political parties genuinely *want* to revive democracy on the basis of giving effective voice to a wider range of citizens. Governments increasingly seek to deflect popular unrest but without undermining their own control or power in any far-reaching sense. To the extent that Europe's problem has in recent years been framed more often as one of populism than of democratic erosion, elites have been as concerned to limit popular sovereignty as to open up to it.

This has reframed the long-standing debate between consensual and competitive forms of democracy in Europe, with those doubling down on a familiar pro-liberal consensus casting themselves as democracy's guardians against those advocating less cosy consensus-preservation and more vibrant pluralism.

The situation has been far more complex than the picture often painted of mainstream, liberal governments battling to save democracy from 'the populists'. Government approaches often have a flavour of pinning the blame for democracy's problems on others, on those somehow external to the mainstream democratic system – outside powers, social-media companies, populists. The threats these actors bring are of course real and serious, but this framing rather takes the focus away from faults intrinsic to the democratic system itself or those related to political elites' own actions. Elites have framed the democracy challenge as one involving 'good democrats' against 'bad populists' in part to legitimize their own relatively modest reforms that fall short of radically opening up democracy to allow citizens the possibility of co-creating policy agendas.

Much bottom-up citizen participation has had a tinge of democratic resistance against oligarchic parties and parliament, even if sometimes it has less clearly democratic connotations. Overall, despite the many books and articles now pitched against direct democracy, this has not been an excessive element of government or civil society responses to Europe's democratic malaise. The direct-majority popular will is still more contained than unleashed across Europe. Governments limit popular will commonly in the name of liberal democracy, even as many citizens seek more emancipatory forms of popular participation. There remains unfulfilled potential for extending some forms of direct democracy where these can be moulded to the core parameters of liberal-representative processes.

This intricate array of political forces across Europe ensures that the whole debate about democratic decay and renewal is highly charged and contested at a basic analytical level of whether actors' respective strategies actually help or endanger democracy. Debates can feel somewhat schizophrenic: a lament that democracy is not responsive enough to citizens coexists with fears of citizens having *too much* influence. Governments and EU institutions may feel that controlled reform strikes the right balance in this dilemma, but this strategy risks supplying illiberal agendas with the very oxygen that sustains them. This is the paradox that sits at the heart of Europe's mixed dynamic of accumulating but still-subdued democratic reform.

Liberalism and democratic renovation

All this has significant implications for the broader shape of European liberalism. Chapter 2 outlined the way in which Europe's democracy malaise is nested within a broader crisis of liberalism. The relationship between the two – liberalism and democracy – has been the subject of much debate. A standard claim made by analysts, academics and political leaders in recent years is that the populist surge entails a battle between democracy and liberalism, including necessary trade-offs between the two. Many writers have argued that the priority is to defend liberal social values, internationalism, EU integration and economic openness even if this means limiting the sway of majority opinions and returning to a more controlled form of democracy.[6]

However, this book's detailed evidence on real-life reform efforts sheds a different light on the liberalism-democracy relationship and suggests a more nuanced picture. Many actors' democratic strategies have in practice sought to shore up liberalism and democracy together, rather than these being treated as trade-offs. Those leading many strands of democratic innovation are passionate opponents of illiberalism, not its handmaidens. Conversely, the book demonstrates that illiberal national-populists have rarely followed through on their claims to be committed to adding new impetus to democracy. The

---

[6] A. C. Grayling, *Democracy and Its Crisis* (London: Simon and Schuster, 2018); A. Weale, *The Will of the People: A Modern Myth* (Cambridge: Polity Press, 2018).

supposed trade-off between liberalism and democracy that many say has come to define European politics seems too simplistic and stark to capture the dynamics behind these real-world reform efforts.

Through a large number of critiques in recent years, it is now received wisdom that liberalism has become too rigid and intolerant of other views and that democracy needs to rest less in the liberal elite and incorporate other, community-level voices. Many disgruntled citizens have come to see liberalism as part of an unloved status quo rather than as a creed for radical and empowering change, which is what it originally was. They often see elites equating the defence of liberal values with nothing more than a doubling down on existing policies. A common line is that democrats need to make greater effort to reach out and offer inclusion to 'moderate illiberals'.[7]

However valid this criticism is in a general sense, it fails to take on board just how much change citizens, civic groups and other reformers are generating at the level of inclusive and local democratic involvement. Through their actions it can be said that the democratic part of the liberal project has begun to adapt in recent years more than is commonly realized, and this makes the standard arguments against liberals and the liberal project look rather abstract and behind-the-curve. The democracy agenda has moulded itself around local community-building efforts and a wider range of citizen-oriented values. These kinds of democratic actors may be relearning Aristotle's point about a density of moral community and virtue being needed to underpin citizen rights and freedoms.[8]

Still, governments and wider political elites have not been willing to facilitate or extend this incipient liberal adjustment nearly far enough. If the many accounts of political philosophy calling for democratic innovation fail to take on board the practical experimentation going

---

[7] 'A manifesto for renewing liberalism', *The Economist*, 13 September 2018; E. Fawcett, 'The daunting task of repair', *Open Democracy*, 29 May 2018; V-Dem, *Defending Democracy against Illiberal Challengers; A Resource Guide* (Gothenburg: University of Gothenburg, 2020); F. Fukuyama, 'Liberalism and Its Discontents', *American Purpose*, 5 October 2020.

[8] A. Ryan, *On Aristotle* (New York: Norton, 2014); A. Gopnik, *A Thousand Small Sanities: The Moral Adventure of Liberalism* (London: Basic Books, 2019).

on across Europe, practical reform efforts can in turn struggle to convert the new philosophical ethos of a more flexible liberalism into operational reform initiatives. If bottom-up democratic renovation is one part of a broader rethink of liberalism, it remains tentative and bereft of the high-level political support that would help it more fully flourish.

A more ambitious democratic agenda

The policy implications that follow from these analytical assessments are clear: deeper and more ambitious democratic resistance and renewal are still needed across Europe. While the book has focused mainly on conceptualizing the reform trends that have gathered pace in recent years, it contains a more normative message that political reform needs to be less cautious, less restrained, less tame. Europe still needs a more ambitious reworking of democratic practices, with reform agendas that involve far stronger and qualitatively new elements of citizen engagement and influence. Democratic rebuilding needs to be unchained from its current tethers.

This is not to discount the justified fears of overly disruptive and misdirected change. There are legitimate concerns over the need to contain illiberal identities and political projects and prevent deeper polarization. A delicate balance is certainly required between safeguarding liberal constitutionalism and democratic empowerment. Yet European governments have erred in tilting too far towards the former not the latter in recent years. Deeper democratic renewal can be advanced in ways that do not endanger but give more dynamic life to core liberal guarantees and representation. It must be possible to address the frustrations of those who feel stranded by globalization, identity shifts and technological change without giving ground to political illiberalism. A degree of adversarial, political confrontation is a necessary part of this agenda, not something to be avoided or curtailed through a managerial approach to democratic reform. For all the undoubtedly impressive democratic innovations that have accumulated in recent years, more pluralistic and dynamic democratic engagement and open-ended contestation are still required.

To this end, one of the most pressing imperatives is to articulate better connections between the different levels of reform outlined in the book. Different types and levels of democratic resistance and reform fulfil different, vital functions. Analysts have long made the case that different types of democratic accountability and participation need to work more closely in tandem with each other. A familiar staple of democratic theory is the contention that direct and representative democratic dynamics need to be complementary to each other. Analysts have argued that emerging forms of citizen participation need to feed into a better use of direct democracy, and these in turn need to foster new types of party politics.[9] Prominent theorists call for innovative democratic redesign focused on such practical linkages rather than a quest for discreet, abstract models of democracy.[10]

To a modest degree, European democratic actors at multiple levels have begun to explore such linkages. The book shows how increasingly protests have linked to civil society, participative initiatives have linked to parliaments, parties have linked down to social movements, online activism has linked to offline activism and EU ideas have linked to local community concerns. However, overall different reform efforts have remained relatively disconnected from each other and often have even seemed to cut across one another. The proliferation of local initiatives, protests and civic-tech constitute a loose cluster of democratic innovation that have not linked together well into a coherent whole. The twin dynamics of democratic resistance and renewal rarely work in tandem with each other. The policies detailed throughout this book mostly embody a scattergun of partial initiatives.

---

[9] From a large literature on these, see for example D. Lazer, K. Esterling and M. Neblo (eds), *Politics with the People: Building a Directly Representative Democracy* (Cambridge: Cambridge University Press, 2018); A. Lieninger, 'Direct democracy in Europe: Potentials and pitfalls', *Global Policy*, 6 (2015), 17–27 p. 16.

[10] D. Innerarity, *Democracy in Europe* (London: Palgrave Macmillan, 2018); M. Saward, *Democratic Design* (Oxford: Oxford University Press, 2021).

There has been no united or comprehensive 'democracy policy' across Europe but rather a fragmented collection of individual policy responses, civil society initiatives, citizen uprisings, political-party adjustments, parliamentary efforts, digital strategies and EU-level reforms. Democratic renovation would benefit from some kind of civic-led and European-level hub to feed in best practice from the myriad national and subnational experiments with assemblies, e-petitions, legislative crowdsourcing, protests and new-style parties. This is not in any way to advocate moves towards a single template of reform, as this is probably neither feasible nor desirable. The appropriate balance between different types of democratic rebuilding will vary across different contexts depending on core processes of political contestation. Yet there is a need to coalesce the many areas of democratic change across Europe and build a picture of how they relate to each other.

Turning tide

In recent years it appears that there has been sufficient democratic renewal at least to help hold democratic erosion at bay. Events have not borne out the large number of warnings that democracy is in terminal crisis, on the road to inexorable demise or in the throes of progressive deconsolidation. For now, these claims seem to have been proven hugely exaggerated. However, while neither the national-populist surge nor a battery of other challenges have swept away the entire edifice of liberal pluralism, democracy's structural fragility remains worrying and Covid-19's impact has added further strains.

Europe's tentative democratic renovation has remained short of a root-and-branch restoration or a really deep recasting of what democracy means. Most reform initiatives have taken shape as responses to fast evolving challenges. Rather than fully predesigned democratic templates, they have a certain feel of rickety ships being built at sea. The changes do not in themselves denote or ensure democratic renewal but can rather been seen as opening up its possibility. Democratic resistance and renewal have gathered momentum in recent years but do not yet represent a fundamental paradigm shift. It is uncertain how robustly they are embedded in Europe's political fabric. The signs that democracy's adverse tide could be turning are clear, but stronger commitment and political action will be needed to make this change decisive.

Bibliography

Albertazzi, D., and S. Mueller (2013), 'Populism and liberal democracy: Populists in government in Austria, Italy, Poland and Switzerland', *Government and Opposition*, 48/3, 343–71

Alemanno, A., and J. Organ (eds) (2020), *Citizen Participation in Democratic Europe: What Next?* London: Rowman and Littlefield.

Altmann, D. (2011), *Direct Democracy Worldwide*. Cambridge: Cambridge University Press.

Amnesty International (2017), *Dangerously Disproportionate: The Ever-Expanding National Security State in Europe*. London: Amnesty International.

Annenberg Public Policy Center of the University of Pennsylvania (2020), 'Freedom and Accountability: A Transatlantic Framework for Moderating Speech Online'.

Appelbaum, A. (2020), *The Twilight of Democracy: The Seductive Lure of Authoritarianism* London: Doubleday.

Aries, Q., 'Europe's failure to protect liberty in Hungary', *The Atlantic*, 29 December 2019.

Avaaz (2019), *Far Right Networks of Deception* London: Avaaz.

Barberà, O., A. Barrio and J. Rodríguez-Teruel (2019), 'New parties' linkages with external groups and civil society in Spain: A preliminary assessment', *Mediterranean Politics*, 24/5, 646–64.

Beck, U., and E. Grande (2007), 'Cosmopolitanism: Europe's way out of crisis', *European Journal of Social Theory*, 10/1, 67–85

Bedock, C. (2017), *Reforming Democracy: Institutional Engineering in Western Europe*. Oxford: Oxford University Press.

Bellamy, R. (2019), *A Republican Europe of States*. Cambridge: Cambridge University Press.

Bellamy, R., and D. Castiglione (2013), 'Three models of democracy, political community and representation in the EU', *Journal of European Public Policy* 20/2, 206–23

Bellamy, R., and S. Kröger (2017), 'A democratic justification of differentiated integration in a heterogeneous EU', *Journal of European Integration*, 39/5, 625–39.

Berggruen Institute (2020), *Renewing Democracy in the Digital Age*, Los Angeles: Berggruen Institute.

Berman, S. (2018), *Democracy and Dictatorship in Europe*. Oxford: Oxford University Press.

Berman, S., and H. Kundnani (2021), 'The costs of convergence', *Journal of Democracy*, 32/1, 22–36.

Bermeo, N. (2016), 'On democratic backsliding', *Journal of Democracy*, 27/1, 5–19.

Bertelsmann Stiftung (2018), *Citizens' Participation Using Sortition*, Gutersloh: Bertelsmann Stiftung.

Bickerton, C. (2014), *European Integration: From Nation-States to Member States*. Oxford: Oxford University Press.

Bickerton, C. (2018), 'Beyond the European void? Reflections on Peter Mair's legacy'. *European Law Journal*, 24/4–5, 268–80.

Blank, G., and E. Dubois (2019), 'The myth of the echo chamber', Oxford Internet Institute, 9 March 2018.

Blauberger, M., and V.van Hüllen (2020) 'Conditionality of EU funds: An instrument to enforce EU fundamental values?', *Journal of European Integration*, published online 8 January 2020.

Blockmans, S., and S. Russack (eds) (2019), *Representative Democracy in the European Union*, London: Rowman and Littlefield.

Bond, I., and A. Gostynska-Jakubowska (2020) *Democracy and the Rule of Law: Failing Partnership?* London: Centre for European Reform.

Bontcheva, K., and J. Posetti (eds) (2020), *Balancing Act: Countering Disinformation While Respecting Freedom of Expression*. Paris: UNESCO.

Boulianne, S. (2019), 'Building faith in democracy: Deliberative events, political trust and efficacy', *Political Studies*, 67/1, 4–30.

Brannen, S., C. Haig and K. Schmidt (2020), *The Age of Mass Protests*. Washington, DC: CSIS.

Brattberg, E., and T. Maurer (2018) *Russian Election Interference: Europe's Counter to Fake News and Cyber Attacks*. Washington, DC: Carnegie Endowment for International Peace.

Butcher, P., and C. Stratulat (2019), *Citizens Expect: Lessons from the European Citizens Consultations*. Brussels: European Policy Centre.

Butler, I. (2018), *Analysis of the Commission's Proposal for a Rights and Values Programme*. Brussels: Civil Liberties Union for Europe.

Butler, I. (2018), *Countering Populist Authoritarians*. Brussels: Civil Liberties Union for Europe.

Caiani, M., and P. Graziano (2019), 'Understanding varieties of populism in times of crises', *West European Politics*, 42/6, 1141–58

Caluwaerts, D., and M. Reuchamps (2016), 'Generating Democratic Legitimacy through Deliberative Innovations: The Role of Embeddedness and Disruptiveness', *Representation*, 52/1, 13–27.

Caporaso, J., M. Kim, W. Durrett and R. Wesley (2015), 'Still a regulatory state? The European Union and the financial crisis', *Journal of European Public Policy* 22/7, 889–907

Capstick, S., C. Demski, C. Cherry, C.Verfuerth and K. Steentjes (2020), *Climate Change Citizens' Assemblies*, CAST briefing paper 03.

Casal Bértoa, F., and T. Weber (2018), 'Restrained change: Party systems in times of economic crisis', *Journal of Politics*, 81/1, 233–48.

Casal Bértoa, F., and Z. Enyedi (2020), *Party System Closure: Party Alliances, Government Alternatives and Democracy in Europe*. Oxford: Oxford University Press.

Casal Bértoa, F., and J. Rama (2021), 'The anti-establishment challenge', *Journal of Democracy*, 32/1, 37–51

Centre for European Policy Studies (2018), *Rethinking the EU's Cyber Defence Capabilities*, Report of CEPS Task Force.

Chenoweth, E. (2020), 'The future of nonviolent resistance', *Journal of Democracy*, 31/3, 69–84.

Chevenal, F. (2016), *European Union and Direct Democracy: A Possible Combination?* Zurich: BEUCitizen project.

Cianetti, L., and S. Hanley (2021), 'The end of the backsliding paradigm', *Journal of Democracy*, 32/1, 66–80.

CitizensLab (2017), *Mapping New Forms of Civic Engagement in Europe*. Berlin: CitzensLab.

Civicus (2015), *State of Civil Society Report 2015*. Johannesburg: Civicus.

Civil Liberties Union for Europe and Greenpeace (2020), *Locking Down Critical Voices*. Hague: Civil Liberties Union for Europe.

Civil Society Europe (2018), *Report on Civic Space in Europe 2017*. Brussels: Civil Society Europe.

Closa, C. (2019), 'The politics of guarding the treaties: Commission scrutiny of rule of law compliance', *Journal of European Public Policy*, 26/5, 696–716.

Cole, A. (2019), *Emmanuel Macron and the Two Years that Changed France.* Manchester: Manchester University Press.

Coleman, S. (2017), *Can the Internet Strengthen Democracy?* Cambridge: Polity Press.

Collin, K. (2019), *Populist and Authoritarian Referendums: The Role of Direct Democracy in Democratic Deconsolidation.* Washington, DC: Brookings.

Cordero, G., and X. Coller (2018), *Democratizing Candidate Selection: New Methods, Old Recepits?* London: Palgrave, p. 141.

Costa Pinto, A., and C. Pequito Teixeira (2018), *Political Institutions and Democracy in Portugal: Assessing the Impact of the Eurocrisis.* London: Palgrave Macmillan.

Costamagna, F., and M. Goldmann, 'Constitutional innovation, democratic stagnation?', *Verfassungsblog*, 30 May 2020.

Council of the European Union (2014), *EU Human Rights Guidelines for Freedom of Expression Online and Offline*, Foreign Affairs Council, 12 May 2014.

Council of the European Union (2019), *Conclusions of the Council and of the Member States on Securing Free and Fair European Elections*, 6753/1/2019.

Council of the European Union (2020), *Conference on the Future of Europe.* Brussels: Council Secretariat.

Council of the European Union, 'Conference on the future of Europe. Council agrees its position', press statement, 24 June 2020.

Counter Extremism Project (2019), *Europe Ethno-nationalist and White Supremacy Groups.* London: CEP.

Crouch, C. (2011), *The Strange Non-Death of Neo-Liberalism.* Cambridge: Polity Press.

Curato, N., and M. Böker (2016), 'Linking mini-publics to the deliberative system: A research agenda', *Policy Sciences*, 49/2, 173–90.

Curtice, J., E. Clery, J. Perry, M. Phillips and N. Rahim (eds) (2019), *British Social Attitudes Survey* 36, 2019 edition, London: National Centre for Social Research.

Daly, T. (2019), 'Democratic decay: Conceptualising an emerging research field', *Hague Journal on the Rule of Law*, 11, 9–36.

Daly, T. and B. Jones (2020), 'Parties versus democracy: Addressing today's political party threats to democratic rule', *International Journal of Constitutional Law*, 18/2, 509–38.

Das Progressive Zentrum Democracy Lab (2017), *Anthology on Democratic Innovation*. Berlin: Democracy Lab.

Dassonneville, R., and I. McAllister (2020), 'The party choice set and satisfaction with democracy', *West European Politics*, 43/1, 49–73.

Dawson, J., and S. Hanley (2019), 'Foreground liberalism, background nationalism: A discursive institutionalist account of EU leverage and democratic backsliding in East Central Europe', *Journal of Common Market Studies*, 57/4, 710–28.

De Cleen, B., B. Moffitt, P. Panayotu and Y. Stavrakakis (2019), 'The potential and difficulties of transnational populism: The case of the Democracy in Europe Movement 2025 (DiEM25)', *Political Studies*, 69/1, 146–66.

De Vries, C., and S. Hobalt (2020), *Political Entrepreneurs: The Rise of Challenger Parties in Europe*. Princeton: Princeton University Press.

Democracy Reporting International (2020), *Phase Two of Covid Responses across the EU: The Rule of Law Stress Test, Continued*. Berlin: DRI.

Deneen, P. (2018), *Why Liberalism Failed*. London: Yale University Press.

Diamond, L. (2019), *Ill Winds: Saving Democracy from Russian Rage, Chinese Ambition and American Complacency*. London: Penguin.

Dijkstra L., H. Poleman and A. Rodriguez-Pose (2018), *The Geography of EU Discontent*. Brussels: European Commission.

Dobler, C. (2020), *The 2019 Grand Debat National in France: A Participatory Experiment with Limited Legitimacy*. Berlin: Democracy Reporting International.

Doorenspleet, R. (2018), *Rethinking the Value of Democracy*. London: Routledge.

Drozdiak, W. (2020), *The Last President of Europe*. New York: Public Affairs.

Dryzek, J. (2006) *Global Deliberative Politics*. Cambridge: Polity Press.

Dunleavy, P., and S. Kippin (2018), 'How democratic are the UK's parties and party system', *Democratic Audit*, 22 August 2018.

Dunleavy, P., A. Park and R. Taylor (eds) (2018), *UK Democratic Audit 2018*. London: LSE Press.

Eatwell, R., and M. Goodwin (2018), *National Populism: The Revolt against Liberal Democracy*. London: Pelican.

Economic and Social Committee (2017), *The Future Evolution of Civil Society in the European Union by 2030*. Brussels: ECSC.

Economist Intelligence Unit (2013), *Rebels without a Cause: What the Upsurge in Protest Movements Means for Global Politics*. London: EUI.

Economist Intelligence Unit (2018), *Democracy Index 2017*. London: EIU.

Economist Intelligence Unit (2019), *Democracy Index 2018*. London: EUI.

Economist Intelligence Unit (2020), *Democracy Index 2019*. London: EUI.

Eichhorn, J., V. Kupsch, L. Multhof and M. Mohr. (2019), *How European Publics and Policy Actors Values an Open Society*. Brussels: Open Society Foundations.

Eiermann, M., Y. Mounk and L. Gultchin (2017), *European Populism: Trends, Threats and Future Prospects*. London: Institute for Global Change.

Eisen, N., A. Kenealy, S. Corke, T. Taussig and A. Polyakova (2019), *The Democracy Playbook: Preventing and Reversing Democratic Backsliding*. Washington, DC: Brookings.

European Alternatives (2020), *Rejuvenating Europe's Democracy*, Report of the Euryka project.

European Civic Forum (2019), *Civic Space Watch Report 2019*. Brussels: ECF.

European Commission (2016), *Justice Scoreboard 2016*. Brussels: Commission.

European Commission (2017), *White Paper on the Future of Europe*, COM.

European Commission (2018), *Action Plan against Disinformation*, COM, 36.

European Commission (2018), Active subsidiarity: A new way of working, Report of the Task Force on Subsidiarity, Proportionality and 'Doing less more efficiently', July 2018.

European Commission (2018), *Citizens' Dialogues and Citizens' Consultations: Progress Report*. Brussels: Commission.

European Commission (2018), *A Europe that delivers: institutional options for making the EU's work more efficient*, COM, 95.

European Commission (2018), *Special Eurobarometer 477 Democracy and elections*, November 2018.

European Commission (2018), *Tackling Online Disinformation: A European Approach*, COM, 236.

European Commission (2019), *Citizens' Dialogues and Citizens' Consultations, Key Conclusions*. Brussels: Commission.

European Commission (2019), 'Europe in May 2019: Preparing for a more united, stronger and more democratic Union in an increasingly uncertain world: The European Commission's contribution to the informal EU27 leaders' meeting in Sibiu on 9 May 2019'. Brussels: Commission.

European Commission (2019), *Further Strengthening the Rule of Law within the Union*, COM, 163.

European Commission (2019), *The Future Government 2030+* Brussels: European Commission.

European Commission (2019), *Justice Scoreboard 2019*. Brussels: Commission.

European Commission (2019), *Strengthening the Rule of Law within the Union: A Blueprint for Action*, COM, 343.

European Commission (2020), *2020 Rule of Law Report: The Rule of Law Situation in the European Union*, COM, 580.

European Commission (2020), *Justice Scoreboard 2020*. Brussels: Commission.

European Commission (2020), On the European democracy action plan, COM, 790/3.

European Commission (2020), Shaping Europe's Digital Future, COM(2020) 67.

European Commission (2020), *A European Strategy for Data*, COM, 66.

European Commission (2020), *Technology and Democracy: Understanding the Influence of Online Technologies on Political Behaviour and Decision-Making*. Brussels: Joint Research Centre.

European Commission and High Representative of the Union for Foreign Affairs and Security Policy (2020), *Tackling Covid-19 Disinformation: Getting the Facts Right*, Join, 8.

European Commission (2016), *Standard Eurobarometer 85*. Brussels: Commission.

European Commission (2020), *Technology and Democracy: Understanding the Influence of Online Technologies on Political Behaviour and Decision-Making*. Brussels: Joint Research Centre, 2020.

European Committee of the Regions (2020), *Future of Europe. From Local to Europeans: Putting Citizens at the Centre of the EU Agenda*, Brussels.

European Court of Auditors (2019), 'Challenges to effective EU cybersecurity policy', ECA briefing paper.

European Economic and Social Committee (2018), *Societies Outside Metropolises: The Role of Civil Society Organisations in Facing Populism*. Brussels: EESC.

European Parliament Research Service (2018), *Prospects for E-democracy in Europe Case Studies*. Brussels: EPRS.

European Political Strategy Centre (2019), 'Rethinking strategic autonomy for the digital age', European Commission, EPSC Strategic Note.

European Regulators Group for Audiovisual Media Services (2019), *Report of the Activities Carried Out to Assist the European Commission in the*

Intermediate Monitoring of the Code of Practice on Disinformation.
Brussels: ERGA.

European Union (2019), *Strategic Agenda 2020–2024*. Brussels: EU.

Expert Group of the Friedrich Ebert Stiftung (2018), *The Other Democratic Deficit: A Toolbox for the EU to Safeguard Democracy in Member States.* Berlin: FES.

Fawcett, E., 'The daunting task of repair', *Open Democracy*, 29 May 2018.

Feenstra R., S. Tormey, A. Casero-Ripollés and J.Keane (2017), *Reconfiguring Democracy: The Spanish Political Laboratory.* London: Routledge.

Feldstein, S. (2019), *The Global Expansion of AI Surveillance.* Washington, DC: Carnegie Endowment for International Peace.

Feldstein, S. (2020), *How to Tackle Europe's Digital Democracy Challenges.* Brussels: Carnegie Europe.

Foa, R., and Y. Mounck (2017), 'The signs of deconsolidation', *Journal of Democracy*, 28/1, 5–16.

Foa, R., A. Klassen, M. Slade, A. Rand and R. Williams (2020), *The Global Satisfaction with Democracy Report 2020.* Cambridge: Centre for the Future of Democracy.

Formina, J., and J. Kucharczyk, 'Populism and protest in Poland', *Journal of Democracy*, 27/4, 58–68.

Fossum, J. 'Addressing the right problems, with the right instruments, at the right time: Reflections on the Conference on the Future of Europe', *Der Europaische Foderalist*, 25 July 2020.

Fossum, J. (2019), 'Democracy and differentiation in Europe', *Journal of European Public Policy*, 22/6, 799–815

Freedom House (2021 due March), *Freedom in the World 2020.* Washington, DC: Freedom House.

Freedom House (2020), *Freedom in the World 2020: A Leaderless Struggle for Democracy.* Washington, DC: Freedom House.

Fukuyama, F. (2018), *Identity: The Demand for Dignity and the Politics of Resentment.* London: Macmillan.

Fukuyama, F. (2020), 'Liberalism and its discontents', *American Purpose*, 3 October 2020.

Fundamental Rights Agency (2018), *Challenges Facing Civil Society Organizations Working on Human Rights in the EU.* Vienna: Fundamental Rights Agency.

Ganesh, B., and C. Froio (2020), 'A "Europe des Nations": Far right imaginative geographies and the politicization of cultural crisis on Twitter in Western Europe', *Journal of European Integration*, published online 19 August 2020.

Garbaudo, P. (2019), *The Digital Party*. London: Pluto Press.

Garton Ash, T., R. Gorwa and D. Metaxa (2019), 'Glasnost! Nine ways Facebook can make itself a better forum for free speech and democracy', Oxford-Stanford Report.

Gastil, J., and K. Knobloch (2020), *Hope for Democracy*. Oxford: Oxford University Press.

Gastil, J., and R. Richards (2013), 'Making direct democracy deliberative through random assemblies', *Politics and Society*, 41/2, 253–81.

Gaston, S. (2020), 'The divided continent: Understanding Europe's social landscape in 2020 and beyond', European Policy Centre working paper.

Gerwin, M. (2018), *Citizens' Assemblies: Guide to Democracy That Works*. Krakow: Otwarty Plan.

Gherghina, S., and V. Stoiciu (2020), 'Selecting candidates through deliberation: The effects for Demos in Romania', *European Political Science*, 19/2, 171–80.

Globsec Trends 2019 (2019), *Central and Eastern Europe 30 Years after the Fall of the Iron Curtain*. Bratislava: Globsec.

Gobierno de España (2019), Consultas Ciudadanos sobre Europa celebradas en España 2018, Madrid: Gobierno de España

Goodhart, D. (2017), *The Road to Somewhere*. London: Penguin.

Gopnik, A. (2019), *A Thousand Small Sanities: The Moral Adventure of Liberalism*. London: Basic Books.

Gostyńska-Jakubowska, A. (2016), *The Role of National Parliaments in the EU: Building or Stumbling Blocks?* London: Centre for European Reform.

Gostyńska-Jakubowska, A. (2019), *Boosting the Role of National Parliaments in EU Democracy*. Brussels: Carnegie Europe.

Grayling, A. C. (2018), *Democracy and Its Crisis*. London: Simon and Schuster.

Griessel, B. (2019), 'Democratic innovations in Europe', in S. Elstub and O. Escobar (eds), *Handbook on Democratic Innovation and Governance*. London: Elgar.

Guerot, U. (2019), *Why Europe Should Become a Republic! A Political Utopia*. Bonn: J.H.W.Dietz.

Habermas, J. (2012), *The Crisis of the European Union*. Cambridge: Polity Press.

Hamburger, J. (2018), 'Whose populism? The mixed messages of la France insoumise', *Dissent*, Summer.

Hansard Society (2019), *Audit of Political Engagement: 2019 Report*. London: Hansard.

Helbing, M. (2013), 'Nationalism and democracy: Competing or complementary logics?', *Living Reviews in Democracy* 4.

Hendricks, C., S. Ercan and J. Boswell (2020), *Mending Democracy: Democratic Repair in Disconnected Times*. Oxford: Oxford University Press.

Hendriks, F. (2019), 'Democratic innovation beyond deliberative reflection: The plebiscitary rebound and the advent of action-oriented democracy', *Democratization*, 26/3, 444–64.

Hessel, S. (2010), *Indignez-Vous*. Montpelier: LP.

Hobson, C., D. Hodson and U. Puetter (2015), 'The new intergovernmentalism: European integration in the post-Maastricht era', *Journal of Common Market Studies*, 53/4, 703–22.

Hüller, T. (2016), 'Out of time? The democratic limits of EU demoicracy', *Journal of European Public Policy*, 23/10, 1407–24.

Hume, M. (2017), *Revolting!* London: William Collins.

Hutter, S. and H. Kries (eds) (2019), *European Party Politics in Times of Crisis*. Cambridge: Cambridge University Press.

Ignatieff, M. (2017), *The Ordinary Virtues: Moral Order in a Divided World*. Cambridge, MA: Harvard University Press.

Independent Commission on Referendums (2018), *Report of the Independent Commission on Referendums*, Constitution Unit. London: UCL.

Innerarity, D. (2015), 'Transnational self-determination: Resetting self-government in the age of interdependence', *Journal of Common Market Studies*, 53/5, 1061–76.

Innerarity, D. (2018), *Democracy in Europe*. London: Palgrave Macmillan.

Innerarity, D. (2020), *Una teoría de la democracia compleja: gobernar en el siglo XXI*. Barcelona: Galaxia Gutenberg.

Innerarity, D. (2015) 'What must be democratized? The European Union as a complex democracy', in S. Champeau, C. Closa, D. Innerarity and M. Poaires Maduro (eds), *The Future of Europe: Democracy, Legitimacy and Justice after the Euro Crisis*. London: Rowman and Littlefield.

International Civil Society Centre (2013), *Riding the Wave*. Berlin: International Civil Society Centre.

International IDEA (2019), *Global State of Democracy 2018*. Stockholm: International IDEA.

International IDEA (2020), *Global State of Democracy 2019*. Stockholm: International IDEA.

International Trial Watch (2020), Spain: The right to protest in Spanish Courts, Barcelona: Internatioal Trial Watch.

Jacoby, W. (2017), 'Grand coalitions and democratic dysfunction: Two warnings from Central Europe', *Government and Opposition*, 52/2, 329–55.

Jacquet, V. (2019), 'The role and the future of deliberative mini-publics: A citizen perspective', *Political Studies*, 67/3, 639–57.

Jenkins, S. (2018), *A Short History of Europe from Pericles to Putin*. New York: Viking.

Jungherr, A., G. Rivero and D. Gayo-Avello (2020), *Retooling Politics: How Digital Media are Shaping Democracy*. Cambridge: Cambridge University Press.

Kaldor, M., and S. Selchow (2012), *The Bubbling Up of Subterranean Politics in Europe*. London: LSE.

Kaye, D. (2019), *Speech Police, The Global Struggle to Govern the Internet*, Columbia Global Reports, Columbia University.

Keane, J. (2020), *The New Despotism*. Cambridge, MA: Harvard University Press.

Klineberg, E. (2018), *Palaces for the People*. London: Penguin Random House.

Kolster, C., and H. von Homeyer (2019), *Pan-European Parties in a Time of Resurgent Nationalism*. Brussels: German Marshall Fund.

Kosiara-Pedersen, K., and P.Kurrild-Klitgaard (2018), Change and stability in the Danish party system', in M. Lisi (ed.), *Party System Change, the European Crisis and the State of Democracy*. London: Routledge.

Krastev, I. (2017), *After Europe*, Pennsylvania: University of Pennsylvania Press.

Krastev I., S. Dennison and M. Leonard (2019), *What Europeans Really Wanted: Five Myths Debunked*. London: ECFR.

Krause, L., and J. Gagne (2019), *Fault Lines: Germany's Invisible Divides*. Berlin: More in Common.

Kreuder-Sonnen, C. (2018), 'An authoritarian turn in Europe and European Studies?', *Journal of European Public Policy*, 25/3, 452–64.

Kriesi, H. (2018), 'The implications of the euro crisis for democracy', *Journal of European Public Policy*, 25/1, 59–82.

Kuczerawy, A. (2019), 'Fighting online disinformation: Did the EU Code of Practice forget about freedom of expression?', in E. Kużelewska, G. Terzis, D. Trottier and D. Kloza (eds), *Disinformation and Digital Media as a Challenge for Democracy*, European Integration and Democracy Series, 6, Intersentia.

Kundnani, H. (2020), *The Future of Democracy in Europe: Technology and the Evolution of Representation*. London: Chatham House.

Kyle, J., and Y. Mounk (2018), *The Populist Harm to Democracy: An Empirical Assessment*. London: Institute for Global Change.

Lacey, N. (2019), 'Populism and the Rule of Law?', LSE International Inequalities Institute working paper 28.

Lambertz, K-H. and L. Jahier (2018), 'Bringing the EU closer to its citizens: The call for a permanent mechanism for structured consultations and dialogues with citizens', European Economic and Social Committee and European Committee of the Regions Non paper, 14 December 2018.

Landemore, H. (2020), *Open Democracy: Reinventing Popular Rule for the Twenty-first Century*. Princeton, NJ: Princeton University Press.

Lazer, D., K. Esterling and M. Neblo (eds) (2018), *Politics with the People: Building a Directly Representative Democracy*. Cambridge: Cambridge University Press.

Legatum Institute (2019), *Prosperity Index 2019*. London: Legatum Institute.

Levi-Faur, D., and F. van Waarden (eds) (2018), *Democratic Empowerment in the European Union*. Cheltenham: Edward Elgar.

Levitsky, S., and G. Ziblatt (2018), *How Democracies Die*. London: Penguin.

Lieninger, A. (2015), 'Direct democracy in Europe: Potentials and pitfalls', *Global Policy*, 6/1, 17–27.

Lisi, M. (2018), 'The impact of the European crisis on party system change: Some comparative reflections', in M. Lisi (ed.), *Party System Change, the European Crisis and the State of Democracy*. London: Routledge.

Luhrman, A., and S. Lindberg (2019), 'A third wave of autocratization is here: What is new about it?', *Democratization*, 26/7, 1095–113.

Magen, A., and L. Pech (2018), 'The rule of law and the European Union', in C. May and A. Winchester (eds), *Handbook on the Rule of Law*. London: Edward Elgar.

Mair, P. (2013), *Ruling the Void: The Hollowing of Western Democracy*. London: Verso Books.

Manent, P. (2013), *Democracy without Nations: The Fate of Self-Government in Europe*. Wilmington: ISI Books.

Marcos-Marne, H., C. Plaza-Colodro and T. Freyburg (2020), 'Who votes for new parties? Economic voting, political ideology and populist attitudes', *West European Politics*, 43/1, 1–21.

Margarit, D. (2020), *Insurgent Conservatism in Romania*. Bucharest: Friedrich Ebert Stiftung.

Margetts, H. (2019), 'Rethinking democracy with social media', in A. Gamble and T. Wright (eds), *Rethinking Democracy*. Chichester: Wiley.

Martinelli, A. (2018), 'Populism and nationalism: The (peculiar) case of Italy', in A. Martinelli (ed.), *When Populism Meets Nationalism: Reflections on Populist Parties in Power*. Milan: ISPI.

MediaLab (2019), *Future Democracies: Laboratory of Collective Intelligence for Participatory Democracy*. Madrid: MediaLab.

Meyer-Resende, M. (2019), *Is German Democracy Back to Normal?* Brussels: Carnegie Europe.

Meyer-Resende, M., and R. Goldzweig (2019), *Online Threats to Democratic Debate: A Framework for a Discussion on Challenges and Responses*. Berlin: Democracy Reporting International.

Mohrenberg, S., R. Hubert and T. Freyburg (2019), 'Love at first sight? Populist attitudes and support for direct democracy', *Party Politics*.

Moller, J., 'Resilient democracies', *American Interest*, 12 November 2018.

Monbiot, G. (2017), *Out of the Wreckage: A New Politics for an Age of Crisis*. London: Verso.

Moore, M. (2018), *Democracy Hacked*. London:Oneworld.

Mouffe, C. (2018), *For a Left Populism*. London: Verso.

Mounk, Y. (2018), *The People vs Democracy: Why Our Freedom Is in Danger and How to Save It*. Cambridge, MA: Harvard University Press.

Mudde, C. (2019), *The Far-Right Today*. Cambridge: Polity Press.

Mudde, C., and C. Kaltwasser (2018), 'Studying populism in comparative perspective: Reflections on the contemporary and future research agenda', *Comparative Political Studies*, 51/13, 1667–93.

Mudde, C., and C. RoviraKaltwasser (2017), *Populism: A very Short Introduction*. New York: Oxford University Press.

Mueller, J. W. (2016), *What is Populism?* Pennsylvania: University of
Pennsylvania Press.

Mungiu-Pippidi, A. (2019), *Europe's Burden: Promoting Good Governance
Across Border.* Cambridge: Cambridge University Press.

Mungiu-Pippidi, A. (2015), *Public Integrity and Trust in Europe,*
Berlin: European Research Centre for Anti-Corruption and State-Building,
Hertie School of Governance.

Narsee, A. (2021), *Europe's Right to Protest Under Threat.* Brussels: Carnegie
Europe.

Negri, G. (2020), 'Civic space under Lockdown, in *European Civic Space
Watch 2020: Stories from the Lockdown.* Brussels: European Civic Forum.

Nicolaidis, K., and R. Youngs (2014), 'Europe's democracy trilemma',
International Affairs, 90/6, 1403–19.

Nodia, G. (2017), 'The end of the postnational illusion', *Journal of Democracy,*
28/2, 5–19.

Norris, P. (2019), 'On dealigning and realigning elections: Is Britain about to
experience a Westminster earthquake?', LSE Blog, 13 November 2019.

Norris, P., and R. Inglehart (2018), *Cultural backlash: Trump, Brexit, and the
Rise of Authoritarian Populism.* Cambridge: Cambridge University Press.

OECD (2020), *Innovative Citizen Participation and New Democratic
Institutions: Catching the Deliberative Wave.* Paris: OECD.

Pabst, A. (2019), *The Demons of Liberal Democracy.* Cambridge: Polity.

Pachl, U., and P. Valenti (eds) (2019), *A Human-Centric Digital Manifesto for
Europe.* Brussels: Open Society European Policy Institute.

Pamment, J. (2020), *The EU Code of Practice on Disinformation: Briefing Note
for the New EU Commission.* Washington, DC: Carnegie Endowment for
International Peace.

Pamment, J. (2020), *The EU's Role in Fighting Disinformation: Taking Back the
Initiative.* Washington, DC: Carnegie Endowment for International Peace.

Pappas, T. (2019), 'Populists in power', *Journal of Democracy,* 30/2, 70–84.

Parkinson, J. (2020) 'The role of referendums in deliberative systems',
Representation, published online, 6 February.

Pech, L., and D. Kochenov (2019), 'Strengthening the rule of law within
the European Union: Diagnoses, recommendations, and what to avoid',
Reconnect policy brief.

Pech, L., V.Perju and S. Palton, 'How to address rule of law backsliding in
Romania', *Verfassungsblog,* 29 May 2019.

Pedder, S. (2018), *Revolution Francaise: Emmanual Macron and the Quest to Reinvent a Nation*. London: Bloomsbury.

Persson, T., and K. Edholm (2018), 'Assessing the effects of European Union funding of civil society organisations: Money for nothing?', *Journal of Common Market Studies*, 56/3, 559–75.

Pew Research Center (2017), *Globally, broad support for representative and direct democracy*. Washington, DC: Pew.

Pew Research Center (2018), 'Eastern and Western Europeans differ on importance of religion, views of minorities, and key social issues', Washington DC: Pew.

Pew Research Center (2018), *In Western Europe, Populist Parties Tap Anti-establishment Frustration but Have Little Appeal across Ideological Divides*. Washington, DC: Pew.

Pew Research Center (2019), *European Public Opinion Three Decades After the Fall of Communism*. Washington, DC: Pew.

Polletta, F. (2016), 'Social movements in an age of participation', *Mobilisation*, 21/4, 485–97.

Pomerantsev, P. (2019), *This Is Not Propaganda: Adventures in the War Against Reality*. London: Public Affairs.

Pysgkas, A. (2017), *From the 'Democratic Deficit' to a 'Democratic Surplus': Constructing Administrative Democracy in Europe*. Oxford: Oxford University Press.

Qvortrup, M. (2017), 'Demystifying direct democracy?', *Journal of Democracy*, 28/3, 141–52.

Raunio, T. (2015), 'The role of national legislatures in EU politics', in O. Cramme and S. Hobolt (eds), *Democratic Politics in a European Union under Stress*. Oxford: Oxford University Press.

Reigh, G. (2019), 'What's next for Romania?', *Open Democracy*, 10 July 2019.

Ricard-Nihoul, G. (2020), *Representation Et Participation: Reinventer La Democratie Europeenne*. Paris: Notre Europe.

Rodríguez-Teruel, J., and A.Barrio (2016), 'Going National: Ciudadanos from Catalonia to Spain', *South European Society and Politics*, 21/4, 587–607.

Rodríguez-Teruel, J., A. Barrio and O. Barberà (2016), 'Fast and furious: Podemos' quest for power in multi-level Spain', *South European Society and Politics*, 21/4, 561–85.

Rodriguez-Teruel, J., O. Barbera, A.Barrio and F. Casal Bértoa (2018), 'From stability to change? The evolution of the party system in Spain', in M. Lisi (ed), *Party System Change, the European Crisis and the State of Democracy*. London: Routledge.

Rosanvallon, P. (2008), *Counter-Democracy: Politics in an Age of Distrust*. Cambridge: Cambridge University Press.

Runciman, D. (2019), *How Democracy Ends*. London: Profile.

Rupnik, J. (2018), 'The crisis of liberalism', *Journal of Democracy*, 29/3, 24–38.

Russack, S. (2019), 'EU parliamentary democracy: How representative?', in S. Blockmans and S. Russack (eds), *Representative Democracy in the European Union*. London: Rowman and Littlefield.

Ryan, A. (2014), *On Aristotle*. New York: Norton.

Sanchez-Cuenca, I. (2019), 'A vueltas con España (y su democracia)', *Revista CTXT*, Numero 214.

Saward, M. (2021), *Democratic Design*. Oxford: Oxford University Press.

Scheppele, K. (2018), 'Autocratic legalism', *University of Chicago Law Review*, 85, 545–83.

Schiller, T. (2018), 'Local referendums: A comparative assessment of forms and practice', in L. Morel and M. Qvortrup (eds), *Routledge Handbook on Direct Democracy and Referendums*. London: Routledge.

Schimmelfennig, F. (2015), 'What's the news in "new intergovernmentalism"? A critique of Bickerton, Hodson and Puetter', *Journal of Common Market Studies*, 53/4, 723–30

Schimmelfennig, F. (2015), 'Liberal intergovernmentalism and the euro area crisis', *Journal of European Public Policy*, 22/2, 177–95.

Schimmelfennig, F. (2019), 'Is differentiation the future of European integration?', in B. Fagersten and G. von Sydow (eds), *Perspectives on the Future of the EU*. Stockholm: Swedish Institute for European Policy Studies.

Schmidt, V. (2006), *Democracy in Europe: The EU and National Politics*. New York: Oxford University Press.

Seabrooke, L., and E. Tsingou (2019), 'Europe's fast- and slow-burning crises', *Journal of European Public Policy*, 26/3, 468–81.

Seddone, A., and G. Sandri (2020), 'Primary elections and party grassroots: Participation, innovation and resistance', *European Political Science*, published online.

Sgueo, G. (2016), 'Participatory budgeting. An innovative approach', European Parliament Research Service.

Shackelford, S., 'The battle against disinformation is global', *The Conversation*, 20 March 2020.

Shapiro, I. (2017), 'Collusion in restraint of democracy: Against deliberation', *Daedaleus*, 146/3, 77–84.

Simon, J., T. Bass, V. Boelman and G. Mulgan (2017), *Digital Democracy: The Tools Transforming Political Engagement*. London: Nesta.

Sintomer, Y. (2018), 'Deliberative Polls and the Systemic Democratization of Democracy', *Good Society*, 27/1–2, 155–64.

Slavov, A. (2020), 'National referendums: Between legitimate popular decision-making and populist take-over', in S. Blockmans and S. Russack (eds), *Deliberative Democracy in the EU: Countering Populism with Participation and Debate*. London: Rowman and Littlefield.

Smith, G., and R. Bechler, 'Citizens assembly towards a politics of considered judgement. part-2', *Open Democracy*, 27 November 2019.

Snyder, T. (2019), *The Road to Unfreedom*. London: Vintage.

Solijonov, A. (2016), *Voter Turnout Trends Around the World*. Stockholm: International IDEA.

Stasavage, D. (2020), *The Decline and Rise of Democracy*. Princeton: Princeton University Press.

Stoiciu, V. (2017), 'Romanian social movements – between repoliticization and reinforcement of the status quo, 2012-1017', Studia Universitatis Babes-Bolyai.

Stratulat, C., and P. Butcher (2018), *The European Citizens' Consultations: Evaluation Report*. Brussels: European Policy Centre.

Susskind, J. (2018), *Future Politics*. Oxford: Oxford University Press.

Szczerblak, A. (2019), 'Can Poland's opposition win this year's election?', EUROPP Blog, LSE.

Taggart, P., and C. Kaltwasser (2016), 'Dealing with populists in government: Some comparative conclusions', *Democratization*, 23/2, 1–21.

Taylor, C., P. Nanz and M. Beaubien Taylor (2019), *Reconstructing Democracy: How Citizens are Building from the Ground Up*. Cambridge, MA: Harvard University Press.

TIMBRO (2019), *Authoritarian Populism Index*. Stockholm: TIMBRO.

Topaloff, L. (2017), 'The rise of referendums: Elite strategy or populist weapon?', *Journal of Democracy*, 28/3, 127–40.

Tormey, S. (2015), *The End of Representative Politics*. Cambridge: Polity Press.

Tucker, A. (2020), *Democracy against Liberalism*. Cambridge: Polity Press.

UK Government (2019), *Online Harms White Paper*. London: HMG.

UK House of Commons (2015), *Open Up! Speaker's Digital Democracy Commission*. London: House of Commons.

UK Parliament (2020), *The Government's Response to COVID-19: Human Rights Implications*, UK Parliament Committees.

UK Parliament Intelligence and Security Committee (2020), *Russia*. London: House of Commons.

United Nations General Assembly, Human Rights Council Working Group on the Universal Periodic Review, Compilation of Information, A/HRC/WG.6/35/ESP/2, 18 November 2019.

Van Ham, C., J. Thomassen, K. Aarts and R. Andeweg (2017), *Myth and Reality of the Legitimacy Crisis: Explaining Trends and Cross-National Differences in Established Democracies*. Oxford: Oxford University Press.

Van Hecke, S., et al. (2018), *Reconnecting European Political Parties with European Union Citizens*. Stockholm: International IDEA.

Van Middelaar, L. (2020), *Alarums and Excursions: Improvising Politics on the European Stage*. London: Agenda.

Van Reybrouck, D. (2018), *Against Elections: The Case for Democracy*. New York: Seven Stories Press.

Vandor, P., N. Traxler, R. Millner and M. Meyer (2017), *Civil Society in Central and Eastern Europe: Challengers and Opportunities*. Vienna: ERSTE Stiftung Studies.

Varieties of Democracy (2020), *Defending Democracy against Illiberal Challengers: A Resource Guide*. Gothenberg: University of Gothenburg.

Varieties of Democracy (2020), *Structure of V-Dem Indices, Components and Indicators*. Gothenberg: University of Gothenburg.

Varieties of Democracy (2018), *Annual Democracy Report 2018*. Gothenberg: University of Gothenburg.

Varieties of Democracy (2019), *Annual Democracy Report 2019*. Gothenberg: University of Gothenburg.

Varieties of Democracy (2020), *Annual Democracy Report 2020*. Gothenberg: University of Gothenburg.

Vidal, G., and I. Sanchez-Vitores (2019), 'Spain – out with the old: The restructuring of Spanish politics', in S. Hutter and H. Kries (eds), *European Party Politics in Times of Crisis*. Cambridge: Cambridge University Press.

Von der Leyen, U. (2019), *A Union That Strives for More: My Agenda for Europe: Political Guidelines for the Next European Commission 2019–2024*. Brussels: European Commission.

Vospernik, S. (2017), 'Referendums and consensus democracy: Empirical findings from 21 EU countries', in L. Morel and M. Qvortrup (eds) (2018), *Routledge Handbook on Direct Democracy and Referendums*. London: Routledge.

Warren, M. (2017), *The Handbook of Deliberative Democracy*. Oxford: Oxford University Press.

Weale, A. (2018), *The Will of the People: A Modern Myth*. Cambridge: Polity Press.

Wike, R., and S. Schumacher (2020), *Democratic Rights Popular Globally but Commitment to Them Not Always Strong*. Washington, DC: Pew.

Wilson, R., and C. Mellier (2020), *Getting Climate Assemblies Right*. Brussels: Carnegie Europe.

World Justice Report (2020), *Rule of Law Index 2019*. Washington DC: World Justice Report.

Youngs, R. (2019), *Civic Activism Unleashed: New Hope or False Dawn for Democracy?* Oxford: Oxford University Press.

Youngs, R. (2019), *Six Ideas for Rejuvenating European democracy*. Brussels: Carnegie Europe.

Zielonka, J. (2018), *Counter-Revolution: Liberal Europe in Retreat*. Oxford: Oxford University Press.

Zuboff, S. (2019), *The Age of Surveillance Capitalism*. London: Profile Books.

Zulianello, M. (2020), 'Varieties of populist parties and party systems in Europe: Form state-of-the-art to the application of a novel classification scheme to 66 parties in 33 countries', *Government and Opposition*, 55/2, 327–47.

Index

www.ingramcontent.com/pod-product-compliance
Lightning Source LLC
Chambersburg PA
CBHW070400270326
41926CB00014B/2630

* 9 7 8 0 7 5 5 6 3 9 7 2 4 *